P9-AGH-940

Building
Social Security:
The Challenge of
Privatization

International Social Security Series

In cooperation with the
International Social Security Association (ISSA)
Neil Gilbert, Series Editor

Targeting Social Benefits:
International Perspectives and Trends
Neil Gilbert, editor

Social Security at the Dawn of the
21st Century: Topical Issues and New Approaches
Dalmer D. Hoskins, Donate Dobbernack, and
Christiane Kuptsch, editors

Activating the Unemployed: A Comparative
Appraisal of Work-Oriented Policies
Neil Gilbert and Rebecca A. Van Voorhis, editors

Recent Health Policy Innovations in
Social Security
Aviva Ron and Xenia Scheil-Adlung, editors

Who Returns to Work and Why: A Six-Country
Study on Work Incapacity and Reintegration
Frank S. Bloch and Rienk Prins, editors

Building Social Security:
The Challenge of Privatization
Xenia Scheil-Adlung, editor

Building Social Security: The Challenge of Privatization

Xenia Scheil-Adlung
editor

International Social Security Series
Volume 6

Transaction Publishers
New Brunswick (U.S.A.) and London (U.K.)

368.4
B932

Copyright © 2001 by Transaction Publishers, New Brunswick, New Jersey.

The International Social Security Association (ISSA) was founded in 1927. It is a nonprofit international organization bringing together institutions and administrative bodies from countries all over the world dealing with all forms of compulsory social protection. The objective of the ISSA is to cooperate at the international level, in the promotion and development of social security throughout the world, primarily by improving techniques and administration in order to advance people's social and economic conditions on the basis of social justice.

The responsibility for opinions expressed in signed articles, studies, and other contributions rests solely with their authors, and publication does not constitute an endorsement by the International Social Security Association of the opinions expressed by them.

All rights reserved under International and Pan-American Copyright Conventions. No part of this book may be reproduced or transmitted in any form or by any means, electronic or mechanical, including photocopy, recording, or any information storage and retrieval system, without prior permission in writing from the publisher. All inquiries should be addressed to Transaction Publishers, Rutgers—The State University, 35 Berrue Circle, Piscataway, New Jersey 08854-8042.

This book is printed on acid-free paper that meets the American National Standard for Permanence of Paper for Printed Library Materials.

Library of Congress Catalog Number: 2001027203
ISBN: 0-7658-0878-1
Printed in the United States of America

Library of Congress Cataloging-in-Publication Data

Building social security: the challenge of privatization / edited by Xenia Scheil-Adlung.
    p. cm.— (International social security series ; v. 6)
    Includes bibliographical references and index.
    ISBN 0-7658-0878-1 (pbk. : alk. paper)
    1. Social security—Finance. 2. Privatization. 3. Individual retirement accounts. 4. Social security—Finance—Case studies. I. Scheil-Adlung, Xenia. II. Series.

HD7101 .B85 2001
368.4—dc21   2001027203

Contents

Foreword   ix
Dalmer D. Hoskins

Introductory Overview   xi
Xenia Scheil-Adlung

Part 1: Privatization: Visions, Effects, and Challenges

1. Social Security Privatization: Different Context—   3
Different Discourse
Christiane Kuptsch

2. Privatization: More Individual Choice in   19
Social Protection
Monika Queisser

3. Africa: Implications of Privatization Measures   31
Initiated by International Financing Organizations
Théopiste Butare

Part 2: Privatization: An Organizing Principle for Financing Social
Security?

4. The Case for Funded, Individual Accounts in   45
Pension Reform
Robert Holzmann and Robert Palacios

5. Individual Accounts Versus Social Insurance: 63
A United States Perspective
Alicia Munnell

6. Strengthening Public Pensions with
    Private Investment—Canada's Approach
    to Privatization Pressures
    Monica Townson
                                                            83

Part 3: Privatization: A Tool for Governance?

7. Germany: Efficiency and Affordability in
    Social Security through Partial Privatization
    of Provision for Risks
    Jürgen Husmann
                                                            95

8. Privatization: From Panacea to Poison Pill—
    The Dutch Paradigm
    Dik Hermans
                                                            101

9. Healthy Markets—Sick Patients?
    Effects of Recent Trends on the Health Care Market
    Xenia Scheil-Adlung
                                                            113

10. Social Health Insurance Development in Low-Income
    Developing Countries: New Roles for Government
    and Nonprofit Health Insurance Organizations
    in Africa and Asia
    Guy Carrin, Martinus Desmet, and Robert Basaza
                                                            125

Part 4: The Empirical Framework: National Experiences of
        Privatization in Various Branches of Social Security

11. The Privatization of Pensions in Latin America and
    Its Impacts on the Insured, the Economy, and
    Old-Age People
    Carmelo Mesa-Lago
                                                            157

12. First Experiences with the Privatization of the Polish
    Pension Scheme: A Status Report
    Ewa Borowczyk
                                                            169

13. Austria's Discussion on Social Security   175
    Privatization: Some Notes Focusing on
    Old-Age Insurance
    Walter Geppert

14. The Evolution of Public and Private Insurance in   185
    Sweden during the 1990s
    Edward Palmer

15. Tunisian Health Insurance: Towards Complementarity   201
    of Public and Private Sector
    Mohamed Ridha Kechrid

16. Impact of Private Sector Involvement in Health   209
    Insurance in Uruguay: A Status Report
    Julio Pilón

17. China: From Public Health Insurance to a   215
    Multi-Tiered Structure
    Aidi Hu

18. Impacts of Private Sector Involvement in Health   223
    Insurance in Indonesia
    Sonja Roesma

19. Trends in Private Sector Involvement in the   233
    Delivery of Workforce Development Services
    in the United States
    Stephen A. Wandner and Janet O. Javar

20. Changes in Employment Services through   247
    Deregulation
    Regina Konle-Seidl and Ulrich Walwei

21. The Privatization of Accident Compensation   259
    in New Zealand
    John Miller

22. The Advantages of Statutory over Private Employment   269
     Accident Insurance: The Example of Germany
       Günther Sokoll

23. The Danish Experience with Privatization: 283
     New ways of Solving Tasks
       Karen Sejersdal Christensen

     List of Authors   291

     Index   295

Foreword

The International Social Security Association (ISSA) has for several decades published a report, usually once every three years, on the principal developments in social security programs around the world. The primary purpose of this report, customarily published on the occasion of the ISSA's General Assembly, is to highlight significant social security reforms and innovations that have recently occurred in the different regions of the world and in the various branches of social security, including old age, disability, health, unemployment, occupational risks and family allowances.

Whereas the previous reports focused on significant changes within the different geographical regions and branches of social security, this first report of the new century addresses a single development affecting all regions and branches: the trend toward the privatization of social security protection. Private provision is hardly a new phenomenon, since illustrations are to be found in the very origins of social security. However, examples of privatization have increased in number and frequency in recent years and the intensity of the debate about the implications of this trend has increased sharply almost everywhere.

Whereas, in the past, privatization could often be seen as being associated with the charitable efforts of religious organizations and community associations or as a complement to basic social security protection, today we find that in many countries it is related to market forces which have a significant impact on government decisions concerning social security protection as a whole.

What is the role of privatization today in the development of national social security systems? This is the critical question this publication tackles from different points of view, expressed by administrators, researchers, social protection experts, and representatives of international financial organizations, non-governmental institutions and other sectors. While the perspective of each of the contributors to this publication is markedly different, the overall objective cuts across differences: namely, to develop the most efficient and cost-effective system of social security protection.

The Authors

The ISSA is very grateful to all the authors who contributed to this publication. The different chapters have been written by well-known international experts and practitioners who analyze the pros and cons of various developments related to privatization in the different branches of social security.

The authors' views and knowledge are derived from their first-hand experiences with social security in Africa, Asia, the Americas and Europe. Representatives of the leading international organizations dealing with social security issues—the International Labour Organization, the OECD, the World Bank, and the World Health Organization—further expand the parameters of the viewpoints and experiences expressed.

Acknowledgments

I would like to thank the members of the project team whose efforts led to the successful conclusion that this publication represents. Xenia Scheil-Adlung was the editor, and developed the publication from its inception to its final outcome. She provided both policy and technical guidance to the project. Renate Schmitz was the administrative assistant who accurately supervised the work involved in the production of the four language editions of the publication.

The translators and many other persons whose names do not appear here also made significant contributions to the different language versions. A multilingual publication of this importance obviously requires a high degree of teamwork and coordination, and I profoundly appreciate the contributions made by all the ISSA staff members and other persons involved in the realization of the volume.

The debate over the respective roles of the public and private sectors in the provision of social security protection will continue for many years to come, with varying degrees of intensity, in all parts of the world. The ISSA fully intends to take part in this important debate which will inevitably influence the future direction of social security in the years to come.

Dalmer D. Hoskins
Secretary General
International Social Security Association

Introductory Overview

X. Scheil-Adlung

In recent years, in both the specialist press and the tabloids, the idea of *privatization in social security* has become a shimmering catch phrase, leitmotif, trendy. Politicians base election campaigns on promises of more or less privatization in social security. Many governments introduce private business management methods into their social security systems, representatives of social security institutions and academics prepare theory papers on the possible outcomes of privatization and international financial organizations describe doomsday scenarios based on the premise of failure to privatize.

Depending on one's political standpoint, the concept of privatization is often indirectly related to and defined as

- more freedom of choice in social security

- "new stewardship"

- new partnership between the public and private sector

- introduction of three or more conceptual pillars

- regulation of the second pillar

- introduction of individual accounts and funding methods

- emphasis on benefits (rather than contributions).

The debate about "privatization" in social security concerns all branches of social security: old age, sickness, unemployment, accident insurance, family allowances, etc., without so far any detailed exchange of experiences between the individual branches. Far more frequently, "privatization in social security" is equated with "privatization of old-age pensions."

In this regard, depending on the point of view, the "state" or "privatization" or the "market" are attributed with mythical properties and the debate is polarized as poor versus rich or efficiency versus bureaucracy. Often a lack of conceptual clarity hampers the understanding of different positions.

Thus, the worldwide controversy suffers not only from a lack of clear ideas and concepts of "privatization," but also reflects regional, historical and cultural differences over the meaning of social security in a modern state. At the forefront is the question as to how far the state should solve social problems and in which areas non-state solutions should be given priority.

In that regard, there is a fundamental consensus that the state is responsible for social needs and the collaboration of public and private components of social security. What is not agreed, however, is to what extent it is acceptable for social needs to be subject to financial constraints.

For countries without distinct welfare state traditions, the controversy over privatization of social security is often confined to commercial aspects such as improved cost effectiveness and management.

Conversely, other countries strive for higher levels of welfare services and financial resources, especially in order not to endanger the greater social uniformity of their societies compared with others. The debate over the privatization of social security is for these countries a cultural challenge that extends far beyond the cost aspects of social security. It is closely related to:

- the importance and role of the state in welfare provision

- the importance and role of private (commercial and non-profit) sectors in achieving social goals

- the role of social protection in prevention before and at the onset of social risks

- redistribution within society and inclusion and exclusion of its members.

It has long been apparent in the trend towards privatization of social security that solutions to financial, economic, social and cultural problems cannot be expected from either state or private models alone. In practice, there is increasing evidence of a new cooperation between these sectors, which also envisages the involvement of *civil society*. Thus,

- state policy is supported by the methods of the commercial private sector, both in management and financing

- responsibility for achieving the goals of the welfare state is transferred to the regulated private sector, in the form of insurance or commercial presence within the state system and

- non-profit and family welfare provision, including care and childcare, are envisaged within state social security systems.

Through this publication, the *International Social Security Association* hopes to contribute to the current debate on *Privatization of Social Security* and shed light on the wealth of possible forms and effects of privatization. This multifaceted book allows the reader to learn about the challenge of privatization in the various forms of social security by assembling a set of highly up-to-date, technically complex and legal issues based on practical analysis and actual experience.

Next comes an overview of the various positions of supporters and opponents of privatization in the main branches of social security, followed by national experience of privatized or part-privatized social security systems.

The publication is divided into the following parts:

- Privatization: Visions, Effects and Challenges

- Privatization: An Organizing Principle for Financing Social Security?

- Privatization: A Tool for Governance?

- The Empirical Framework: National Experiences of Privatization in Various Branches of Social Security.

Privatization: Visions, Effects, and Challenges

The first part of the publication sets out the predominant aspects of privatization in social security: visions of privatization, its effects and challenges are the main focus.

The contrasting visions of privatization in social security are presented in the theoretical and analytic chapter of *Christiane Kuptsch* through various definitions and concepts. Her contribution addresses the limits and significance of the impact of privatization in different branches of social security.

Monika Queisser is concerned in her contribution with the challenge that the social security systems and their standard benefit packages are no longer regarded as adequate. The author's view is that social security must be supplemented through non-public systems, in order to achieve greater individual freedom of choice and ultimately greater efficiency.

Théopiste Butare, in his contribution, addresses the effects and challenges of privatization in Africa. Developments in privatization in this part of the world were mainly driven by major international finance institutions such as the World Bank and the International Monetary Fund, whose policies must now be measured in terms of their results. What effects were achieved in terms of the economy, unemployment and combating poverty and what influence was there on social security? The author sees only limited benefits in this regard.

Privatization: An Organizing Principle for Financing Social Security?

The question of how far privatization can be seen as an organizing principle in the financing of social security is considered in the following chapters by authors with different experiences and conclusions.

Thus, *Robert Holzmann* and *Robert Palacio* consider that individual accounts can have significant advantages compared with public pensions insurance. The central arguments in favor of this are relieving the financial burden on the state budget and the wider spread of risk.

Conversely, *Alicia Munnell* maintains that the introduction of individual accounts is not compatible with the fundamental goals of social security, particularly as fluctuations in the financial markets and investment decisions do not offer a reliable basis for income in old age. The author also points out that the major finance institutions are now toning down their initial unequivocal support for individual accounts, questioning in particular the management and control costs of entrepreneurial success.

Monica Townson is also skeptical about the World Banks proposals. She also points to very high management and control costs and transitional costs of changing methods from pay-as-you-go to funding. Furthermore, according to the author, any further withdrawal of the state would lead to increased poverty and inequality of incomes in Canada. This conflicts with the social policy goals that were pursued under state pension programs.

Privatization: A Tool for Governance?

Can the management and control of social security be improved through privatization? This is the question addressed in this part of the publication by representatives of the employers, the social security administrations and international organizations.

The employer's view is presented by *Jürgen Husmann*. His comments center on the possibility of part-privatization to supplement social security and its enormous significance for the financing of public health and old-age pension insurance.

Dik Hermans describes in his contribution the developments and background to privatization and subsequent de-privatization of parts of his country's social security system. In the author's view, a paradigm change has occurred, which raises problems of management as well as control of the social security system.

Xenia Scheil-Adlung's contribution focuses on new developments in the health care market and effects on equality of treatment, quality and developments in infrastructure.

Guy Carrin, Martinus Desmet, and Robert Basaza examine the potential for nonprofit health insurance in Bangladesh, the Congo and Uganda. The role of government is seen, in particular, as providing such insurance for the poor and subsidizing their contributions.

The Empirical Framework: National Experiences of Privatization in Various Branches of Social Security

What is the experience in different countries and branches of social security of privatization? In this part of the publication the whole range of approaches to privatization is described: private commercial and nonprofit sector is thus discussed, as is the part-privatization of social security systems, through outsourcing of management or benefits payments or "traditional" private insurance.

The area of *old-age pensions* is addressed, among others, by the contribution of *Carmelo Mesa-Lago*. The author analyses the effects of pensions reform in *Latin America* from the point of view of the insured, including freedom of choice, cover and financial burden. He goes on to survey the effects on the economy, such as competition and cost savings, and the elderly population.

Experiences of privatization of pensions in *Europe* are presented from the viewpoint of Poland, Austria and Sweden. *Ewa Borowczyk*, in her contribution, describes positive and negative experiences with the privatization of the Polish pension system. Greater justice and personal responsibility were offset by administrative problems and concerns about pension levels.

Walter Geppert points in his contribution to the advantages and disadvantages of funding in old-age pension insurance. The author pleads for country-specific solutions, reflecting the respective values and constraints of the economy and employment.

Edward Palmer describes the radical changes that the Swedish old-age pension insurance system has undergone since the 1990s. The development of new financial instruments and the involvement of capital markets are at the forefront.

What is the significance of privatization in risk of *health*? More than in other branches of social security, it has long been a matter here of striking a reasonable balance between the public and private sector. Thus the private sector is not only involved in commercial private insurance, but also non-profit insurance, such as mutual benefit societies. Moreover, both sectors are interrelated in the organization and management of health systems

Mohamed Ridha Kechrid sets out the historical development and current reforms of the health system in Tunisia. A focal point of his contribution is the analysis of the differing roles of the public and private sector.

Julio Pilón describes Uruguay's experience with private non-profit mutual benefit societies. The author states that a grading of benefits, based on basic needs, average needs and extended requirements can only be achieved with great difficulty for health care. Moreover, the growth of the health sector, as a result of rising life expectancy and technical progress demands solutions based on solidarity rather than the profit motive. Properly managed and controlled mutual benefit societies can satisfy these demands with a high level of service.

Aidi Hu analyses China's latest health insurance reform. Here an individual health insurance account was opened for each insured person and a collective health insurance fund established. The author describes the reform as the middle way between social insurance and private provision, and points to advantages, such as the extension of coverage, as well as weaknesses.

Sonja Roesma describes the extensive role of privatization in various stages of the development of Indonesian health insurance. She also addresses the recent economic crisis in Asia and the influence of the World Bank and International Monetary Fund.

What is the significance of the trend towards privatization in *employment services*? This issue is addressed by authors from the viewpoint of the United States and Germany.

Stephen A. Wandner and *Janet O. Javar* give an overview of the trend towards privatization of employment services in the United States. This trend can be seen on various levels: in the involvement of employers and private employment agencies in program implementation, in competition between private service providers and automated Internet employment databases as well as training and other services, and lastly welfare services. The importance of private agencies, "mediating" between state and job-seekers, is thus becoming increasingly important.

Regina Konle-Seidl and *Ulrich Walwei* are concerned in their contribution with the consequences of deregulation, or liberalization, of employment services in Europe. The authorization of private employment agencies resulted in parallel public and private agencies which, however, has not yet led to faster job placements.

The question of how far privatization of *accident insurance* can be judged as a good or bad thing is considered by *John Miller* and *Günther Sokoll*.

John Miller's contribution is based on the latest experience of privatization of accident insurance in New Zealand and the reintroduction of the previous accident compensation scheme after one year. The reason for that was the conviction that profit-oriented private insurance would inevitably lead to higher costs, and more disputes with injured employees whose claims were contested.

Günther Sokoll also sees no advantage in the privatization of accident insurance. On the contrary: privatization would, among other things, lead to poorer prevention and loss of efficiency and quality. The author's view is that social accident insurance is unbeatable, for accident victims, employers and society.

What possibilities are to be found in the privatization of *welfare services* and what experience is there of this? This question is addressed by *Karen Sejersdal Christensen*. The author highlights the importance of voluntary social work in her presentation. The role of the state is primarily seen as taking responsibility for the weakest members of society, while the private sector should be more strongly involved in areas such as the labor market, training and housing.

Part 1

Privatization: Visions, Effects, and Challenges

1

Social Security Privatization: Different Context—Different Discourse

C. Kuptsch

1. Introduction

"Let's plant a tree!" A woman from the taiga hearing this sentence would most probably think of a birch tree rather than a coconut palm, while a man from the Caribbean would think of mangroves rather than alders.

"Let's privatize social security!" Just as the woman from the taiga and the man from the Caribbean will not think of the same type of tree, so a financial consultant from the Chilean Ministry of Economic Affairs and an accident insurer from New Zealand are unlikely to have the same ideas about privatization. Even if the term "privatization" has fewer associations than there are types of trees, we can still assume that not everyone is thinking of the same thing. In a single discussion about privatization in the social security field you might hear the following statements:

- "Privatization leads to capital formation and stimulates the economy."

- "Privatization could cut costs and make things more customer-friendly."

- "Privatization helps to combat absenteeism."

- "Privatization leads to social exclusion for a lot of people."

The person responsible for the first sentence is thinking about how social security is financed, which he/she associates with private institutions (though this is not necessarily the case, since public social security institutions can also, in principle, operate through funded schemes). The second sentence looks at privatization from the point of view of the provision of social security benefits. The third sentence links privatization with the direct payment of social security costs by employers. In the last sentence the term "privatization" is used to mean the redistribution of responsibilities between the public and private sectors.

This chapter focuses on meanings given to the words "social security privatization," in order to prevent misunderstandings and confusion. It presents a number of fundamental considerations on the concept of privatization in social security, and it attempts to systematize the different aspects from which "privatization" can be approached. Examples from recent discussions on privatization or of privatization processes will be used to show how context-dependent the term privatization is, in other words how differently people talk about privatization in various branches of social security and in various social protection systems, and what different forms it can take. Finally, the chapter looks at what the term privatization can mean as a synonym for other terms.

2. Definitions: The Terms "Privatization" and "Social Security"

"Privatization" is a rather blurred concept, which is inevitable, since it is really nothing more than a pointer. "Privatization" is a process that can have various different starting points. What people mean by "privatization" thus depends on the context and can only be defined in relation to the starting point. To begin with, "privatization" simply means that something will be organized more "privately" in the future than it has been before.[1]

"Social security" too does not have a clear-cut, internationally accepted definition. It is a term which carries different associations in literature and in everyday parlance, and particularly from one social protection system to another. Some countries define "social security" very narrowly (such as the United States, where it is only understood to be social insurance for old-age, survivors and disability), and this then tends to mean that in international discussions the terms "social security" and " social protection" are often used synonymously.

This chapter follows the definition used by the International Labour Office, as set out in the *World Labour Report 2000*,[2] since it attempts to cover the situations in all regions and social protection systems. The *World Labour Report 2000* defines "social security" as the *protection which society provides for its members through a series of public measures*. The ILO definition covers:

- social insurance (i.e., contributory systems);

- social assistance (i.e., tax-financed benefits for those on low incomes); and

- universal benefits (i.e., tax-financed benefits paid regardless of income and need).

3. Possible Meanings of the Term Privatization Derived from Starting Points for Privatization Processes in Social Security

"Social security privatization," therefore, is all about making public benefits which are available to individuals in insecure circumstances more "private" in future. In principle this can be achieved, (a) by transferring state responsibility to non-state actors and (b) by more closely involving the private sector in areas for which the state is still responsible. One can therefore speak of "privatization"

- where *tasks are redistributed* between the public and private sectors, with the private sector given greater weight; or

- where existing arrangements are *reorganized*, with the state remaining responsible for providing benefits when certain risks occur (in particular situations).

Privatization as a Redistribution of Tasks

Different societies have different ideas about the tasks that the state should be responsible for, and those ideas can change with time. The fact that a particular task is important for public welfare, in other words that it is a "public" responsibility, does not mean that it has to be carried out or even regulated by the state. Supplying food and clothing would be one example. On the other hand, a constitutional state may carry out only public responsibilities; anything else would have to be seen as interfering with the freedom of the individual. The usual justification for state action is that individual citizens and social groups are not in themselves capable of satisfying public welfare needs. If circumstances change, the justification for certain state activities may no longer apply, or else a new justification may emerge.[3]

Some legal systems draw a distinction between "exclusive state responsibilities," which as things stand are solely matters for the state and thus cannot, in principle, be privatized, and "competitive state responsibilities," which may be legitimately carried out by private bodies. Where such a distinction is made, the privatization issue may take the form of a social debate about the extent of or even whether it makes sense to have exclusive state responsibilities, or about which state responsibilities are to be classified as exclusive and which as competitive. In some countries the constitution contains information or instructions on which responsibilities the state itself must assume and cannot privatize; in others this issue is not addressed.[4]

These differences in themselves mean that social security privatization is regarded differently from one country to another. The *starting point* for privatization in the sense of the redistribution of responsibilities between the state and the private sector may not just be historically different, there may also be other "*taboo areas*."

At the very least it must be assumed that the privatization debate will vary greatly from one social protection system to the next, particularly since people living in different types of welfare state will clearly give different answers to the question of *who* should be allocated responsibility under privatization. Those living in welfare states which set great store by the principle of subsidiarity and the role of the family and social groups are more likely to think that "social security privatization" means the transfer or restoration of responsibility to families and welfare associations than those from countries where the emphasis is on the individual.[5]

We cannot go into the debate about the different types of welfare state and their typologies in this chapter,[6] nor can we consider how many ideal types of welfare state there are, what criteria should be used to distinguish between them and which countries should be classified where. Yet the debate in literature on these issues shows that there is at least agreement that "welfare state" does not always mean the same thing. This is why it should not simply be assumed that "social security privatization" can only mean a shift from state regulation to market regulation. The distinction often drawn in other contexts between the public and private sectors, which defines the public sector in terms of state regulation and the elimination of market forces and considers the market to be the regulating element in the private sector, appears too narrow when applied to the question of "social security privatization" and therefore inappropriate.[7]

The state may, in principle, give responsibility for social security to the following non-state actors:

- individuals (by encouraging the individual to look after him/herself);

- families;

- nonprofit-making organizations, the "voluntary sector" (including charities, church/religious organizations, self-help groups, mutual benefit societies, etc.);

- social groups (e.g., trade unions);

- employers; and

- profit-orientated institutions (referred to, generically, as "the market"; e.g., private insurance companies).

"Formally Identified Privatization" and "Creeping Privatization." The redistribution of responsibilities may be actively pursued and formally identified, such as in changes to legislation, or it may result from the unplanned and possibly unintentional withdrawal of the state from a particular field.[8]

One of many examples of "formally identified privatization" was the abolition of the Supplementary Social Benefits Fund for Civil Servants (*Fondo Complementario de Prestaciones Sociales para los Servidores Públicos*) in Panama. This supplementary scheme, which provided pensions on the basis of special laws (for teachers, nurses, etc.) and benefits in addition to pensions under the Social Insurance Fund (*Caja de Seguro Social*), was replaced under a law introduced in February 1997 by the Pensions Savings and Funding Scheme for Civil Servants (*Sistema de Ahorro y Capitalización de Pensiones para los Servidores Públicos*).[9] Unlike the supplementary scheme, the new scheme is based on voluntary membership. Only those who have made voluntary payments into individual accounts receive benefits. The state, therefore, has officially—through the legislative process—withdrawn from an area of benefits. It also no longer guarantees that the benefits which it previously paid can continue to be claimed through other channels.

"Creeping privatization" takes many different forms. For example, cuts in benefits under public schemes which have the effect of increasing demand for private provision may be classified as creeping privatization. This covers not just direct reductions in social benefits, but also indirect measures such as tightening up eligibility criteria. The following are just a few examples—for once not from Europe or North America—where "creeping privatization" in the form of direct and indirect reductions in benefits is, however, anything but unusual.

In 1999 social benefits were reduced in Hong Kong (China); the maximum rent allowance, for example, was cut by 2.6 percent on 1 April.[10] In Trinidad and Tobago conditions for receiving invalidity benefits were tightened up in May 1999.[11] Jordan is considering increasing the minimum contribution period for receiving a disability pension and making it more difficult to take early retirement.[12] Under the Islamic Republic of Iran's draft Third Economic, Social and Cultural Development Plan, the minimum retirement age is to be gradually increased from 50 to 60 for men and from 45 to 55 for women.[13] In Japan, a pension reform of March 2000 introduced a progressive increase in the retirement age from 60 to 65 over the period 2013-2025 for men and 2018-2030 for women.[14]

"Creeping privatization" may also result from an increase in the demand for private provision because of the growing number of people who are no longer covered by statutory insurance schemes. These are mainly people who, under schemes which assume full-time employment as the norm for the purpose of receiving benefits, are in atypical jobs or alternative forms of employment (part-time work, job-sharing, shorter working week or year, special periods of leave, etc.), or people who do not have full social protection because they lack sufficient qualifying periods of residence or legal resident status. The increase in the numbers of such people is often the result of measures to combat unemployment and efforts to reduce labor costs.[15]

This type of "creeping privatization" mainly affects industrialized countries where population structures are changing. In developing countries, where a large proportion of the population earn a living in the informal sector and are not covered by public social security schemes, most risks are already "privatized." Here the trend is in the opposite direction, with efforts being made to extend public benefits to a wider circle of people. "Creeping privatization" in this context involves cuts in benefits, if anything at all.

Privatization as Reorganization

"Social security privatization" also means different things in different contexts because social protection schemes are organized differently from one country to another and even from one sector to another. It is usually the case that each scheme already has private elements, but by no means the same ones as in a different branch within the same country, and also not necessarily the same ones as in a parallel scheme in another country.

There are three organizational levels in social security schemes where private elements can be incorporated or where state action can be replaced or supplemented by private action. Social security can be organized "more privately" in terms of:

- its institutions;

- its administration; and

- the payment of its costs.

Public and Private Institutions

Social security can be provided by both public and private institutions. Private institutions (such as private insurance companies and employers) can share responsibility with or even completely take the place of public institutions. If the state entrusts private institutions with certain tasks, it usually meets its social responsibilities by at least laying down minimum requirements for carrying out the activity in question and by monitoring compliance with them.

The pension insurance schemes in Latin America are excellent examples of different organizational models with regard to institutions. While the pension insurance schemes in Chile, Bolivia and Mexico are almost entirely in the hands of the private sector (except for supervision and certain guarantee functions), Peru and Colombia have state and private pension insurance institutions operating along-side each other, and those insured have to choose between them. Argentina and Uruguay have set up mixed systems in which state institutions are responsible for the first pillar of the system and private insurers administer the second; members are required to participate in both components.[16]

Private institutions also play a major role in work accident insurance in some countries, with employers required to obtain insurance cover from a private insurer. Sometimes it is also possible to obtain insurance from a state institution which is competing with private providers. Examples here include Kenya, Tanzania, Uganda, Dominica, Singapore, Finland and Portugal.

The picture is very similar in the field of healthcare, where there are also social security schemes handled by private bodies. As with pensions insurance, private institutions often serve to provide supplementary benefits in this field, too.

The United States is probably the most famous example of a private health insurance model, but other countries also operate through private institutions.

For example, under legislation introduced in 1996 in Switzerland, compulsory health insurance may be provided by nationally recognized public or private health funds and by private insurance companies on the basis of insurance contracts under the law on insurance contracts.[17] Those required to have insurance are free to choose between the recognized health funds and the authorized private insurers and can change from one to another as they wish. The insurers are under an obligation to contract for basic insurance and must offer clients uniform conditions, with regional differences in premiums allowed, but not risk selection. The premiums for top-up insurance, on the other hand, are calculated in relation to the risk. Top-up insurance here is not subject to social health insurance law, but to the law on insurance contracts, and is therefore governed by private rather than public law.

In Germany private insurance firms are responsible, among other things, for providing care insurance for people who are not subject to statutory health insurance. However, the law forbids private insurers from carrying out risk assessment in this field, and requires them to provide the same benefits as statutory care schemes. The maximum private insurance premium must also not exceed the maximum contribution rate for social care insurance.[18]

These examples from various branches of social security show that "privatizing" a social security scheme by more heavily involving private institutions can take very different forms. Private institutions may be made responsible for implementing entire schemes, or they may run parts of a scheme. They may also compete with state institutions. "Privatization" may also mean a combination of the last two options. Pertaining to institutions, "privatization" may also simply mean modifying an institution's legal form, with the state as it were "changing into private dress."[19] Depending on the context, this is sometimes referred to as "formal privatization" and sometimes as "artificial privatization."

Administration of Social Security

The picture becomes even more complex when we consider that those receiving social security benefits do not necessarily have to receive them directly from the institution in charge of a system. A benefit provider may operate between the institution and the recipient. This set-up is particularly common with social benefits that are not paid in cash, but are benefits in kind or services. So social security institutions and benefit providers can be, but do not have to be, one and the same.

Like the social security institutions the benefit providers may also be public (state) bodies—such as state and municipal hospitals—or private, such as private clinics and private doctors and pharmacists.

"Social security privatization" can therefore mean new ways of organizing the provision of benefits, with state benefit providers being converted into private bodies or the state withdrawing entirely or in part from the direct provision of benefits.

Selling a state hospital to a charity or a profit-making HMO is therefore just as much a "privatization" as if family doctors are allowed to purchase the practice in which they have been operating as state doctors, as has been happening recently in Hungary.[20]

One example of the "privatization" of previously state-provided services is the *Ticket to Work and Self-Sufficiency Program* in the United States. Under this program, disabled beneficiaries of Disability Insurance (DI) or Supplemental Security Income (SSI) are allowed to obtain vocational rehabilitation services, employment services and other support services from state or private providers, as they choose. Private firms are thus in competition with state bodies, and they receive a proportion of the benefits saved if a disabled person finds work through their placement services and achieves substantial earnings.[21]

Certain developments in the health field in Australia can be seen as the state indirectly withdraws from the direct provision of benefits and thus also can be classified as "privatization." In order to reduce expenditure on public health care in the long term the Australian government began offering tax incentives in January 1999 to those taking out private health insurance.[22] Since July 2000 favorable premiums have been offered under the *Lifetime Health Cover* program for those taking out insurance for treatment in private hospitals, and especially low premiums are guaranteed for life if they maintain their cover.[23]

On the subject of state and private benefit provision it should also be mentioned that it is sometimes called "privatization" when social security institutions encourage greater competition among benefit providers. From this perspective, "social security privatization" can thus derive from the relationship between social security institutions and benefit providers, not just from how the benefit providers are organized[24] (for the whole aspect of competition as privatization see section 4. below).

It can also be regarded as "social security privatization" when state authorities or public bodies make private suppliers responsible for administrative activities other than the provision of benefits. These would include a wide range of activities from accountancy to the collection of contributions. This sub-contracting—with the state always retaining responsibility in principle—can take various forms, such as works and services contracts.

Payment of Costs

Finally, social security can be organized "more privately" in that the state obliges private individuals or employers to directly pay costs that were previously (state/publicly) financed by taxes or social contributions. This situation is also sometimes called "social security privatization."

A very common form of "privatization" in the sense of the direct payment of costs by private *individuals* are higher co-payments in the health sector; on medicines, transport, etc.

In the Netherlands there is an extreme example of the transfer of costs to the *employer*. Since 1996 employers there have been required to make up the income lost by workers who fall ill; they have to pay 70 percent of the sick worker's wage for up to 52 weeks. This measure was introduced to reduce absenteeism, since it was assumed that employers were in a better position than the social funds to identify abuses. It also created a financial incentive for employers to take preventive measures in their own firms.[25]

"Privatization" in the payment of social security costs is not just limited to the health sector, as can be seen from the fact that employers in Algeria are now required to pay a proportion of family benefits, for which the state alone was responsible up to 1999.[26]

In the field of invalidity insurance, employers in the Netherlands have, since 1998, been allowed to pay invalidity benefits themselves, in other words to leave the state scheme. They themselves are able to take out their own private insurance to cover this.[27] This has given employers the option, but not a fundamental obligation, to pay their own benefits. Nevertheless, this too can be labeled as "social security privatization."

4. Possible Meanings of the Term Privatization as a Synonym for Other Terms

The wealth of meanings that the term privatization has in social security is further boosted by the fact that "privatization" is also sometimes used as a synonym for other expressions.

Competition and Market Mechanisms

"Privatization" is often used to mean the introduction of competition, the strengthening of competitive elements or the use of market mechanisms, probably originally as a result of economic theories which, for reasons of parsimony, equate state action with monopoly and private action with competition.

The terms "privatization" and "competition" are probably also used synonymously because certain situations can be viewed both from the point of view of a shift from "public" to "private" and from the point of view of the surrender of a monopoly and the introduction of competition. For example, the privatization of previously state-provided services under the USA's *Ticket to Work Program*, described earlier, can be seen as a partial withdrawal by the state and a shift from "public" to "private," and also as "opening up the market" and allowing competition in this field. The same applies for the co-existence of state and private pension insurance institutions or sickness funds where previously the state had a "monopoly," to take more general examples.

Taking the original equation one step further, as it were, it is sometimes even claimed that the main problem with "privatization" lies not in the contrast between "public or private," but in the dichotomy between "monopoly or competition," and the competition is just as likely to be between public institutions as between private institutions.[28]

This chapter cannot go into whether it really makes sense to call every increase in competition "privatization." The fact is that even the use of competitive instruments (such as reduced premiums and advertising campaigns) by national authorities or public social security institutions are sometimes classified as privatization. The same is true of the use of market mechanisms (such as tax and other incentives). In such cases privatization is seen as bringing the public sector closer to the private in terms of the approaches and instruments used.

Deregulation and Liberalization

Deregulation means the removal of state rules which directly interfere with competition; it mainly involves opening up markets by eliminating restrictions on access, and cutting down on state intervention.

If restrictions on market access are removed at international level, this is usually referred to as liberalization.[29]

The term "privatization" is also occasionally used in these two meanings, probably for similar reasons to those given earlier in connection with the term "competition."

Commercialization

Finally, the term "privatization" is quite often associated with a movement towards profit-making, in other words commercialization, particularly as many privatization processes involve a transition to profit-making.

On further consideration, however, the idea that "privatization" equals "commercialization" is usually rightly dismissed, since privatization does not necessarily involve a switch to profit-making.

For example, selling a hospital run on a nonprofit-making basis by a charity to a profit-making institution may well be commercialization, but it is not privatization. It is a transaction within the private sector.

5. Conclusions

As we have demonstrated, "privatization" is a rather blurred concept which merely serves as a pointer. "Social security privatization" has so many meanings because the starting points for privatization in this field vary so greatly from one context to another. The starting situation in each case is characterized by the existing division of responsibilities between the public and private sectors, by inherent taboo areas and by existing private elements at the level of institutions, administration and payment of costs. In addition, "social security privatization" can start on all these levels simultaneously or take place on just one sub-level. There are also interdependencies involved, in other words some privatization can, but do not have to, trigger others.

"Social security privatization" takes many different forms, and the term "privatization" means very different things in different contexts, not least because it is used as a synonym for other terms. So it is not surprising that discussions on privatization, particularly at international level, almost inevitably generate misunderstandings. The same term is being used, but to mean very different things.

Any debate on privatization will also probably be influenced by the observer's "ideological" viewpoint, since some people will see the privatization of social security as giving the individual greater freedom of choice and liberating him/her from the "nanny state," while others will see it as abandoning the individual in difficult circumstances.

Disagreements in discussions on privatization can certainly be defused if those involved spell out what they understand by "privatizing social security." However, this sometimes means having to explain very complex ideas. Giving an explanation will certainly be a lot more difficult than just pointing to a tree to identify the type one wants to plant.

Notes

1. The general meaning of the term privatization (not in relation to social security) is discussed in detail by Paul Starr, who sees it as an idea, a theory, rhetoric, political practice and policy movement: Paul Starr. 1988. "The Meaning of Privatization," *Yale Law and Policy Review*, No. 6, pp. 6-41.

2. ILO. 2000. *World Labour Report 2000: Income security and social protection in a changing world*, p. 29, Geneva, International Labour Office.

3. Deutscher Beamten Bund (DBB—German Civil Service Association), *DBB-Positionen, Verwaltung 2000, http://www.dbb.de/positionen/ verwaltung_2000_1.html.*

4. Laws, too, may provide information here (though they are usually more easily amended than constitutions). For example, in the United States there is a federal law requiring the states to have a state plan for child support and to set up a state authority to administer the plan. See Office of Child Support Enforcement, The Administration for Children and Families, Department of Health and Human Services, *A Guide to Developing Public-Private Partnerships in Child Support Enforcement*, Chapter 2: Privatization, Competition and Partnership; *http:// www.acf.dhhs.gov/programs/cse/rpt/pvt/ch2.htm.*

5. It should be stressed here that these are merely assumptions and that no statements can, of course, be made about what people actually associate with the term privatization.

6. A recent overview of this debate is given by Peter Abrahamson. 1999. "The Welfare Modelling Business," *Social Policy and Administration*, Vol. 33, No. 4, December, pp. 394-415.

7. It is even debatable whether the "market" is a public or private place. It is mainly economists who use the equations "state = public" and "market = private," whereas for sociologists and anthropologists examining cultural phenomena the market tends to be a public place. The market as well as politics are viewed, particularly when it comes to roles and gender relations, as being the antithesis of the private sphere of the family. See Starr, op.cit., for a broader discussion of these issues.

8. We cannot go into the reasons for privatizing social security in this essay. See, inter alia, on this subject Bernd von Maydell. 1999. "Privatisierung sozialer Sicherheit—Erscheinungsformen und Entwicklungsperspektiven," *Arbeit und Sozialpolitik*, No. 7-8, pp. 12-20.

9. ISSA. 1999. *Trends in Social Security*, No. 2, Geneva, International Social Security Association.

10. ISSA. 2000. *Trends in Social Security*, No. 1, Geneva, International Social Security Association.

11. ISSA. 1999. *Trends in Social Security*, No. 3, Geneva, International Social Security Association.

12. ISSA. 2000. *Trends in Social Security*, No. 2, Geneva, International Social Security Association.

13. ISSA. 2000. *Trends in Social Security*, No. 2, Geneva, International Social Security Association.

14. ISSA. 2000. *Trends in Social Security*, No. 3, Geneva, International Social Security Association.

15. Von Maydell, op.cit., p. 15.

16. Bernd Aichmann. 1998. "Pension insurance, health care, poverty alleviation: Recent developments in Latin America," *Developments and Trends in Social Security 1996-1998*, Geneva, International Social Security Association.

17. Andreas Hänlein. 2000. "Soziale und private Krankenversicherung—Konkurrenz und Konvergenz: Eine rechtsvergleichende Skizze," *Schweizerische Zeitschrift für Sozialversicherung und berufliche Vorsorge/ Revue suisse des assurances sociales et de la prévoyance professionnelle (SZS/RSAS)*, Vol. 44, pp. 214-231.

18. Xenia Scheil-Adlung. 1995. "Social Security for dependant persons in Germany and other countries: Between tradition and innovation," *International Social Security Review*, Vol. 48, No. 1, pp. 21-37.

19. Institute for International Research, *www.iir-technology.at/opensite4.html.*

20. ISSA. 2000. *Trends in Social Security*, No. 2, Geneva, International Social Security Association.

21. ISSA. 1999. 2000. *Trends in Social Security*, Nos. 1/1999 and 3/2000, Geneva, International Social Security Association.

22. ISSA. 1999. *Trends in Social Security*, No. 2, Geneva, International Social Security Association.

23. ISSA. 2000. *Trends in Social Security*, No. 3, Geneva, International Social Security Association.

24. See von Maydell, op.cit., p. 18.

25. Details of the measures contained in the Law on the employer's extended obligation to continue to pay wages in the event of illness (WULBZ) together with background information are given in *Trends in Social Security* No. 11/June 1996.

26. ISSA. 1999. *Trends in Social Security*, No. 2, Geneva, International Social Security Association.

27. Renée van Wirdum. 1998. "The context of change: Social security reform in the Netherlands," *International Social Security Review* (Worldview, Netherlands), Vol. 51, No. 4, pp. 93-103.

28. See, for example, Demetra Smith Nightingale/Nancy Pindus. 1998. *Privatization of Public Social Services: A Background Paper*, The Urban Institute, *http://www.urban.org/pubman/privitiz.html.*

29. Institute for International Research, *www.iir-technology.at/opensite4.htm.*

2

Privatization: More Individual Choice in Social Protection

M. Queisser

1. Introduction

Social protection policies in many countries around the world are undergoing a process of rapid change. Current arrangements are no longer regarded as adequate for the realities of today's labor markets, employment careers, family compositions and life-course designs. Increasing financial pressure on many social security systems is undermining the trust and confidence of the population in these systems, which in turn precipitates the decline of traditional social protection. In many countries, citizens are dissatisfied with the traditional package of social services and demanding a larger range of options from which to choose. Governments are exploring ways of increasing the efficiency of service delivery by introducing choice and competition into social protection while, at the same time, trying to ensure that this will not lead to an erosion of the level, coverage and distribution of social protection.

Extending individual choice does not necessarily mean individualization of rights or privatization of social protection. Choice can be offered at many different levels within existing systems of social protection. Individuals may be given the right to opt out completely from the social protection system, they may be free to choose the composition of their individual package of goods and services, or they may be offered a choice among different providers within a given menu. This chapter discusses the reasons why citizens and government may be interested in having more elements of individual choice in social protection. It examines whether more choice could lead to more efficient results and discusses the preconditions that individuals need to make informed choices as well as the implications for the role of the state.

2. Why Allow More Individual Choice?

Most systems of social protection are publicly organized and, in many countries, based on the principles of social insurance. The main reason for state intervention in social protection is information failure in insurance markets due to moral hazard and adverse selection. Moral hazard occurs when individuals have control over the probability that the insured event occurs. Private insurers may be unable to calculate a premium for such cases and insurance will thus not be available. Adverse selection is caused by a lack of information about the true individual risk which will result in insurance companies charging a uniform premium for all clients, thus making it impossible for a person with low risks to purchase insurance at an "actuarially fair" price. Mandatory social insurance enables risk pooling and the inclusion of risks that would be difficult or prohibitively expensive to insure in private insurance schemes. Compulsory membership is further justified by myopia: many individuals would not take out any insurance voluntarily but would still require some form of public assistance in cases of illness, old age or during spells of unemployment. Finally, most systems of social protection aim at "social solidarity" and redistribution of resources, which could not be achieved in a purely private system.

The first question to ask in exploring the issue of individual choice in social protection thus concerns its rationale: Why would governments be interested in allowing the individual more choice given the important reasons for government involvement in social protection? And why would consumers be interested in exercising more choice in social protection?

In the public debate, the different dimensions of individual choice are often not spelled out, leading to confusion and an unnecessary polarization of views along ideological lines. One dimension refers to individual choice within existing systems of social protection, for example, by mandating a certain level of protection but giving individuals the choice among different providers of services. This type of individual choice leaves the overall design of the system untouched and does not change the redistribution or solidarity elements of social protection. The other dimension relates to giving individuals the choice of opting out of the system. If such individual choice is allowed in systems which aim at redistribution, the net losers can be expected to opt out which will have both distributional effects and undermine the solidarity objectives of the system. In practice, however, the two dimensions of individual choice cannot always be clearly separated. Allowing individuals to partially opt out, for example, affects both dimensions.

Advocates of opting out often see individual choice as an end in itself and usually equate choice with market solutions. In this view, individuals should be free to choose from private markets as the market is the most efficient, self-adjusting information system for matching demands and supplies.[1] Further, they emphasize the problems of decision-making in public administrations. Social protection institutions in many countries are governed by tripartite bodies, which are supposed to represent the interests of all parties engaged in the provision and consumption of social protection. In practice, however, these bodies may not properly represent the interests of individuals and decisions may be taken on the grounds of other motivations, such as maximization of budgets, power considerations, or self-interest of the concerned bureaucrats.[2]

Advocates of individual choice within existing systems argue that choice may be employed as an instrument to improve efficiency in the production of social services. Citizens are demanding more diversified and sophisticated services from government. Meanwhile, public debt and fiscal imbalances limit governments' room to maneuver. One option for coping with those difficulties is enhancing the role of private and nonprofit sectors and focussing more closely on the needs of citizens as clients, in terms of efficiency, effectiveness and quality of service.[3] Allowing public sector activities to be contested by other providers may also lead to quality improvements and cost reductions. Thus, giving individuals the option of partially exiting the systems and purchasing services from private providers may increase the responsiveness of a system. Policy-makers would be alerted to changing needs of the population more quickly and able to react. Transferring full responsibility to the market would not be necessary.

A better responsiveness of social protection systems may also be achieved by other means, for example using "voice" rather than "exit" mechanisms. Customer surveys, monitoring and evaluation of satisfaction with the services provided and increased empowerment and involvement of the clients in the administration of services could be an alternative to transferring more responsibility to the individual and to the private sector. Thus, a careful evaluation of the merits and demerits of introducing elements of individual choice in social protection is required.

Approaching the extension of individual choice from a consumer perspective, the following dimensions of choice can be distinguished:

- Volume/level: People may want to consume (and thus pay for) more or less social protection.

Social protection systems which offer high levels of benefits or packages of services and accordingly charge high contribution or tax rates may force individuals to devote more of their resources to social protection than they wish. This constraining nature of compulsory systems is particularly clear-cut in systems with little or no redistribution, such as retirement schemes with a very close link between contributions and benefits. Allowing individual choice above a determined minimum level enables people to make other provisions, for example investing in housing or education rather than spending their money on pensions or health insurance. Especially for lower-income households such freedom to choose may be important. Increases in take-home pay through lower contribution rates have a larger impact on their ability to choose other goods and services than for higher-income households.

- Products: People may want to consume different products and services according to their preferences.

Traditional social protection systems provide citizens with a set menu of standard, universal products and services. This supply may not correspond to peoples' needs or preferences any longer in the light of economic and social changes. In some cases, policy makers and service providers may not be aware of changes in preferences and demand. Giving people the possibility of making their own decisions can reveal such shifts in preferences. Assuming that providers—public or private—will react to new demand, individual choice will lead to the supply of previously not offered products and expansion of the standard menu to a wider range of options.

- Pattern: People may want to buy and consume social protection at different paces and different moments over their life-course.

Most existing systems of social protection assume that people demand certain products and services in certain phases and circumstances of their lives. As changes take place in people's life-course and career designs as well as in family structures, consumption patterns change and different types and levels of social protection are demanded at different stages of the life cycle.

From a state/government perspective, there is an interest to allow more individual choice for the following reasons:

- Volume/level of provision: Save resources by providing only a basic level for all and avoiding "overprovision."

Financial pressure on social protection systems is increasing due to demographic trends and labor market changes, particularly in the areas of pensions and health care. Governments in many countries are looking at ways to reduce the levels of publicly mandated schemes in order to reduce or at least stabilize payroll taxes and public subsidies to these systems. Reducing mandated public provision of social protection to a basic level and leaving the remainder to the individual enables governments to alleviate the pressure on existing systems.

- Efficiency of provision: Improve product/service quality by letting consumers choose products and providers.

Governments have an interest in increasing the efficiency of social protection and may therefore want to introduce *contestability* in the provision of social protection. Under pressure to do more with less, they can make more effective use of the networks and skills of non--government organizations. Existing products and services may be produced and offered at lower cost and/or the quality of products and services may be improved at constant costs. Competition could be introduced between public and private providers, exclusively between private providers in a fully privatized system or also between different public providers.

- Targeting: Use individual choice to focus public provision on the most vulnerable groups.

Letting individuals opt out of existing systems can reveal economic differences between the various groups of clients and thus help to identify the most vulnerable groups of society. If the provision of services is scaled down in the public systems and opting out of the systems is made possible, it is likely that only the poorer groups will remain in the public systems. Public resources for social protection can then be reallocated to them. In the context of increasing financial pressure on social budgets, this can help governments to target social protection towards the most vulnerable groups. At the same time, however, the pooling of poorer clients, i.e.,, "bad risks" in the terminology of insurance, risks undermining the functioning of solidarity-based social insurance systems.

From the perspective of service providers, the interest in giving individuals more choice is straightforward: Private companies enter the market to make profits; in the case of nonprofit organizations such as mutual insurance companies, co-operatives or charity organizations, responsiveness to their clients' or constituency's needs would be the primary interest. Public providers, on the other hand, might be less interested in giving their clients a choice to opt out or turn to other providers since the competition from private providers could endanger their existence.

3. Regulating Individual Choice

Offering more individual choice in existing systems of social protection means that the state moves from being the main or even exclusive provider of social protection to being one of several providers. It also means that the government has to take on the additional role of regulating and supervising the other providers in the market. Best practices and guidelines for regulatory reforms have been developed by the OECD for several sectors, such as telecommunications, financial services or electricity.[4] Taking into account these guidelines, several implications and responsibilities for the role of government can be identified:

- First, it needs to be determined what the adequate level of mandatory basic protection should be and what part of the current benefit package constitutes "overprovision" and should thus be opened to individual choice.

- Second, the appropriate rules of the game need to be established and the roles and responsibilities of the various actors need to be defined clearly.

- Third, the government has a responsibility to ensure that all players have access to reliable and independent information.

- Fourth, it needs to be determined to what extent the government will assume the role of the guarantor of last resort over and above any mandated basic level of social provision.

The definition of what the level of basic mandatory participation in public systems should be depends on value judgements of the society concerned and is subject to a political decision. The basic participation can be defined in different ways. Governments may offer a universal basic protection level to the population and leave everything beyond this to individual choice. They may define income thresholds above which individuals may opt out of public systems partially or completely. Or they may allow individual choice only for certain dimensions of social protection, such as the administration of service provision, and leave the overall level of mandated protection uniform for all participants of the system.

Once the areas and degrees of individual choice have been defined, the question of appropriate government regulation arises. In most countries, there is a broad consensus that social protection should not be left entirely to market forces. Markets can only be expected to produce an efficient outcome if there are no public goods, no external effects nor increasing returns to scale.[5] If any of these conditions is violated, government interventions may be able to improve efficiency. In the social sectors, government intervention is primarily justified by the existence of public goods (e.g., public health) and external effects (e.g., vaccination programs, reduction of air and water pollution). Intervention can take the forms of regulation, financing or public production of goods and services. All of these measures directly interfere with the market mechanism. A fourth, more indirect form of intervention consists of income transfers from the state to the clients that they can then use to purchase goods and services produced in the market.

4. Information and Empowerment

A basic and general requirement for individual choice is that people understand what their options are and what the consequences of alternative choices are likely to be. This means that the individual must have access to information on products and services that is comprehensive, comprehensible and, most importantly, reliable. The customer cannot assess, for example, the quality of medical services or the financial soundness of an insurance company. Individual choice thus has to be made on the basis of trust in the government's ability to regulate and supervise the providers. Building a framework of trust is thus an important task for governments as they involve the markets more in social protection. As will be discussed below, some governments also use guarantees as an instrument to build trust and confidence in private providers and thereby encourage individuals to make use of the choices offered.

But while transparency of product and service information is usually sufficient for people to make informed choices in markets for consumer goods, such as food, televisions, or cars, choices in social protection are far more difficult to make, even if the range of options is clearly understood. This is due to the fact that most individuals cannot easily assess risks, particularly as far as decisions on health care and retirement provision are concerned. Such decisions have to be made over a long time horizon and are costly, sometimes even impossible, to reverse. Even in a well-regulated environment, individuals will be uncertain with respect to both the future evolution of the quality and price of the product or service purchased and the extent of their future needs.[6]

Providing transparent and reliable information is not an easy task. Sometimes, the information necessary for adequate functioning of the market simply does not exist. In the absence of accurate information providers will base their pricing on estimates which may or may not turn out to be correct. One such example of consistent errors is the mortality assumptions used by life insurance companies in many countries. As increases in longevity turn out to be much higher than assumed, life insurance companies are forced to increase their premiums and adjust the benefits. Insurance companies' pricing policies at market entry also influence premium evolution. In a system where individual choice is newly allowed, there is both a lack of information and a tendency of companies to offer below-market rates to attract new business; inevitably, rates will have to be adjusted later. Individuals who chose to opt out of the public system can suddenly be confronted with conditions under which opting out would have been less beneficial than remaining in the public system.

Moderate increases of premiums are part of the risk that individuals chose to take and thus have to bear. But strong and unforeseen increases of premiums may seriously jeopardize the effectiveness of social protection to a point where governments may feel obliged to intervene, particularly in systems which rely predominantly on private sector provision. In public insurance systems, premium, i.e., contribution rate, adjustments are subject to the political process and are usually undertaken more gradually than in private insurance companies. In public systems, governments can decide to distribute the financial burden of rate adjustments among different groups of the population and among several generations by using different ways of financing necessary revenue increases. Private insurance companies are likely to do this only to a very limited extent. The question then arises how governments should react to price increases in the private sector. Should there be limits on increases and how would such caps or other regulatory measures affect the private insurance companies' ability to operate?

5. Monitoring Process and Outcomes

Another important issue that is subject to considerable debate, is the question of government guarantees. To what extent should the state seek to protect individuals beyond the mandated basic minimum? There is broad agreement that governments should try to devise mechanisms to prevent failure of process by monitoring providers and intervening in cases where providers are violating the rules of the game. The rules of the game are laid down in the regulatory and supervisory framework. If a government decides to introduce market elements into the system of social protection, it needs to ensure that real competition between providers takes place. Public monopolies should not be replaced with cartels of private providers as this may result in a situation where consumers pay even higher costs for the same products and services. Regulation should also seek to limit the potential for so-called "cream-skimming" among providers as much as possible, i.e., there should be no incentives for providers to discriminate in favor of those consumers who are judged to be the "best risks" in an insurance sense of the term. Regulation and supervision have to be designed in a way to prevent, detect and sanction fraudulent behavior of the various players engaged in the market.[7]

More problematic is how to deal with failure of outcome. What happens when people make bad choices? Should government limit the choices available to exclude bad ones as much as possible or will such interventions distort the markets in a way that efficiency is severely affected? Should additional safety nets, for example through reinsurance or guarantee funds, be introduced to help individuals who find themselves with inadequate protection because they chose a high-risk strategy?

This dilemma is encountered particularly in the pensions sector. For example, in the United Kingdom, the issue became relevant in the context of pensions mis-selling. When contracting out of the public earnings-related pension scheme in exchange for personal pensions was introduced, the financial sector was judged to be sophisticated and safe enough. But the providers of financial services entered into a fierce competition for customers. They used high-pressure sales tactics to convince participants of occupational schemes, older workers and other persons for whom their existing arrangements were more beneficial to switch to inappropriate personal pension plans. The government decided to undo the "bad choices" of individuals by obliging financial service providers to compensate individuals for the losses. The assessment of who was to be compensated was based on whether it would have been better for people to stay in their occupational scheme rather than opt for a personal pension. Thus, despite giving workers individual choice, the government ended up determining which choices were good choices for which group of people. Other countries have learnt from this experience and dealt with this problem by imposing minimum rate-of-return guarantees on pension funds or regulating in detail which assets the private funds may invest in. There is debate, however, whether such guarantees lead to distortions of the market and will result in much less efficient outcomes.

Notes

1.   See Nozick, R. 1974. *Anarchy, State and Utopia*, Oxford: Hayek, F. von. 1960. *The Constitution of Liberty*, Chicago; and Friedman, M. 1962. *Capitalism and Freedom*, Chicago.
2.   See Downs, A. 1957. *An Economic Theory of Democracy*, New York; Tullock, G. 1970. *Private Wants and Public Means*, New York; and Niskanen, W. 1971. *Democracy and Representative Government*, Chicago.
3.   See OECD. 1999. *A Caring World: The New Social Policy Agenda*, Paris.

4.   See OECD. 1997a. *The OECD Report on Regulatory Reform: Summary*, Paris.
5.   See Barr, N. 1998. *The Economics of the Welfare State*, Oxford.
6.   See Arrow, K. 1963. "Uncertainty and the welfare economic of medical care," *American Economic Review*, No. 53, pp. 941-73.
7.   See OECD. 1997a. *The OECD Report on Regulatory Reform: Summary*, Paris; and 1997b. "Best Practice Guidelines for Contracting-Out Government Services,"*PUMA Policy Brief*, Paris.

Bibliography

Adema, W. 1999. "Net Social Expenditure," *OECD Labour Market and Social Policy Occasional Papers*, No. 39, Paris.

Arrow, K. 1963. "Uncertainty and the welfare economic of medical care,"*American Economic Review*, No. 53, pp. 941-73.

Barr, N. 1998. *The Economics of the Welfare State*, Oxford.

—. 1992. "Economic Theory and the Welfare State: A Survey and Interpretation," *Journal of Economic Literature*, Vol. XXX, pp. 741-803.

Casey, B. 1998. "Mandating private pensions--the public finance implications," *International Social Security Review*, No. 4, pp. 57-70.

Considine, M. 1999. "Markets, Networks and the New Welfare State: Employment Assistance Reforms in Australia,"*Journal of Social Policy*, Vol. 28, No. 2, pp. 183-203.

Downs, A. 1957.*An Economic Theory of Democracy*, New York.

Fay, R. 1997. "Making the public employment service more effective through the introduction of market signals," *Labour Market and Social Policy, OECD Occasional Papers*, No. 25, Paris.

Friedman, M. 1962. *Capitalism and Freedom*, Chicago.

Green paper. 1998. "A New Contract of Welfare: Partnership in Pensions," London.

Hayek, F. von. 1960. *The Constitution of Liberty*, Chicago.

Hirshman, A. 1981. *Essays in Trespassing, Economics to Politics and Beyond*, London.

Legrand, J. and Bartlett, W. 1993. *Quasi-markets in Social Policy*, London.

Lowenstein, G. 1999. "Costs and Benefits of Health- and Retirement-Related Choice," *Paper prepared for the Eleventh Annual Conference of the National Academy of Social Insurance*, 27–28 January.

Murthi, M.; Orszag, J.M. and Orszag, P. 1999. "The Charge Ratio on Individual Accounts: Lessons from the U.K. experience,"*Birkbeck College Working Paper 99-2*, London.

National Academy of Social Insurance. 1998. *Report of the Panel on Privatization of Social Security*, Washington, D.C.

Niskanen, W. 1971. *Democracy and Representative Government*, Chicago.

Nozick, R. 1974. *Anarchy, State and Utopia*, Oxford.

OECD. 1997a. *The OECD Report on Regulatory Reform: Summary*, Paris.

—. 1997b. "Best Practice Guidelines for Contracting-Out Government Services," *PUMA Policy Brief*, Paris.

—. 1999. *A Caring World: The New Social Policy Agenda*, Paris.

Taylor-Gooby, P. 1999. "Markets and Motives, Trust and Egoism in Welfare Markets," *Journal of Social Policy*, Vol. 28, No. 1, pp. 97-114.
Tullock, G. 1970. *Private Wants and Public Means*, New York.

3

Africa: Implications of Privatization Measures Initiated by International Financing Organizations

T. Butare

1. Social Security Systems in Africa

As a general rule, social security schemes in Africa, most of which were established between 1960 and 1965, cover only that part of the population in the formal sector of the economy, which in most of the countries of the African continent accounts for less than 20 percent of the active population. The majority of workers in those countries belong to the informal urban sector or the traditional agricultural sector, where they engage in subsistence activities, in isolation from organized structures and established social protection systems.[1]

The extension of social protection to sectors not yet covered has for many years encountered difficulties of various kinds. The principal difficulty relates to the fact that incomes generated in those sectors are low and difficult to measure; this further aggravates the delicate nature of designing a form of social security contribution for persons in those sectors. It is easy to imagine that workers in those sectors, faced with a proposal for membership in a social security scheme, will inevitably refer energetically to their short-term needs, pointing out that they can hardly satisfy the priorities essential for survival.

The other problems faced by African countries in the field of social security are, as regards the sectors already covered, linked to the difficulty of collecting contributions, to deficient skills in the various fields of specialization in social security management, as well as the insufficient use of actuarial analyses as a decision-making tool.

Today many social security schemes in sub-Saharan Africa are experiencing increasing difficulties of an administrative and financial nature which are threatening to jeopardize their very existence. Reforms are thus urgently necessary. One approach to the needed reforms, relating specifically to pension regimes, consists of setting up structures within which the public retirement schemes would confine themselves to paying small uniform benefits, leaving the responsibility for payment of the earnings-related part of pensions to private commercial pension funds within defined-contribution compulsory savings systems.[2] In the following two sections we shall examine the debate on privatization in Africa, beginning with a study of the impact of privatization measures falling within the overall framework of structural adjustment programs, and then turning to questions relating to the total or partial privatization of social security systems.

2. Structural Adjustment Programs: Their Objectives and Impact

Since the beginning of the 1980s most countries in Africa, and particularly those south of the Sahara, have been introducing macroeconomic reforms as part of structural adjustment programs. Reforms had become necessary following severe and damaging shocks of external origin (deterioration of terms of trade, rises in real interest rates on debts contracted, etc.). The principal origin of those shocks was the second leap in oil prices and the ensuing recession in the industrialized countries; they plunged many African countries into a state of lasting economic crisis.

It can be stated that, all in all, the period 1960-1980 was marked by a high rate of economic expansion and the consolidation of state authority and the machinery of government. To finance their development the countries with prosperous economies secured credit facilities from private, bilateral and multilateral lenders. During those two decades the ratio of debt to gross national product (GNP) averaged approximately 47 percent—still an acceptable situation.[3] During that period the production sector was dominated by publicly-owned enterprises, which had been established in considerable numbers and were creating large numbers of jobs as a result of the investment they were receiving.

In a number of countries in the region the implementation of structural adjustment policies began at the start of the 1980s in a general context of relative economic stagnation in a long-term perspective, permanent indebtedness and rapid population and urban growth. By the end of the 1980s the level of indebtedness in some countries exceeded that of GNP. With the help of the IMF and the World Bank, no less than 240 stabilization and adjustment programs were launched in Africa between 1980 and 1989.[4]

The initial phase in the adjustment process for countries undertaking reforms of this type is generally the restoration of the major equilibria (budget equilibrium, equilibrium in the balance of payments). The next stage consists of structural adjustment programs as such, the aim of which is to reform the relative prices system and the incentives structure in order to set the economy once again on the road to competitiveness and growth. The general framework for economic recovery favored by the international financing institutions for the implementation of these programs is one of regulation by the market and openness to the international economy.

The "social dimension" of adjustment was introduced some time later. The avowed purpose of this new dimension is the protection of the most vulnerable groups and the introduction of measures to compensate groups affected by the adjustment process. In addition, a certain measure of attention to institutional aspects and aspects of governance has been observed recently. However, it must be made clear that, notwithstanding these initial moves to take into account social aspects and questions of governance, the principal aim of the programs initiated by the IMF and the World Bank is to seek the macro-economic stability which will provide the preconditions for an environment favorable to growth. This means that only limited resources are devoted to social programs, because a maximum of resources must be invested in projects designed to accelerate economic growth.

The principal measures to be taken within the framework of structural adjustments affecting public enterprises have frequently consisted of privatization of those which still appear economically viable and, in certain cases, their rehabilitation or closure.

Until now the implementation of structural adjustment measures, and in particular those involving disengagement of the state from enterprises deemed to be unprofitable, or the penalization of the latter, has led to a fall in employment in the formal sector as a result of staff reductions or closures. The consequence has been a reduction in the volume of contributions collected by the social security institutions, which thus suffer a drop in their principal source of income. The combined effect of the fall in the total volume of contributions and the increase in life expectancy aggravates still further the difficulty of maintaining financial stability in medium- and long-term pension schemes. Furthermore, in a considerable number of countries the reserves of social security institutions have sometimes been wiped out as a result of liquidations of banks following economic restructuring or in loans made by the state and never repaid.[5]

As regards the ongoing process of globalization, it can be said that from the very beginning the African countries have been determined to participate in order not to remain marginalized. To promote exports and to attract more direct foreign investment these countries are endeavoring to improve their international competitiveness by adopting new structural adjustment programs and even, in certain cases, establishing free zones for the production of exportable manufactured goods.

In some cases the pressure exercised by the search for competitiveness leads to attempts to reduce labor costs, sometimes by noncompliance with certain labor standards or by reducing social security benefits and coverage. The reasoning behind the latter method is that compulsory employer contributions increase production costs and thus constitute an obstacle to optimum performance. This approach leads to a situation in which countries might be tempted to reduce the scale of social security in order to attract foreign firms. It must, however, be pointed out that the relationship between social security costs and productivity is highly complex and difficult to determine. But it can also be observed that in many cases international investors do not seek to study the true nature of that relationship but rather let themselves be guided by the manner in which they perceive social security costs in the country concerned; they also consider the level of social security to be a measure of the bargaining power of the workers.[6]

Another remark which may be made about globalization is that it makes for convergence of economic policies throughout the world. Emphasis is laid on competitiveness and the liberalization of markets—and especially capital markets—a scaling-down of state intervention in the economy, the privatization of a wide range of enterprises and the reduction of public expenditure (which frequently implies cuts in social services). The difference, where African countries are concerned, is that these changes are often the result of pressures from international creditors applied through the instrument of structural adjustment programs.

It must also be pointed out that the social consequences of reforms based on the free play of markets have so far been extremely negative for the populations of the African countries. As a rule the primary incomes of the poor have declined, the numbers of persons living below the poverty line have increased and access to public services and social security benefits has lessened. Moreover, measures taken to protect the poor and the vulnerable from the worst aspects of adjustment never reach all the poor and usually do not even reach the majority of them.[7]

3. Aspects Relating to the Privatization of Social Security Systems

In addition to the fact that privatization measures in various sectors of the economy form an integral part of structural adjustment measures with, as explained earlier, significant indirect repercussions in the field of social security, voices are being raised—particularly that of the World Bank—explicitly arguing that the method of organization of social security based on the social insurance principle is now obsolete and should be replaced by a system more conducive to growth (World Bank, 1994). In a number of parts of the world, including Africa, the question is thus being asked as to whether consideration might be given to introducing into the social protection system of a country certain elements based on private enterprise side by side with a basic scheme of a public type.[8]

The argument generally advanced in support of an enhanced role for the private sector in the area of social protection rests primarily on the need to improve management. However, it should be observed that there is a priori no reason why a public service should not function just as well as a private one, especially in the social sphere, provided that there is a genuine will to rationalize management.

The difficulty of collecting contributions experienced by many African institutions managing public social security schemes is also a problem which has led some people to think that the task might be carried out more efficiently by the private sector; but here again, there is as yet no empirical evidence supporting this assumption.

As for the argument that the privatization of pension systems would permit the development of capital markets and thus be beneficial to growth, one observation which may be made on the subject is that such a step would lead many countries into an impasse on account of the lack of professional expertise in the techniques of market regulation.

It thus appears, in the light of the difficulty of finding a theoretical basis to support a change in the status of social security systems from that of public institutions to one of partially or completely privatized structures, and in the absence of any significant and conclusive empirical observations relating to successes observed in other fields and in similar conditions, that the arguments in favor of privatization rest on essentially ideological bases.

In résumé, and generally speaking, it may be said that the choice between public and private administration rests on a range of value judgments rather than on a clear and unequivocal choice between two situations, one of them being more advantageous than the other. One of these judgments involves expressing a preference for the state as a regulator rather than as an administrator or vice versa. In African countries in particular, where only limited expertise in the field of market regulation is available, direct administration by the state seems simpler and more manageable. But it may also be the case that private enterprises such as insurance companies or pension management firms are the only institutions to possess expertise in fields such as record-keeping over long periods or investment portfolio management. The challenge thus consists of finding the "right" functions to be assigned to each type of management (public or private), bearing in mind both needs and the resources available.[9]

4. The Socioeconomic Context and the Future of Social Security in Africa

Recourse to structural adjustment programs and the situations of worsening poverty and deterioration of social protection systems in

Africa resulting from the implementation of those programs cannot be fully described without reference to the general outlines of the development policies followed in most countries on the African continent since the 1960s. The most frequently held opinion at the time was that the modern sector of the economy would continue to absorb an ever-increasing proportion of the economically active population, with the result that from the outset very little interest and investment were directed toward the traditional agricultural sector and the urban informal sector. Initially the modern urban sector experienced a measure of development, and for twenty years or so no major problems arose.[10]

As a result of the combined effects of a high rate of population growth, the inadequacy of existing educational facilities, the economic crisis which began towards the end of the 1970s in a context of large-scale migration of young people from the rural areas into the towns and other factors, the absorption capacity of the modern sector was soon overwhelmed, and many African countries entered the spiral of indebtedness and structural adjustment programs. The jobs created up to then by the modern sector and covered by formal social protection systems were only sufficient in number to provide employment for a small proportion (generally less than 20 percent) of the economically active population; and, for the reasons already mentioned, in many sub-Saharan countries of Africa the situation has still not improved.

Moreover, according to some sources, between 1980 and 1995 economic performance in the wake of the implementation of adjustment programs was frequently characterized by a fall in GNP *per capita*, stagnation of exports and direct foreign investment and a decline in public-sector employment which was not offset by the creation of jobs in the formal private sector. The result was that in most parts of sub-Saharan Africa the informal sector of the economy increased in size.[11] This relative decline in formal employment also means that the proportion of the economically active population with access to social security benefits has decreased since the beginning of the 1980s; and the levels of performance observed during the last five years seem unlikely to have brought about any improvement in this situation.

The survey of the economic situation in Africa prepared in 1999 states that since 1996 GDP has, on the average, been rising faster than the population, in contrast to the situation during the previous fifteen years.[12] This is certainly gratifying news. However, the report goes on to say that, generally speaking, growth has created few jobs and is precarious, inasmuch as it is based on a process of stabilization requiring cuts in public expenditure which should have served to develop human capital and institutions necessary for sustainable growth.

These considerations naturally lead us to speculate on what types of reforms should be introduced in order to achieve growth established on a viable basis, i.e., lasting growth during which there would be a sustained increase in the numbers of suitable jobs and in social protection.

One of the principal defects in the reforms introduced under structural adjustment programs is that those reforms focus excessively on cuts in public expenditure, leaving little room for policies concerning improvement of the use of skills and capacities, which are more complex. Policies of this kind in fact require greater knowledge of the economy and more thought on the question of the sequencing of the instruments of adjustment policies should be introduced and the conception of measures specific to individual countries which must be taken into account during the stabilization phase; this would subsequently permit an improvement in the utilization of capacities and skills. One cannot help thinking that some countries should have made every effort to improve their infrastructures and their production capacities during the years in which their economies were expanding (1960-1980); they might thus have been able to escape the experience of painful reforms.

One area of capacity in which inequalities deleterious to growth are frequently observed is that resulting from investment in education and training. It is generally recognized that inequalities with regard to knowledge and information problems, the two often coexisting, have a considerable negative impact on development; that impact is likely to become much more severe as the process of globalization advances. The struggle against social exclusion and inequalities in education and training also presupposes that greater heed be given to the needs and possibilities of the urban informal sector and the rural sector, these being the sectors which have suffered most from the harmful effects of the crisis and the absence of social protection.

Unfortunately, the outlook in the area of social protection for the next ten to twenty years appears far from bright for many African countries, in which the average annual population growth rate is 3 percent and job creation is still insufficient.[13] To maintain the percentage of the working population currently covered by compulsory social security schemes, the number of workers covered would have to rise at an annual rate of 3 percent. But in present circumstances employment in the formal sector is actually declining. This highlights the urgent need for major reforms which, rather than focusing primarily on a search for economic efficiency based on the market and the private sector, would also leave adequate room for the rehabilitation of public services catering to the most disadvantaged groups and for the reinforcement of certain forms of solidarity.

It is widely recognized that in many African countries there exists an informal system of collective solidarity which, together with a high incidence of poverty, gives individuals little incentive to enter voluntarily a system offering social insurance for the long term. This explains the relative insignificance of schemes offering voluntary private insurance against long-term risks in African countries and justifies the importance attached in a number of countries to solidarity-based compulsory collective protection systems of various kinds. It might also be said that, because the solidarity principle is still held in high regard in societies, particularly in Africa, during the last few years countries such as Nigeria, Ghana and Tanzania have replaced their former provident fund schemes by compulsory defined benefit schemes based on the solidarity principle.

Another current trend in Africa is that several countries are studying means of extending social security coverage to the great majority of the labor force currently excluded from coverage. In addition, increasing attention is being given to the improvement of administrative performance in social security institutions, to the strengthening of skill training in the different specialist branches of social security management, to the establishment of suitable statistical tools permitting reliable management forecasting and to more regular use of actuarial analyses as an auxiliary decision-making tool.

The foregoing broadly outlines a series of measures which have the potential to bring considerable benefits to the African peoples if the economic recovery becomes firmly established and can be maintained on a solid basis. In the view of the author, these measures could be complementary together with the privatization of certain functions of social security systems with a view to enhancing performance. However, privatization does not appear to be a necessary precondition for the introduction or the success of these measures. Whether or not such privatization would make a significant positive contribution would depend on the specific situation in any given country.

Notes

1. See Gruat, J.-V. 1990. "Social security schemes in Africa. Current trends and problems," *International Labour Review*, Vol. 129, No. 4, pp. 495-422; and Butare, Th. 1998b. *Secteur traditionnel et moderne dans un processus de développement*, Geneva and Cambridge, Mass. INU Press (exists in French only).
2. See World Bank. 1994. *Averting the old age crisis: Policies to protect the old and promote growth*, New York, Oxford University Press.
3. See ILO. 2000a. *Réflexions sur les stratégies de réforme de la protection sociale en Afrique francophone du Sud du Sahara*, Geneva (exists in French only).
4. The book by van der Hoeven and van der Geist (1999) contains detailed information on the nature and scope of the adjustment measures implemented in Kenya, Malawi, Uganda, Zambia and Zimbabwe. Reference may also be made to the paper produced by Hugon and Pagès (1998) on the cases of the French-speaking countries of West Africa and the study by Butare (1993) on Ghana and Mauritius.
5. See ISSA. 1994. "The impact of structural adjustment programmes on social security in African countries," *African series, Social Security Documentation*, No. 15, Geneva.
6. See ILO. 2000b. *Reflections on reform strategies for social protection in English-speaking African countries*, Geneva.
7. See UNRISD. 1995. "Adjustment, globalization and social development," International Seminar on Economic Restructuring and Social Policy, 11-13 January, New York.
8. The ISSA has produced a number of studies on aspects relating to the privatization of social security systems in Africa. In particular, the subject was placed on the agenda of the meeting organized for directors of social security institutions in English-speaking Africa, held in Kampala on 19-21 August 1997 (ISSA, 1998).
9. For a detailed analysis of the manner in which these questions are approached in the context of pensions systems, see for example Butare (1998a) or ILO (2000b).
10. See Butare (1998b) for a relatively comprehensive critical analysis of this development strategy and the interactions between the modern and the informal sectors which must be taken into account.
11. See van der Hoeven, R., and van der Geist, W. 1999. *Adjustment, employment and missing institutions in Africa*, Oxford, James Currey Ltd.
12. Economic Commission for Africa, United Nations. 1999. "Economic Survey of Africa, 1998," Addis Ababa.
13. ILO. 2000a. *Réflexions sur les stratégies de réforme de la protection sociale en Afrique francophone du Sud du Sahara*, Geneva (exists in French only).

Bibliography

Butare, Th. 1993. "Ajustement structurel, croissance et réduction de la pauvreté en Afrique subsaharienne," *PECTA working paper*, Addis Ababa, ILO (exists in French only).

—. 1998a. "Social needs and the role of governments and markets; the case of retirement pensions," *International Social Security Review*, Vol. 51, No. 3, pp. 37-62.

—. 1998b. *Secteur traditionnel et moderne dans un processus de développement*, Geneva and Cambridge, Mass. INU Press (exists in French only).

Gruat, J.-V. 1990. "Social security schemes in Africa. Current trends and problems," *International Labour Review*, Vol. 129, No. 4, pp. 495-422.

Hoeven, R. van der, and Geist, W. van der. 1999. *Adjustment, employment and missing institutions in Africa*, Oxford, James Currey Ltd.

Hugon, Ph., and Pagès, N. 1998. "Ajustement structurel, emploi et rôle des partenaires sociaux en Afrique francophone," *Cahiers de l'emploi et de la formation*, No. 28, Geneva, ILO (exists in French only).

ILO. 2000a. *Réflexions sur les stratégies de réforme de la protection sociale en Afrique francophone du Sud du Sahara*, Geneva (exists in French only).

—. 2000b. *Reflections on reform strategies for social protection in English-speaking African countries*, Geneva.

ISSA. 1994. "The impact of structural adjustment programmes on social security in African countries," *African series, Social Security Documentation*, No. 15, Geneva.

—. 1998. "Social security issues in English-speaking African countries," *African series, Social Security Documentation*, No. 19, Geneva.

United Nations Economic Commission for Africa. 1999. "Economic Survey of Africa, 1998," Addis Ababa.

UNRISD. 1995. "Adjustment, globalization and social development," International Seminar on Economic Restructuring and Social Policy, 11-13 January, New York.

World Bank. 1994. *Averting the old age crisis: Policies to protect the old and promote growth*, New York, Oxford University Press.

Part 2

Privatization: An Organizing Principle
for Financing Social Security

4

The Case for Funded, Individual Accounts in Pension Reform

R. Holzmann and R. Palacios

1. Introduction

The trend toward including individual accounts as part of the mandatory pension system continues unabated. Nine Latin American countries have introduced individual accounts (Chile, Peru, Argentina, Colombia, Uruguay, Bolivia, Mexico, El Salvador and Nicaragua) and several more are preparing to do so (Ecuador, Dominican Republic). A similar trend has emerged in Europe where the former socialist countries are taking the lead: Hungary, Kazakhstan, Latvia and Poland have already passed reform legislation and many others including Croatia, Estonia, Macedonia, Romania and the Ukraine are preparing their own versions. There is also movement in this direction in Western Europe, even in countries with large, state-defined benefit plans like Sweden. Several Asian versions of the individual accounts strategy are also emerging, ranging from the gradual liberalization of Singapore's Central Provident Fund to Hong Kong's new, employer-based, defined contribution scheme. In fact, reforms that assign an important role to individual accounts are being discussed in dozens of countries in every region of the world.

Some observers consider such a reform approach as a shift away from a social insurance concept, and the tacit solidarity across and within generations. A discussion about individual accounts versus social insurance has recently taken center stage again in the U.S. with the proposals to replace part of the existing unfunded, defined benefit scheme with prefunded, defined contribution accounts. But in many ways, the U.S. discussion is of little relevance for most countries. The fiscal sustainability problem pales in comparison to most other advanced economies, coverage is practically universal and private pensions are well developed and play a healthy role in that country's capital markets. Contribution rates for pensions in many European and even a large number of developing countries are double those in the U.S. In short, the potential social and economic gains of systemic reform are much greater in the rest of the world. This is especially true in poor countries, where the costs and inequities of "traditional" public pension schemes have led to their demise and low credibility.

This brief note states the broad arguments for individual accounts.[1] The structure of the chapter is as follows: section 2 provides some needed clarification on "individual accounts," section 3 outlines the main arguments for individual accounts while section 4 concludes.

2. Some Clarifications about Individual Accounts

In the popular pension discussion, "individual accounts" are often used as short hand for funded, privately managed, defined-contribution type pension arrangements. However, this can be misleading since each of the main characteristics of a mandated pension system—benefit type, financing and management—can be combined in essentially any form and often are. Of the eight possible combinations shown in Table 4.1, the two cases not found in practice are fully funded and publicly managed, defined benefit plans and unfunded, privately managed defined contribution schemes. This fact is interesting in itself and suggests some natural selection process for pension systems that leads some combinations to become extinct or irrelevant.

While the distinction between the three main pairs—DB/DC, UF/FF and GM/PM may seem apparent, the distinctions are actually less clear-cut.

Defined Benefit vs. Defined Contribution

It is easy to distinguish between polar cases, but in actual systems the differences are harder to pin down. A typical polar case of a DB plan provides x percent of final pay for each year of participation,

Table 4.1
Examples of Mixing Benefit Types, Financing, and Administration

	Publicly managed (GM)	Privately managed (PM)
Defined benefits (DB)		
Unfunded (UF)	Germany, France (basic scheme)	France (supplementary scheme)
Fully funded (FF)		Netherlands (supplementary scheme)
Defined contribution (DC)		
Unfunded (UF)	Latvia, Poland and Sweden (1. Pillar)	
Fully funded (FF)	Singapore, Malaysia	Chile, Mexico, Poland and Sweden (2. Pillar)

e.g., 60 percent of final pay for 40 years in the scheme. A typical polar case of a DC system provides the accumulated contribution payments plus accrued interest at retirement, which may be then transformed into an annuity. However, if we consider a DB system based on lifetime earnings (such as the German and the French point system) and compare it with an unfunded individual account system or "notional defined contribution" (such as in Latvia, Poland and Sweden), the two kinds of benefit schedules are not very different at all. Indeed, a DB point system which takes account of the remaining life expectancy at retirement and an unfunded IA scheme with earnings growth are algebraically identical.[2]

The other possible distinction between DB and DC concerns who bears the income risk, which is said to be the plan sponsor in a (funded and unfunded) DB scheme, and the insured in a funded DC scheme. However, as witnessed by the many contribution increases, benefit changes and special taxes on retirees in pension reforms over the last decades, neither contributors nor retirees are immune to risks under a funded or unfunded DB schemes. The risk under a notional accounts system is equivalent or potentially lower than in an unfunded DB scheme (assuming that the former has an automatic mechanism for adjusting the annuity value with changes in life expectancy that the DB scheme does not). It is also worth noting that in many funded DC schemes the government reduces risk to the individual through guarantees (of a minimum rate of return and/or minimum pension), and/or acts as a guarantor of last resort.

Unfunded vs. Funded Schemes

The typical and often politically flavored distinction is that in one scheme the contribution revenues are used to pay current benefits (and hence exhibits solidarity between generations), while in the other, claims on future retirement income are prefunded (i.e., money is put aside). But such a distinction may not be very relevant at the macroeconomic level (depending on various factors). In the end, both schemes require a subsequent generation to fulfill the generational contract, either in the form of current contributions (in unfunded schemes) or through the purchase of accumulated assets (in funded schemes). Money put aside for retirement alone does not change this fact and even the idea of investing in demographically younger countries (i.e., emerging markets) can probably help only at the margin to cope with an aging population.[3]

Prefunding of demographic bulges (such as preparing for the retirement of the baby boom generation) may help somewhat to achieve more intergenerational equity. But from a macroeconomic perspective, a similar outcome can be achieved by reducing the public debt, creating public assets, or even by leaving the next generation a lower environmental liability (e.g., nuclear waste cleanup). Managing a large reserve fund of a public scheme on the other hand creates problems of its own: How can investment decisions be insulated from political interference, how will the power of a large state pension fund to move markets be wielded, and how will the government behave as a shareholder in terms of corporate governance? While a few international experiences may hold out hope, (e.g., the Canadian investment board experiment begun in 1998) the experience is short and may not be easily transferred to other countries, in particular developing countries. The past experience with public management of public reserve funds is not encouraging.[4]

Publicly vs. Privately Managed Schemes

Again such a distinction is easy for polar cases. At one extreme, a monopolistic public administration can handle contribution collection, record-keeping, benefit disbursement, and asset management. At the other extreme, these functions are performed by competing, private financial institutions subject to the discipline of individual consumer choice of product and firm. In reality, most systems lie along this spectrum. For example, the public sector increasingly outsources functions such as filing and record keeping (information technology), asset management and benefit disbursement. On the other hand, the function of the private sector in a funded system can be reduced to asset management since contribution collection, filing, and benefit disbursement may be done by clearinghouses (such as in Mexico and Sweden).

In summary, equating "individual accounts" with a scheme in which the individual bears the entire risk, which is fully funded, and in which all functions are performed by the private sector is simply wrong. There are many cases in which such an approach is sensible. However, individualization of accounts at different points along the spectrum can provide critical advantages which are discussed next.

3. A Case for Individual Accounts

There are many arguments for moving from typical unfunded, government managed and defined benefit scheme toward individual accounts—unfunded and/or funded, publicly and/or fully or partially privately managed. The main arguments for individual accounts have to do with political economy; population aging and incentive effects. There are additional arguments for considering a move toward funding and the use of the private sector for most or all of the administration.

Individualization—Breaking the Reform Deadlock

The attempt to reform a public pension scheme is typically triggered by short-term financial disequilibria which are further reinforced by concerns for long-term population aging, perceived distortionary incentives of the current scheme, and unequal treatment between occupational groups, gender and generation. In principal, all of these concerns can be addressed by a comprehensive but nevertheless parametric reform of the unfunded DB system. Standard measures include the use of lifetime earnings instead of final or best years, reduced accrual rates, actuarial decrements/increments for earlier/postponed retirement, increase in the standard/ minimum retirement age, a shift to price from wage indexation, etc. These parametric reform solutions have been known for many years and were[5] and are still proposed in many circumstances[6] by advisors from international organizations like the World Bank and the International Monetary Fund. They were also intensively discussed in Latin America and the transition economies of central and Eastern Europe, before systemic reforms were eventually implemented, and continue to be discussed in many EU countries. These reform discussions are often protracted and years often go by with little or no progress. Where major reforms have taken place, in countries such as in the U.K. or Sweden, they are characterized by individualization and a shift toward full funding of part of the system.

The reason behind the reform deadlock and the possibility to overcome it through individualization plus funding is essentially political. First, reforms to the existing schemes inevitably fall short of putting systems on a financially sustainable basis. Politicians have little incentive to do so, creating a credibility problem for the reform and hence an incentive to oppose any reform from the very beginning. Second, in most countries there is not only one but several public schemes which need to be reformed and agreeing on the financially sustainable lowest denominator hits the opposition of all others scheme which provide more generous benefits in a non-transparent manner. In contrast, proposals for individual accounts that are based on individual equity—i.e., you get what you pay in—are more difficult to reject. Last but not least, mixing individual accounts with some change in funding creates coalitions and support among younger cohorts.[7] As long as credible guarantees to leave existing benefits for those close to retirement or already in receipt of a pension can be made, the opposition from older cohorts can be successfully defused.

Individual accounts, plus expectations of higher rates of return for part of the contributions which is funded, creates a paradigm shift which is able to break the reform deadlock.[8] The alternative is protracted debate and delayed reform, with major strains on the relationship between generations and occupational groups and a weakening of social cohesion. It is the unreformed schemes, with their high and rising contribution rates, past and prospective ad hoc benefit cuts, and unequal treatment between different groups of the population which are a threat to "solidarity," not individual accounts and funding. Furthermore, individual accounts provide a more transparent setting for meeting redistributive or "social insurance" objectives, in contrast to the old scheme with its opaque benefit formulas and non-transparent cross-subsidies between schemes.

Matching public contributions (such as in Mexico) or minimum pension guarantees for low income groups (such as in Latvia) can be used to guarantee higher replacement rates and redistribution, protect against poverty in old age, and provide incentives for formal labor market participation.[9] Second, subsidiary social objectives can be pursued through compensating contribution payments for periods of maternity, unemployment or military service. The requirement to make the payment from other social insurance budgets or general revenues enhances transparency.

Individualization—A Better Concept to Cope with Population Aging

Confronted with an aging population, both unfunded and funded schemes will be forced to make difficult choices. Either contribution rates will have to rise during active life, benefits will have to be reduced after retirement, the ratio of working years to retired years will have to be increased or some combination of all of the above.

Much of the current and future aging problem will be due to a positive trend, namely increasing life expectancy. Assuming that individuals prefer a smooth consumption profile over their life cycle, they will have to work longer in order to maintain a certain level of income during their old age. In addition, the possibilities for more flexible labor market options in the future, the increased importance of the service industries and increased labor mobility (including international) all point to the need for new thinking on retirement and pension provision.

Broadly speaking, this kind of flexibility is more difficult in a defined benefit framework. Benefit rules must be extremely complicated in order to avoid labor supply distortions. For example, adjusting the retirement age to changes in life expectancy to keep the DB system financial sustainable requires a political decision, as does the provision of decrements and increments for earlier and later retirement. The international evidence shows that actuarially fair principles are extremely difficult to apply in public schemes.[10] In contrast, DC systems can provide this flexibility without resorting to a series of contentious political decisions to increase the retirement age or to implement actuarial benefit adjustments for advanced or deferred retirement. Since the accumulated amount and the remaining life expectancy essentially determine pension level through the annuity calculation, decrements and increments are calculated automatically, and when life expectancy increases, individuals receive lower pensions and react accordingly to a lengthening of their work life. Also, partial retirement and reentering full employment at later age can be easily accommodated with fewer distortions according to individuals' preferences.

Individualization—A Better Way of Dealing with Labor Market Incentives and Changing Family Patterns

Funded and unfunded individual accounts are not only able to render retirement decisions more neutral compared to traditional DB schemes, they have also less distortionary effects on labor supply during work periods. Since in traditional DB schemes the link between contributions and benefits is generally not very tight, a significant part of the contributions are considered taxes. Even if it is tight, the link is not very transparent with a similar effect on labor supply and tax evasion. An individual account does not eliminate all tax aspects of mandated contributions since imperfect credit markets, shortsightedness, etc., would lead individuals to a different voluntary savings pattern. But the perceived tax component under individual accounts will probably be considerably reduced, and the labor market outcome and the incentives to join the formal labor market will be improved.

Individual accounts also allow higher mobility of labor between professions and nations. DB systems are often differentiated between occupations (such as civil servants and the private sector), impeding labor mobility especially as a worker gets older. Similar mobility restrictions exist between countries with different DB systems. Even if the same benefit structure under two DB system does exist, the mobility between the schemes will generally lead to a benefit loss. These impediments can be eliminated in a DC regime.

Individual accounts are also better equipped to handle changes in family patterns, i.e., the increase in divorce, multiple marriages or relationships over the life cycle, widowhood, and the resulting need for independent old-age security for women. Under an individual account system, accumulated resources (actual or notional) can easily be split after a divorce for the period marriage, aggregated with own and prior contributions and interest received, and supplemented by public resources in a transparent manner (e.g., for periods of child rearing, etc.).

Why Add Funding to Individual Accounts

Unfunded individual accounts can go a long way towards providing income security for old age. Yet unfunded DB and DC schemes both share the same problem since they are exposed to the same fiscal and political risks. At the same time, funding may contribute to increased saving, capital accumulation, and output under certain conditions.[11]

The internal rate of return of an unfunded scheme depends on the growth of the wage bill while the rate of return of a funded scheme depends on returns on capital. These returns are imperfectly or even negatively correlated so that the income risk can be diversified under a mixed system that consists of an unfunded (DB or DC) pillar, and a funded (DB or DC) pillar.[12] The diversification can and should be further increased by investing part of the funded scheme internationally. Full international investment (e.g., according to the proportion of countries' market capitalization), however, is an interesting but only theoretical benchmark since many conditions to make it optimal do not hold in reality.

Prefunding part of retirement income is also a means of coping with the political risk. No pension system is fully immune to political risk and thus political decisions which negatively influence retirement income through contribution and benefit changes, taxation, or inflation. However, individualized and funded provisions create a strong political constituency against such changes, and international financial markets are a check against unsound economic policies.

As evidenced by recent reforms, problems with individual and funded provisions can emerge, but they are not insurmountable: These problems relate to the administrative costs and the potential for reducing the net rate of return for members during the accumulation period (discussed below) as well as the possibility for high costs in the annuitization process, if the market is not functioning properly. The provision of annuities is important in order to insure against uncertain longevity and outliving one's resources but poorly regulated markets and uninformed consumers can lead to high costs. Appropriate regulation and information in a competitive market environment can address these problems, and mandatory annuitization can reduce the potential for adverse selection issues.[13] Clearly however, this is an area where more analysis and new approaches are required.

Why Consider Private Management of Funded Accounts

Since individual and funded accounts—alone or mixed with unfunded retirement provisions—seem to go a long way, one may correctly ask why private management of these funds should be considered at all. Would not centralized public funds be cheaper due to potential economies of scale and the reduced need for marketing? Perhaps, but does public management provide the best risk-adjusted rate of returns, and is it conducive to economic development?

High administrative costs of privately managed individual accounts have been criticized and in some cases, there does appear to be ample room for improvement.[14] However, the real problem with high costs is the potential that the net returns on investments will be reduced to levels that make the individual accounts poor vehicles for long-term savings.[15] In addition, recent reforms have introduced innovations to keep a lid on costs, such as competitive tender arrangements in Bolivia, checks on marketing costs, or clearinghouse arrangements which can reduce private sector involvement to a mere asset management function (such as in Sweden). But the discussion of costs versus individual choice is far from finished.[16]

But from an individual and societal point of view, higher costs have to be compared with the rate of return as well as the quality of services delivered. And in both cases public management does not fair well. Most public pension funds are subject to a series of restrictions and mandates that lead to poor returns. Political objectives often lead to social and economically targeted investments and forced loans to the government to finance its deficits. These investments yield returns that are often below bank deposit rates and almost always below the growth of incomes. This contrasts with privately managed pension fund returns, which generally exceed income growth (see Figures 4.1 and 4.2).

Figure 4.1
Difference between Real Annual Compounded Returns for
Publicly Managed Pension Funds and Real Income
Per Capita Growth in Selected Countries

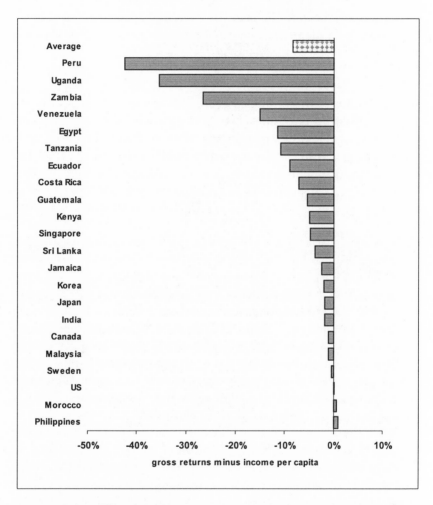

Source: Iglesias and Palacios (2000).

Figure 4.2
Difference between Real Annual Compounded Returns
for Privately Managed Pension Funds and Real Income
Per Capita Growth in Selected Countries

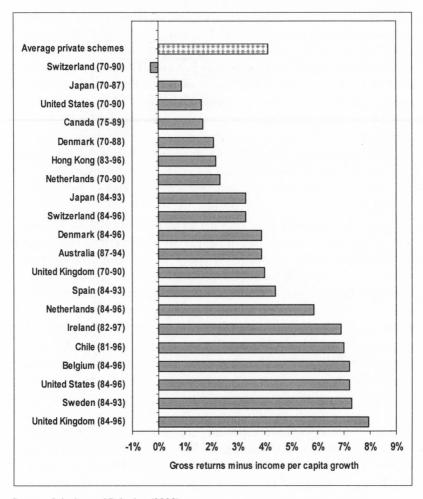

Source: Iglesias and Palacios (2000).

The low rates of return found in many publicly managed schemes over the last few decades have direct and indirect negative consequences. Direct consequences are felt by members of partially funded schemes that must pay higher contributions during their lifetimes or receive lower benefits. For provident fund members, poor returns (or prescribed yields) directly reduce their retirement savings and make it impossible to maintain pre-retirement consumption levels. Indirectly, the presence of these reserves may lead to higher non-pension government deficits if target deficit levels are based on the consolidated budget.[17] Also, the diversion of an important pool of long-term savings to projects with low returns or for higher government consumption implies an important opportunity cost for the economy. Private capital markets are robbed of liquidity and good projects do not find financing. The larger the fund relative to the capital markets, the greater is this cost.

Public management also creates problems with regard to corporate governance. Large public funds would become the largest shareholders in the economy. In many developing countries, this would imply a significant renationalization of private industry. On the other hand, private management can produce positive effects on corporate governance and enterprise performance. The divergence of continental European and U.S. economic development is increasingly linked to difference in governance structure due to differences in financial market structure and pension fund activities.[18]

Equally important, private pension funds as institutional investors can make an important contribution to financial market development which in turn can contribute to more sustainable economic growth. These effects are especially important for developing countries where pension funds and insurance companies can lead to quantitative and qualitative improvements in capital markets. There is increasing evidence of the positive growth effects of adding liquidity and depth to stock markets in particular.[19] The Chilean experience of pension reform, financial market development and high economic growth lends further empirical evidence to this hypothesis.[20] Recent cross-country analysis lends further support to the close link between contractual saving and high equity financing (compared to debt financing) of enterprises, longer maturity of debt instruments, and higher liquidity.[21]

4. Conclusion

Individualization of pension accounts can significantly improve the social insurance aspect of public pension schemes. Since on a global basis, many of these schemes need urgent and comprehensive reforms, individualization can help to make them financially sustainable, more equitable and even more redistributive than the current arrangements.

Individualization of pension accounts is not equivalent to funding or private management. While partial or full funding and partial or full privatization can add value to the individualization approach, individual accounts which are unfunded and publicly managed have advantages of their own: They can break the deadlock in reform, allow a better way of coping with aging, and provide a better way of dealing with labor market distortions and changes in the family structure. Adding full or partial funding can reduce the political and income risks while having positive impact on saving and financial market development. Adding full or partial private management can increase options and individual choice, enhance corporate governance and improve the rate of return of the managed assets.

These perceived or actual advantages of an individualized account approach are the reason why an increasing number of countries are making it part and parcel of their reform effort. Clearly, any new reform approach is confronted with new problems, such as initially high administrative costs of funded and individually managed accounts. But innovations which are undertaken as part of these reforms cause optimism that the net gains, in particular in the context of developing countries, are positive and large.[22]

Notes

1. More detailed discussion of specific reforms and issues can be found at *www.worldbank.org/pensions*.
2. An unfunded DC system, or notional accounts system, mimics a funded DC system, but remains unfunded. As in a conventional DC plan, individuals accrue their contributions and interest payments, but the interest rate is linked to a return consistent with its source of financing and unfunded status (i.e., wage growth related). At retirement, the notionally accumulated amount is converted into a pension taking into account the remaining life expectancy and, possibly, the notional interest rate. See Disney, 1999, and Valdes-Prieto, 2000, for a critical assessment, and Palmer, 2000, for a presentation of main principals of notional accounts based on the Swedish reform.

3. See Holzmann, R. 2000b. *Can Investments in Emerging Markets Help to Solve the Aging Problem?* Social Protection Paper Series, Discussion Paper No. 0010, March, Washington, D.C., World Bank.
4. See Iglesias, A., and Palacios, R. 2000. *Managing public pension reserves: Evidence from the International Experience*, Holzmann, R., and Stiglitz, J., op. cit.
5. See Holzmann, R. 1988. *Reforming Public Pensions*, Paris, OECD.
6. See Chand, S., and Jäger, A. 1996. *Aging Populations and Public Pension Schemes*, IMF Occasional Paper No. 147.
7. Strong evidence of this support can be seen in the voluntary switching process whereby younger cohorts disproportionately vote with their feet for individual accounts in reforming countries (Palacios and Whitehouse, 1999).
8. See Holzmann, R. 2000a. *The World Bank Approach to Pension Reform*, International Social Security Review, Vol. 53, No. 1, pp. 11-34.
9. Simulations for the U.S. indicate that matching contributions can emulate the same distributive effects as the current, progressive pension scheme (Kotlikoff; Smetters and Walliser, 1998).
10. For a survey of rules for early or late retirement, see Palacios and Whitehouse, 1999.
11. There is an extensive literature on this topic which cannot be discussed in this brief note. For a review, see World Bank, 1994. *Averting the old-age crisis: Policies to protect the old and promote growth*, New York, Oxford University Press.
12. See Holzmann, R. 2000a. *The World Bank Approach to Pension Reform*, International Social Security Review, Vol. 53, No. 1, pp. 11-34.
13. See Walliser, J. 2000. *Regulation of Withdrawals in Individual Account Systems*, in Holzmann, R., and Stiglitz, J., op. cit.
14. See Rofman, Rafael. 2000. Regarding costs in Argentina, for example: *The pension system in Argentina: Six years after the reform*, Primer paper, June.
15. See Whitehouse, E. 2000. *Paying for pensions: An international comparison of administrative charges in funded retirement-income systems*, Social Protection Paper Series, Discussion Paper No. 0021, Washington D.C., World Bank.
16. See James, E., Smalhout, S., and Vittas, D. 2000. *Administrative Costs and the Organization of Individual Account Systems: A Comparative Perspective*, in Holzmann, R., and Stiglitz, J., op. cit.
17. See Buchanan, J. 1990. *The Budgetary Politics of Social Security*, Weaver, C. (ed.), *Social Security's Looming Surpluses*, American Enterprise Institute, Washington, D.C.
18. See Boersch-Supan, A., and Winter, J. 1999. *Pension Reform, Saving Behavior and Corporate Governance*, University of Mannheim/NBER (mimeo).
19. See for example Levine and Zervos, 1996, and Levine, 1997.
20. See Holzmann, R. 1997. *Pension Reform, Financial Market Development and Endogenous Growth–Preliminary Evidence for Chile*, IMF Staff Papers 1997, June, pp. 149-178.
21. See Catalan, M., Impavido, G., and Musalem, A. 2000. *Contractual Savings or Stock Market Development: Which Leads?* World Bank, Financial Sector Development Department (mimeo), July.
22. See Holzmann, R., and Stiglitz, J. (eds.). 2000. *New Ideas about Social Security*, Washington, D.C. World Bank (in print).

Bibliography

Boersch-Supan, A. and Winter, J. 1999. *Pension Reform, Saving Behavior and Corporate Governance*, University of Mannheim/NBER (mimeo).

Buchanan, J. 1990. *The Budgetary Politics of Social Security*, Weaver, C. (ed.), Social Security's Looming Surpluses, American Enterprise Institute, Washington, D.C.

Catalan, M.; Impavido, G. and Musalem, A. 2000. *Contractual Savings or Stock Market Development: Which Leads?*, World Bank, Financial Sector Development Department, (mimeo), July.

Chand, S. and Jäger, A. 1996. *Aging Populations and Public Pension Schemes*, IMF Occasional Paper No. 147.

Disney, R. 1999. *Notional Accounts as a Pension Reform Strategy: An Evaluation*, Social Protection Paper Series, Discussion Paper No. 9928, Washington, D.C., World Bank.

Disney, R. and E. Whitehouse. 1999. *Pension Plans and Retirement Incentives*, Social Protection Paper Series, Discussion Paper No. 9924, Washington, D.C., World Bank.

Holzmann, R. 1988. *Reforming Public Pensions*, Paris, OECD.

—. 1997. *Pension Reform, Financial Market Development and Endogenous Growth–Preliminary Evidence for Chile*, IMF Staff Papers 1997, June, pp. 149-178.

—. 2000a. *The World Bank Approach to Pension Reform*, International Social Security Review, Vol. 53, No. 1, pp. 11-34.

—. 2000b. *Can Investments in Emerging Markets Help to Solve the Aging Problem?*, Social Protection Paper Series, Discussion Paper No. 0010, March, Washington, D.C., World Bank.

Holzmann, R. and Stiglitz, J. 2000, (eds.), *New Ideas about Social Security*, Washington, D.C. World Bank (in print).

Iglesias, A. and Palacios, R. 2000. *Managing public pension reserves: Evidence from the International Experience*, Holzmann, R. and Stiglitz, J., op. cit.

James, E.; Smalhout, S. and Vittas, D. 2000. *Administrative Costs and the Organization of Individual Account Systems: A Comparative Perspective*, Holzmann, R. and Stiglitz, J., op. cit.

Kotlikoff, L.; Smetters, K. and Walliser, J. 1998. *Opting out of Social Security and Adverse Selection*, NBER Working Paper Series, Working Paper 6430, February, Cambridge, Massachussetts.

Levine, R. 1997. *Financial Development and Economic Growth—Views and Agenda*, Journal of Economic Literature, Vol. XXXV, pp. 688-726.

Levine, R. and Zervos, S. 1996. *Policy, Stock Market Development, and Long-Run Growth Part I*, The World Bank Economic Review, Vol. 10, No. 2, pp. 323-39.

Palacios, R. and Whitehouse, E. 1999. *The role of choice in the transition to a funded pension system*, Social Protection Paper Series, Discussion Paper No. 9812, Washington, D.C., World Bank.

Palmer, E. 2000. *The Swedish Pension Reform Model—Framework and Issues*, Social Protection Paper Series, Discussion Paper No. 0012, Washington, D.C., World Bank.

Rofman, Rafael. 2000. *The pension system in Argentina: Six years after the reform*, Primer paper, June.

Valdes-Prieto, S. 2000. *The Financial Stability of Notional Account Pensions*, Scandinavian Journal of Economics (in print).

Walliser, J. 2000. *Regulation of Withdrawals in Individual Account Systems*, in Holzmann, R. and Stiglitz, J., op. cit.

Whitehouse, E. 2000. *Paying for pensions: An international comparison of administrative charges in funded retirement-income systems*, Social Protection Paper Series, Discussion Paper No. 0021, Washington D.C., World Bank.

World Bank. 1994. *Averting the old-age crisis: Policies to protect the old and promote growth*, New York, Oxford University Press.

5

Individual Accounts Versus Social Insurance: A United States Perspective

A.H. Munnell

The United States social security system is in better shape than most public pension systems around the world. The aging of the population is less dramatic in the United States than elsewhere, more older workers remain in the workforce, and the benefit promises are comparatively modest. The system currently faces a deficit over the 75-year projection period, but this financing gap can be closed by small changes within the structure of the existing program.

While dramatic change is unnecessary, proposals abound to transform some or all of the United States social security system from a defined benefit plan where benefits are based on lifetime earnings to a defined contribution plan where benefits depend on contributions and investment returns. These proposals are gaining currency even though careful analytical work has shown that individual accounts will not raise returns on social security contributions for most people currently alive. Moreover, individual accounts are risky, costly, and are likely to hurt the disabled, women, and low earners generally. The real concern, however, is that individual accounts would create the mechanism for eventually undermining the social security program.

This chapter explores these points in more detail. The first section describes the demographics and economics facing the United States compared to other countries. The second section explores the sources of the current enthusiasm for individual accounts in the United States. The third section looks at the problems and risks associated with replacing part of the current social security system with individual accounts.

1. The Demographics and Economics of Social Security

During the first half of the twenty-first century, the populations of most developed countries are projected to become smaller and older as a result of below-replacement fertility and increased longevity. As shown in Table 5.1, the population in all but three major developed countries—the United States, Canada, and France—will be smaller in 2050 than it is today. Populations that are simultaneously aging and declining will experience a dramatic increase in the population 65 and older.

Table 5.1
Changes in the Total Population and the Proportion
Aged 65 Years or Older, 2000 and 2050

Country	Population (thousands)		Population change		Per cent 65 years or older	
	2000	2050	thousand	percent	2000	2050
Belgium	10,161	8,918	-1,243	-12	17	28
Canada	29,512	34,394	4,882	17	12	24
France	59,080	59,883	803	1	16	26
Germany	82,220	73,303	-8,917	-11	16	28
Italy	57,298	41,197	-16,101	-28	18	35
Japan	126,714	104,921	-21,793	-17	17	32
Netherlands	15,786	14,156	-1,629	-10	14	28
Spain	39,630	30,226	-9,404	-24	17	37
Sweden	8,910	8,661	-249	-3	17	27
United Kingdom	58,830	56,667	-2,163	-4	16	25
United States	278,357	349,318	70,961	25	12	22

Source: United Nations Secretariat, Population Division, Department of Economic and Social Affairs. 2000. *Replacement Migration: Is it a Solution to Declining and Ageing Populations?* Table I.1, p. 6, Table A.2, p. 106, and Table A.16, p. 134. Canadian numbers are from Eduard Bos, My T. Vu, Ernest Massiah, Rodolfo A. Bulatao. 1994. *World Population Projections 1994-95.* The World Bank.

The aging of the population is a serious problem for most public pension systems. With some exceptions, these systems offer defined benefits and are financed on a pay-as-you-go basis. That is, benefits are calculated as a percent of past wages, and contributions from workers are used to pay benefits for current retirees. Under these systems, the cost is the product of two ratios: the dependency ratio, which is the number of beneficiaries per worker, and the replacement rate, which is the ratio of benefits to pre-retirement earnings.

The Dependency Ratio

The dependency ratio in the United States is lower today and is projected to remain lower than in other developed countries for two reasons: (1) the population is not projected to age as significantly in the United States as elsewhere, and (2) more older people continue working in the United States than elsewhere.

Population Aging

One important reason for the more moderate demographic shifts in the United States is that the fertility rate in the United States remains at two children per woman—the level required to keep the population from declining. It is significantly below that level for a large number of developed countries (Table 5.2). At the same time, life expectancy at age 65 in the United States is roughly the same as the average for the other countries for men and less than average for women. Higher fertility and roughly average life expectancy means that the population shifts will be less dramatic in the United States than elsewhere.

This pattern is evident in Table 5.3, which shows the current and projected ratios of the population 65 and over to the population 15-64. In 2000, the dependency ratio was 19 percent for the United States, while it was well above 20 percent for most European countries and Japan. By 2020, this ratio will have increased to 43 percent in Japan, 38 percent in Italy, and 35 percent in Germany and Sweden; the projected ratio for the United States is 28 percent. By 2050, Italy and Spain are projected to have dependency ratios in excess of 60 percent, Germany and Japan in excess of 50 percent, compared to 38 percent for the United States.

Table 5.2
Total Fertility Rate and Life Expectancy at Age 65 for Selected Countries, 1996

Country	Total fertility rate[a]	Life expectancy at age 65	
		Men	Women
Belgium	1.5	14.0	18.3
Canada	1.7	15.7	19.9
France	1.7	15.9	20.3
Germany	1.3	14.6	18.3
Italy	1.2	15.3	19.1
Japan	1.4	16.5	20.9
Netherlands	1.5	14.8	19.1
Spain	1.2	15.5	19.2
Sweden	1.9	16.0	19.8
United Kingdom	1.7	14.6	18.3
United States	2.0	15.5	19.0

Source: United Nations Department of Economic and Social Affairs. 1996. *Demographic Yearbook 1996.* United Nations.
[a] Total fertility rate is the number of children that would be born to a woman if she were to live to the end of her childbearing years and bear children in accordance with current age-specific fertility rates.

In short, while the public debate in the United States focuses intensively on the retirement of the baby boom generation and the rising ratio of retirees to workers, the problem in the United States is modest compared to that faced by other developed countries.

Labor Force Participation

Although demographics determine the ratio of working-age population to the population 65 and over, the support burden on workers depends on when individuals retire.

With the exception of Japan, the decline in the labor force participation of older persons is one of the most dramatic features of labor force change in developed countries over the past several

Table 5.3
Population 65 and Over as a Percent of Population 15-64

Country	2000	2010	2020	2030	2050
Belgium	25.1	25.6	31.9	41.1	44.7
Canada	18.2	20.4	28.4	39.1	41.8
France	23.6	24.6	32.3	39.1	43.4
Germany	23.8	30.3	35.4	49.2	51.9
Italy	26.5	31.2	37.5	48.3	60.0
Japan	24.3	33.0	43.0	44.5	54.0
Netherlands	20.8	24.2	33.9	45.1	45.7
Spain	22.0	25.9	30.7	41.0	60.3
Sweden	26.9	29.1	35.6	39.4	38.6
United Kingdom	24.4	25.8	31.2	38.7	41.2
United States	19.0	20.4	27.6	36.8	38.4

Source: Eduard Bos, My T. Vu, Ernest Massiah, Rodolfo A. Bulatao. 1994. *World Population Projections 1994-95*. The World Bank.

decades. In the 1960s, the participation rates for men age 60-64 were above 70 percent in all eleven countries in the survey and above 80 percent in several.[1] By the mid-1990s, the rate had fallen to below 20 percent in Belgium, Italy, France and the Netherlands, to about 35 percent in Germany, and to 40 percent in Spain. Although United States analysts often emphasize the dramatic fall here, the decline from 82 percent to 53 percent in the United States is modest compared to the decline in European countries. Table 5.4 presents a summary measure of the extent to which men aged 55-65 have dropped out of the work force for a sample of countries. This measure is the percent of men not in the labor force at each age averaged over the 11-year period. With the exception of Japan and Sweden, the United States clearly has more older men in the labor force than other countries. This increased labor force participation eases the burden in a pay-as-you-go system.

Table 5.4
Average Percentage of Workers Age 55-65 Out of the Labor Force, 1999

Country	Unused labour capacity 55-65
Belgium	67
Canada	45
France	60
Germany	48
Italy	59
Japan	22
Netherlands	58
Spain	47
Sweden	35
United Kingdom	55
United States	37

Source: Jonathan Gruber and David Wise (eds.). 1999. *Social Security and Retirement Around the World.* National Bureau of Economic Research. Chicago: University of Chicago Press, Table 1, p. 29.

The low labor force participation reflects the availability of pension benefits and the incentive to claim them once offered. Table 5.5 shows the retirement age for full benefits and for early benefits and an implicit tax on earnings after eligibility for benefits. The United States clearly has the latest statutory ages for both full and early benefits at 65 and 62, respectively. Although the statutory retirement ages are the most critical of plan provisions, many countries effectively provide early retirement at younger ages through generous unemployment and disability programs. For example, at age 59, 22 percent of men are receiving unemployment or disability benefits in Belgium, 21 percent in France, 27 percent in the Netherlands, and 37 percent in Germany, compared to 12 percent in the United States. Because of the ambiguity created by the availability of disability and unemployment benefits, the retirement ages in Belgium, Italy and the Netherlands are shown with quotation marks.

Table 5.5
Availability of Public Pension and Incentive to Claim Benefits, 1999

Country	Retirement age		Implicit tax on earnings in the next year (per cent)
	For full benefits	Early retirement age	
Belgium[a]	65	"60"	82
Canada	65	60	8
France	60	60	80
Germany	63	60	35
Italy[a]	64	"55"	81
Japan	60	60	47
Netherlands	65	"60"	141
Spain	65	60	-23
Sweden[b]	65	60	28
United Kingdom[a]	65	60	75
United States	65	62	-1

Source: Jonathan Gruber and David Wise (eds.). 1999. *Social Security and Retirement Around the World.* National Bureau of Economic Research. Chicago: University of Chicago Press, Table 1, p. 29 and U.S. Social Security Administration, Office of Policy, Office of Research Evaluation, and Statistics, *Social Security Programs Throughout the World 1999.* SSA Publication No. 13-11805 (August), Table 3, p. xliii.
[a] Retirement for women is 61 in Belgium, 59 in Italy, and 60 in the United Kingdom (gradually rising to 65 over the period 2010-2020).
[b] In Sweden's new pension system, retirement benefits are available at 61.

Replacement Rates

The United States not only faces a less dramatic aging of its population and retains more workers in the labor force, but it also has a relatively less generous pension system than other developed countries. Several studies have examined the replacement rates (ratio of benefits to pre-retirement earnings) for various social security programs throughout the world, and the United States consistently comes out on the low end.[2] Table 5.6 reports the most recent of these re-

Table 5.6
Public Pensions Benefits, 1999

Country	Replacement rate at early retirement age	Adjustments after retirement
Belgium	77	Prices
Canada	20	Prices
France	91	Prices
Germany	62	Wages[a]
Italy	75	GDP
Japan	54	Prices
Netherlands	91	Wages[b]
Spain	63	Prices
Sweden	54[c]	Prices
United Kingdom	48	Prices
United States	41	Prices

Source: Jonathan Gruber and David Wise (eds.). 1999. *Social Security and Retirement Around the World.* National Bureau of Economic Research. Chicago: University of Chicago Press, Table 1, p.29, and U.S. Social Security Administration, Office of Policy, Office of Research Evaluation, and Statistics, *Social Security Programs Throughout the World 1999.* SSA Publication No. 13-11805 (August).

[a] Adjustment based on change in the real value of pensions compared to the changes in earnings.
[b] Adjustment based on change in the net minimum wages.
[c] The replacement rate in Sweden's new system is essentially unchanged.

placement rate comparisons and, with the exception of Canada, the United States shows the lowest benefit levels relative to earnings.

Another dimension of program generosity is the adjustment to benefits after retirement. Most countries adjust benefits to keep pace with the increase in prices. Although adjusting for inflation allows retirees to retain the purchasing power of their benefits, as retirees age their position declines relative to workers whose earnings reflect productivity gains as well as inflation. Three countries adjust benefits by more than prices. Italy keeps benefits in line with growth of GDP, while Germany and the Netherlands adjust benefits with wages. These more generous adjustments allow retirees to retain their relative position as well as purchasing power, but they are quite expensive.

An International Comparison of Financial Status

Later retirement, relatively low replacement rates, and price adjustments after retirement combine to make social security costs relatively low in the United States compared to other countries. Table 5.7 shows current contributions for old-age, disability, and death benefits as a percent of payrolls. These contributions are not a completely accurate way to gauge the cost of the programs, since in many cases the system faces a long-term deficit. Nevertheless, contributions for the United States system are only 12.4 percent of pay-

Table 5.7
Cost for Old-Age, Disability, and Death Benefits

Country	Taxes as a percent of taxable payrolls, 1999	Expenditures as a percent of GDP, 1994-1996
Belgium	16.36	10.1
Canada	7.00	5.2
France	16.45	11.0
Germany	19.50	10.2
Italy	32.70	11.4
Japan	17.34	6.1
Netherlands	37.72	12.4
Spain	28.30	8.7
Sweden	13.35[a]	16.5
United Kingdom	22.20	5.6
United States	12.40	6.9

Source: U.S. Social Security Administration, Office of Policy, Office of Research Evaluation, and Statistics, Social Security Programs Throughout the World 1999. SSA Publication No. 13-11805 (August), Table 3, p. xliii, and International Labour Organisation (http://www.ilo.org/public/english/protection/socsec/publ/css/cssindex.htm).
[a] Under Sweden's new system, the payroll tax rate will be 18.5 percent.

rolls compared to 38 percent in the Netherlands, 33 percent in Italy, 28 percent in Spain, 19.5 percent in Germany, and more than 16 percent in France and Belgium. An alternative measure of program costs is old-age, disability, and death expenditures as a percent of GDP. Table 5.7 shows the figure at 7 percent for the United States compared to nearly twice that level for Belgium, France, Germany, Italy and Sweden.

Not only are United States social security costs relatively low, but the system is also in relatively good financial shape compared to other countries. In a 1996 OECD study, economists estimated the net present value of pension contributions, expenditure and unfunded liability for the major social security systems. Table 5.8 reports those numbers as a percent of 1994 GDP. The United States unfunded

Table 5.8
Unfunded Public Pension Liability (1995-2070) as a Percent of 1994 GDP

Country	Liability/GDP
Belgium	152.6
Canada	100.7[a]
France	102.1
Germany	61.6
Italy	59.7
Japan	70.0
Netherlands	53.3
Spain	108.6
Sweden	132.3[a]
United Kingdom	23.8
United States	23.0

Source: Deborah Roseveare, Willi Leibfritz, Douglas Fore, and Eckhard Wurzel. 1996. "Ageing Populations, Pension Systems and Government Budgets: Simulations for 20 OECD Countries," Economics Department Working Paper No. 168. OECD, Table 2, p. 15.

[a] Both Canada and Sweden have undertaken pension reforms that have reduced their unfunded liability to zero.

liability for social security over the 75-year projection period was equal to 23 percent of GDP, approximately where it remains today. The comparable burden was three or four times larger for most of the other countries studied. Some countries, such as Canada and Sweden, have undertaken major reforms since the 1996 study, so their numbers are no longer relevant. Nevertheless, the message remains the same: the United States social security system faces one of the smallest financing shortfalls of any developed country. A study by the International Monetary Fund[3] came to very similar conclusions.

2. Why the Enthusiasm for Individual Accounts?

Despite these numbers, many otherwise well-informed people believe that the aging population will lead inexorably to the collapse of the program. Replacing at least a portion of the current social security program with individual accounts has become a major issue in this year's presidential campaign. The enthusiasm for individual accounts can be traced to a confluence of events and the lure of higher returns. This section first discusses the events and then examines the potential for individual accounts to offer higher returns.

The Confluence of Events

At least five factors have been driving support for the individual accounts—the emergence of a long-term deficit, the decline in returns or "money's worth" issue, the desire to increase national saving, growing inequality, and Wall Street's interest in this potential market.

- *Emergence of a deficit.* Social security would in all probability not be on the national agenda if the system were in actuarial balance, instead of facing a deficit over the 75-year projection period. The reemergence of a deficit was particularly disconcerting in the wake of the 1983 Amendments that were supposed to keep the social security system solvent for 75 years and produce positive trust fund balances through 2060. Yet, only a year after the 1983 legislation the Trustees began to project a small deficit, and the deficit grew more or less steadily for the next decade. The reemergence of a deficit made social security vulnerable to critics' attacks, and the critics often exaggerated the problems in order to justify dramatic solutions.

- *Money's worth.* A modest deficit by itself would probably not have been enough to stimulate a major movement to restructure social security. The deficit emerged, however, just as the system matured, making apparent the full cost of the program and the low expected returns on social security contributions as compared to those available on market investments—the so-called "money's worth" issue. Since raising taxes or reducing benefits only worsen returns, almost all reform plans involve some form of equity investment.[4] Given that equity investment is desirable, those who do not have confidence in the government-administered investment plans conclude that individual accounts are the only mechanism through which to achieve financial diversification. Supporters of the existing defined benefit structure believe that it is possible for the government to accumulate reserves in the trust funds and hire private sector managers to invest part of those reserves in equities without political interference.[5]

- *Desire to increase national saving.* Longer life expectancies and a rapidly aging population will greatly increase the cost of supporting the aged, and almost everyone agrees that it is prudent to save in anticipation of such an event. Like the debate about government investing in equities, however, the issue is whether saving can be done at the government level. Supporters of the current program argue that it is politically possible to save through social security trust funds in the new budgetary environment; advocates of individual accounts disagree.

- *Growing inequality.* Another development that may have influenced attitudes about redistributive defined benefit social insurance is the growing inequality in income and wealth. The mechanism through which inequality affects the individual account debate is twofold. First, many people who have been able to accumulate wealth believe that they could do much better investing for their own accounts. In part, this self-confidence reflects the run-up in stock market prices that leads people to think they are brilliant investors. In part, it reflects a shift in public attitudes over the 1980s and 1990s towards individual responsibility and self-reliance. Second, some want to offer those at the low end of the income scale, who have not been able to accumulate wealth, access to the high returns of equity investment and believe this can be accomplished only through individual accounts.

- *Wall Street.* The potential for "taking the system private" quickly caught the attention of the nation's financial institutions, and they have been supportive of conservative think tanks leading the charge toward privatization. Interestingly, financial institutions, which once thought that individual defined contribution accounts would be an attractive line of business, now seem to have backed away from wholehearted endorsement of efforts to privatize social security. Their reversal appears to reflect the recognition that the administrative costs associated with setting up and maintaining accounts for millions of low-wage workers would be very high and that the profit potential is much less than originally envisioned. Moreover, such an effort would likely bring increased scrutiny and regulation from the federal government that might harm other aspects of their business. Nevertheless, the initial enthusiasm on the part of financial institutions and the support they provided for conservative think tanks was a major factor behind the push for individual accounts.

This list is in no way exhaustive, however, in that political calculations also entered the picture. For example, several proponents of introducing a small individual account in the current social security program concluded that increasing taxes to support the current system was impossible and introducing a small individual account was the only way to get more money in the program. Many also think that a combined defined-benefit/individual account approach is more politically stable in the long run than the current system. Individual account proponents generally place great weight on the merits of individual control and the ability to match risks to tastes. Therefore, political assessments and value judgments—perhaps more than economics—have brought the individual account debate to the fore.

Can Individual Accounts Produce Higher Returns?

Advocates of privatization often suggest that if participants simply invested their payroll tax contributions in the market instead of sending them to the United States Treasury they could enjoy significantly higher returns. To understand the problem with this simple assertion requires separating three very distinct aspects of privatization proposals. The first pertains to funding: "Should reserves be accumulated in advance of benefit payments?" The second pertains to investments: "To what extent should those accumulated reserves be invested in equities?" The third issue relates to the provision of benefits: "Should benefits be provided under the current defined benefit plan or through individual accounts?" Once these issues are separated, it becomes clear that moving to individual accounts without prefunding will not raise returns on social security contributions, after taking account of transition costs and risks.

It is true that private market returns are high and social security returns are low, but the reason for the low projected return on social security contributions in the United States is a $9 trillion unfunded liability. This liability reflects the fact that, under our pay-as-you-go system, early generations received benefits far in excess of their payroll tax contributions, and later generations have to pay the bill for these large net transfers. If workers invest all their new payroll tax contributions in the market, some mechanism still must be found to pay off promised benefits to current retirees and those nearing retirement (since no one suggests reneging on these commitments). One approach would be to borrow the money and issue recognition bonds to workers and retirees for the full amount of their promised benefits. The government, however, would have to raise new taxes to pay the interest on these bonds, and—for identical portfolios — the new taxes would offset all of the higher returns on individual accounts.[6] In other words, the rate of return in the privatized system, net of new taxes, would be identical to the low returns under the existing system.

Thus, shifting to individual accounts without prefunding would not raise returns from social security. Prefunding either in the trust funds or individual accounts would eventually raise returns, but higher returns to future generations would be gained at the expense of lower returns to current generations who have to pay twice, first to cover promised benefits for others and second to build up reserves in their own accounts. The question of how much to prefund requires weighing the welfare of one generation against that of another. Without prefunding, however, a shift to individual accounts cannot raise returns. Because it is possible to have equivalent amounts of funding in social security trust funds or in a system of defined contribution accounts and because equity investment is possible in either scenario, the question comes down to whether individual accounts or a defined benefit plan are better for people's basic retirement benefits.

3. The Case against Individual Accounts

The basic argument against shifting to individual accounts is that it is inconsistent with the goals of the social security program; it would put people's basic retirement benefits at risk and make them unpredictable. The whole point of having a social security system is to provide workers with a predictable basic retirement income to which they can add income from private pensions and other sources. If it is appropriate for the government to interfere with private sector decisions to ensure a basic level of retirement income, it does not make sense for that basic amount to be uncertain, reflecting one's good luck or investment skills.

Risks and Cost of Individual Accounts

In addition to the fundamental philosophical argument, individual accounts raise a host of practical problems, including potential access before retirement, lack of automatic annuitization, and cost:

- *Access before retirement.* Individual accounts create a very real political risk that account holders would pressure Congress for early access to these accounts, albeit for worthy purposes such as medical expenses, education, or home purchase. Although most proposals prohibit such withdrawals, experience with existing Individual Retirement Accounts and employer-sponsored defined contribution plans suggests that holding the line is unlikely. To the extent that Congress acquiesces and allows early access—no matter how worthy the purpose—many retirees will end up with lower, and in some cases inadequate, retirement income.

- *Lack of automatic annuitization.* Another risk is that individuals stand a good chance of outliving their savings, unless the money accumulated in their individual accounts is transformed into annuities. But few people purchase private annuities and costs are high in the private annuity market.[7] Even if costs were not high, the necessity of purchasing an annuity at retirement exposes individuals to interest rate risk; if rates are high when they retire, they will receive a large monthly amount, if rates are low, the amount will be much smaller. Moreover, the private annuity market does not offer full inflation-adjusted benefits. In contrast, by keeping participants together and forcing them to convert their funds into annuities, social security avoids adverse selection and is in a good position to provide inflation-adjusted benefits.

- *Cost.* The 1994-96 Social Security Advisory Council estimated that the administrative costs for an "Individual Retirement Account (IRA)" approach would amount to 100 basis points per year.[8] A 100-basis point annual charge sounds benign, but it would reduce total accumulations by roughly 20 percent over a 40-year work life. Moreover, while the 100-basis-point estimate includes the cost of marketing, tracking, and maintaining the account, it does not include brokerage fees. If the individual does not select an index fund, then transaction costs may be twice as high. Indeed, the United Kingdom, which has a system of personal saving accounts, has experienced considerably higher costs.[9] Finally, unless prohibited by regulation, these transaction costs involve a flat charge per account that will be considerably more burdensome for low-income participants than for those with higher incomes.

Implications for Benefits over the Long Run

While individual accounts are merely risky and costly for the average and above average worker, they could end up being disastrous for low-income workers in the future. The whole point of shifting funds to individual accounts is to emphasize individual equity— that is, a fair return for the individual saver—rather than adequacy for all. Taking part of what the high earner makes to improve the return for the low earner would be contrary to the spirit of such a plan. To meet this objection many advocates of the defined contribution approach provide either a flat benefit amount or a healthy minimum benefit for low-wage workers. Although such provisions will protect low-income workers in the short term, opponents of these accounts believe that maintaining redistribution within the program is unlikely to be sustainable.

A mixed system with a flat benefit and an individual account is likely to respond very differently to change over time than the existing defined benefit arrangement. For example, suppose that the overall size of social security was viewed as too large as the retirement of the baby boom nears. Benefit cuts under the existing program would likely affect all people at all points in the income distribution proportionately; for example, the extension of the normal retirement age from 65 to 67 in 1983 was a form of across-the-board cut. Congress might even attempt to protect the benefits of workers with low incomes. Cuts under a mixed system are likely to be very different. Congress is likely to view the individual account component as individual saving and see little gain from cutting it back. The more likely target would be the flat minimum benefit, which goes to both those who need it and those who do not. Higher wage workers are going to find they get very little for their payroll tax dollar from such a residual social security program and will withdraw their support. As the minimum is cut repeatedly, it will become inadequate for low-wage workers. In response, Congress is likely to replace the flat benefit with a means-tested program.

Observers sometimes argue that the same economic outcome can be achieved either through means-tested benefits or through social insurance payments that are then taxed back. This conclusion ignores psychological, social, political, and institutional factors in the United States. Means-tested and social insurance programs in the United States grow out of different historic traditions, have different impacts on their recipients, and are viewed very differently by the public. Social insurance reflects a long history of people getting together to help themselves. This self-help approach means that individuals have an earned right to benefits, since they receive payments based on contributions from their past earnings. The programs involve no test of need, and program benefits can be supplemented with income from saving or other sources. Means-tested programs in the United States, on the other hand, grow out of the punitive and paternalistic poor-law tradition, which recognizes only begrudgingly a public responsibility for providing for the impoverished. Means-tested benefits tend to be less adequate than those provided under social insurance programs and have a stigma, which means that many who are eligible never claim their benefits. To the extent that people at the low end of the income distribution are forced to rely on means-tested benefits, they are likely to be worse off than they would be under the existing defined benefit social security system.

4. Conclusion

The irony that emerges from the preceding analysis is that while the United States appears to have the smallest social security financing problem among major developed countries, it is currently engaged in the most extensive debate about a comprehensive restructuring of its system.

The reason that the problems in the United States are less severe than elsewhere is that the United States enjoys a higher fertility rate than other countries where fertility has slipped below replacement. Higher fertility means that the population will not age as rapidly or as much in the United States as in other countries, producing lower dependency ratios. In addition to more favorable demographics, the United States also has more older workers in the labor market than other countries. This means that the support burden on future workers will not be as great. In addition to a higher ratio of workers to retirees, the United States also provides a more modest social security benefit than other public plans. Because of these factors, the United States deficit over the 75-year projection period is less than 2 percent of payroll. This shortfall can be easily closed within the structure of the current program.

Despite the benign outlook for social security, plans abound to dramatically restructure the system. Although enthusiasm for introducing some form of individual accounts have come from both sides of the political aisle over the last several years, the issue has turned sharply partisan in the 2000 Presidential campaign. Enthusiasm for individual accounts sometimes rests on the lure of higher returns, but most analysts agree that higher returns without additional prefunding can never produce higher returns once transition costs and risk are factored into the calculations. Prefunding with or without individual accounts can eventually produce higher returns, but only by placing a greater burden on the current generation who have to pay simultaneously for current benefits and to build up reserves.

The legitimate arguments for private accounts rest on questions of individual control and better matching of portfolios to individual risk preference. Some proponents also believe that individual accounts would be more stable politically over the long run; others think that they might enhance the possibility of getting more funds into the system. The question is whether the possible gains from individual accounts are worth the costs. The answer seems clearly "no." If it is appropriate for the government to interfere with private sector decisions to ensure a basic level of retirement income, it does not make sense for that basic amount to be uncertain, depending on one's investment skills. Individual accounts also are costly, and expose participants to the temptations of early withdrawal and the risks associated with private annuitization at retirement. More fundamentally, separating income support from social insurance in the United States will almost certainly produce less redistribution, which will harm future generations of low-wage workers.

Notes

1.   See Gruber, Jonathan, and Wise, David (eds.). 1999. *Social Security and Retirement Around the World.* National Bureau of Economic Research. Chicago: University of Chicago Press.

2.　See Weaver, R. Kent. 1998. "The Politics of Pensions: Lessons from Abroad," Arnold, A. Douglas, Graetz, Michael J., and Munnell, Alicia H. (eds.), *Framing the Social Security Debate: Values, Politics and Economics.* Washington, D.C.: Brookings Institution Press for the National Academy of Social Insurance.

3.　See Chand, Sheetal K., and Jaeger, Albert. 1996. *Aging Populations and Public Pension Schemes.* International Monetary Fund.

4.　For example, all three proposals emerging from the 1994-1996 Advisory Council on Social Security (1997) advocated equity investment.

5.　Advisory Council on Social Security Reform, 1996, Munnell and Balduzzi, 1998, and Aaron and Reischauer, 1998.

6.　See Geanakoplos, John, Mitchell, Olivia S., and Zeldes, Stephen P. 1998. "Would a Privatized Social Security System Really Pay a Higher Return?" Arnold, A. Douglas; Graetz, Michael J., and Munnell, Alicia H. (eds.), *Framing the Social Security Debate: Values, Politics and Economics.* Washington, D.C.: Brookings Institution Press for the National Academy of Social Insurance.

　　　Projected returns on privatized accounts might appear higher because contributions were invested in stocks rather than bonds. But stocks involve more risk than bonds, so their returns need to be adjusted for risk before comparing them with the safe returns from a conventional social security system. If all households held both stocks and bonds, they should value an additional dollar of stocks the same as an additional dollar of bonds, even though stocks have a much higher expected return before adjusting for their added risk. That is, the risk-adjusted return on stocks and bonds would be identical. In this case, it is appropriate to compare the current system to a privatized system in which the individual accounts were invested only in bonds. This conclusion has to be modified to the extent that some households currently do not have access to equity investment.

7.　The reason for the high costs is adverse selection: people who think that they will live for a long time purchase annuities, whereas those with, say, a serious illness keep their cash. Private insurers have to raise premiums to address the adverse selection problem, and this makes the purchase of annuities very expensive for the average person.

8.　In addition to costs, a study by the Employee Benefit Research Institute (Olsen and Salisbury, 1998) raised real questions about the ability, in anything like the near term, to administer a system of individual accounts in a satisfactory way. Unlike the current social security program that deals with the reporting of wage credits, a system of personal accounts would involve the transfer of real money. It is only reasonable that participants would care about every dollar, and therefore employer errors in account names and numbers that arise under the current program would create enormous public relations problems under a system of individual accounts.

9.　See Murthi, Mamta, Orszag, Michael, and Orszag, Peter R. 1999. "Administrative Costs and Individual Accounts: Lessons from the U.K. Experience," The World Bank (February).

Bibliography

Aaron, Henry J., and Reischauer, Robert D. 1998. *Countdown to Reform: The Great Social Security Debate.* New York, NY: The Century Foundation Press.

Advisory Council on Social Security. 1997. *Report of the 1994-1996 Advisory Council on Social Security.* Washington, D.C.: U.S. Government Printing Office.

Chand, Sheetal K., and Jaeger, Albert. 1996. *Aging Populations and Public Pension Schemes*. International Monetary Fund.

Diamond, Peter A. 1999. *Issues in Privatizing Social Security*. Cambridge, MA: The MIT Press for the National Academy of Social Insurance.

—. 1998. "Economics of Social Security Reform: An Overview," Arnold, A. Douglas, Graetz, Michael J., and Munnell, Alicia H. (eds.), *Framing the Social Security Debate: Values, Politics and Economics*. Washington, D.C.: Brookings Institution Press for the National Academy of Social Insurance.

Geanakoplos, John, Mitchell, Olivia S., and Zeldes, Stephen P. 1998. "Would a Privatized Social Security System Really Pay a Higher Return?" Arnold, A. Douglas, Graetz, Michael J., and Munnell, Alicia H. (eds.), *Framing the Social Security Debate: Values, Politics and Economics*. Washington, D.C.: Brookings Institution Press for the National Academy of Social Insurance.

Gruber, Jonathan, and Wise, David (eds.). 1999. *Social Security and Retirement Around the World*. National Bureau of Economic Research. Chicago: University of Chicago Press.

Munnell, Alicia H., and Balduzzi, Pierluigi 1998. "Investing the Social Security Trust Funds in Equities," Public Policy Institute, American Association of Retired Persons, #9802 (March).

Murthi, Mamta, Orszag, Michael, and Orszag, Peter R. 1999. "Administrative Costs and Individual Accounts: Lessons from the U.K. Experience," The World Bank (February).

Olsen, Kelly A., and Salisbury, Dallas L. 1998. "Individual Social Security Accounts: Issues in Assessing Administrative Feasibility and Costs," Special Report and Issue Brief #203 (November).

Roseveare, Deborah, Leibfritz, Willi, Fore, Douglas, and Wurzel, Eckhard. 1996. "Ageing Populations, Pension Systems and Government Budgets: Simulations for 20 OECD Countries," Economics Department Working Paper No. 168. OECD.

United Nations Secretariat, Population Division, Department of Economic and Social Affairs. 2000. *Replacement Migration: Is it a Solution to Declining and Ageing Populations?*

U.S. Social Security Administration. 1999. *Fast Facts and Figures about Social Security*.

U.S. Social Security Administration, Office of Policy, Office of Research Evaluation, and Statistics. 1999. *Social Security Programs Throughout the World 1999*. SSA Publication No. 13-11805 (August).

Weaver, R. Kent. 1998. "The Politics of Pensions: Lessons from Abroad," Arnold, A. Douglas, Graetz, Michael J., and Munnell, Alicia H. (eds.), *Framing the Social Security Debate: Values, Politics and Economics*. Washington, D.C.: Brookings Institution Press for the National Academy of Social Insurance.

6

Strengthening Public Pensions with Private Investment—Canada's Approach to Privatization Pressures

M. Townson

Like many other industrialized countries, Canada has been debating how best to provide financial security for its aging population. During the 1990s, much of the debate centered on what changes needed to be made to the public-sponsored earnings-related plan, the Canada Pension Plan (CPP), which constitutes the second pillar of Canada's retirement income system.[1] The CPP has been a pay-as-you-go plan since its inception in 1966 and is funded entirely by contributions from workers and their employers, with no allocation from general tax revenues. The focus of the debate was therefore on the need for contribution rate increases and the acceptability of increasingly higher rates over the next 30 to 40 years.

With the objective of limiting future contribution rate increases, changes were implemented at the beginning of January 1998 to move to a system of partial funding, with an arms-length investment board charged with investing the fund in the private capital market. Investment earnings on the fund will be used to supplement contribution revenue so that contribution rates can be maintained at a "steady state" after 2003, with no further increases. The adoption of this form of privatization has generally been seen as a way of strengthening the publicly managed plan so it will continue as a social insurance arrangement for the foreseeable future.

1. A Balanced System at Moderate Cost

Canada's retirement income system has a mix of public and private arrangements that is generally acknowledged to be a reasonable balance between collective and individual responsibility for retirement provision. By the standards of OECD countries, Canadian public expenditures on income security for the elderly are relatively modest and are expected to peak at levels well below those anticipated in most other western countries in the twenty-first century.[2]

Public programs are still the major source of income for the current elderly (see Appendix table). Public pensions—in particular the maturing of the CPP—have been responsible for significant reductions in poverty and inequality among the elderly over the past two decades. Low-income rates among Canadian seniors—defined as those aged 65 or older—measured by the usual international standard based on persons with adjusted incomes less than half the median income, are now among the lowest in the OECD.[3]

2. Changes to the Second Pillar

The escalating cost of the Canada Pension Plan has been the subject of some concern over the past decade or so. As a social insurance program, the CPP includes not only retirement pensions, but pensions for those who become disabled and their dependent children, as well as protection for survivors including dependent children of deceased contributors. Retirement pensions are equivalent to 25 percent of inflation-adjusted average annual lifetime earnings up to the average wage.

In 1985, federal and provincial finance ministers who jointly administered the plan, adopted a 25-year schedule of contribution rates, which allowed for gradual rate increases to accommodate population aging. However, the Chief Actuary's report, produced for the statutory review of the plan in 1995, indicated that for various reasons, contribution rate increases would have to be higher than had been anticipated. It was suggested that combined employer/employee rates might reach close to 14 percent of covered earnings by 2030, compared with a combined employer/employee rate of 5.6 percent in 1996.

A range of possible policy options was presented for public discussion—including various combinations of reduced benefits and increased contribution rates. The possibility of investing most or all future available funds in the market was also raised. The government made no suggestion that contribution revenues might be directed to individual accounts, nor did it propose moving to the kind of second pillar privatization favored by the World Bank. In fact, polling conducted for the federal Department of Finance around the time of the public consultations found "a massive majority of Canadians wants the CPP to continue" and that "this desire cuts across all age groups and all income levels."[4]

A key theme that emerged during the public consultations was a strong desire to see the CPP remain a public pension plan rather than privatized. Most participants wanted the public system preserved, fearing that its many benefits would be lost if the plan were privatized.[5] For example, the "drop-out" provisions of the CPP which protect workers who have periods of illness or unemployment, would be lost if the second pillar defined benefit plan were replaced with private, defined contribution arrangements. Another feature of the CPP that is particularly important for women is the provision which allows a parent to exclude years when they had a child under the age of seven from the calculation of average lifetime earnings on which the retirement pension is based. This protection would also be lost in a system of individual accounts. The social insurance features of the CPP such as disability coverage and provisions for surviving spouses of contributors would also be lost.

However, there was a vocal minority involved in the public consultations, led by two of three participating taxpayer associations, which argued in favor of privatization. They criticized the pay-as-you-go approach and the proposed significant increases in contribution rates. And they suggested the CPP be replaced with a mandatory, defined-contribution, fully-funded, privately managed plan.

3. Investing the CPP Fund in the Market

Ultimately, federal and provincial ministers rejected this form of privatization. Under considerable pressure from the business community, they decided that combined employer/employee contribution rates could not be allowed to exceed 10 percent of covered earnings. They adopted a proposal for a rapid increase in contribution rates over a six-year period to reach a combined employer/employee rate of 9.9 percent of covered earnings by 2003. According to the ministers, this level, known as the "steady-state rate," should sustain the CPP indefinitely—throughout the period when the baby boomers enter retirement and afterwards—so that no further rate increases will be required. Provisions were also implemented to slow the growth in costs by tightening up the administration of benefits—particularly of disability benefits—and by changing the way some benefits are calculated.

The new higher contribution rate will generate more than enough revenue to pay current benefits. The objective in moving to a higher rate so quickly was to use surplus contribution revenue to build up an investment fund equivalent to about five years' worth of benefits. Previously, legislation required the finance ministers to set contribution rates at a level that would generate sufficient revenue to pay current benefits and maintain a contingency reserve equivalent to two years' worth of benefits. The reserve was invested in 20-year non-marketable securities of provincial governments at the federal government's cost of funds—somewhat lower than provinces would pay on their own market borrowing.

Building up a larger fund and earning a higher rate of return through investment in the market, is intended to help pay for the rapidly growing costs that will occur once baby boomers start to retire, around 2010. An arm's length Investment Board has been appointed to manage the invested assets. As a transitional measure, provinces were given the option of rolling over existing CPP borrowings at maturity for another 20-year term. For the first three years, provinces also have access to 50 percent of new CPP funds that the board chooses to invest in bonds. After this three-year period, to ensure the fund's investment in provincial securities is consistent with market practice, new CPP funds invested in provincial securities will be limited to the proportion of provincial bonds held by pension funds in general.

As a result of these transitional arrangements, the share of CPP assets managed by the board is still quite small. In determining its asset mix, the board has taken into consideration the amounts that are already invested in government bonds and as a result, 100 percent of new investments have been allocated to equities. Initially, the board was required to adopt a passive investment program, which substantially replicates one or more broad market indexes by investing in domestic and foreign stock index funds. In December 1999, the federal and provincial finance ministers agreed to expand the investment scope. The board may now invest actively up to 50 percent of the assets that are allocated to domestic securities.

The fund is expected to grow steadily over the coming years, from about $3 billion at the beginning of 2000 to more than $100 billion within 10 years, making it the biggest pension fund in the Canadian marketplace.[6] The president and chief executive officer of the Investment Board says that managing these assets "will inevitably involve exploring a full arsenal of investment strategies...passive and active investing in public equity and debt securities, merchant banking, private equity and debt, infrastructure projects, venture capital opportunities, real estate investments and derivative contracts."[7]

However, the size of the fund and a shift to a more active investment approach is bound to raise issues such as the potential impact of such a large fund on the market; the exercise of proxy voting rights by the fund managers; and the limitation on foreign investments, which are currently restricted to 30 percent of the book value of assets. It remains to be seen how these questions will be addressed.

It must also be emphasized that even when the new investment fund is fully up and running, the CPP will still be essentially a pay-as-you-go plan. At the end of 1997, for example, the plan's assets of $36 billion represented about 8 percent of liabilities. Under the new funding formula, assets will eventually reach 20 percent of liabilities.

However, it is expected that this form of partial privatization will allow the government to avoid significant contribution rate increases over the next 30 years. It has also been seen as a way of improving public confidence in the stability of the plan—in effect, resisting the pressure for more radical measures such as replacing the CPP with mandatory individual savings accounts.

4. Tax Assistance for Other Private Arrangements

Canada's retirement income system also involves a considerable amount of tax assistance to private investments through the third pillar. These are intended to supplement the relatively modest first and second pillar arrangements. For tax purposes, individuals may deduct their contributions to workplace pension plans, generally known as Registered Pension Plans (RPPs), within certain limits. As well, there is a system of Registered Retirement Savings Plans (RRSPs) which are voluntary savings arrangements for which contributors also receive a tax deduction. In both arrangements, taxation of earnings is deferred until funds are withdrawn in the form of pensions, annuities or lump sums. At that time, both interest and principal become taxable income.

The federal government estimates that deductions for contributions to these plans, and the non-taxation of investment income, involved a loss of tax revenue in 1997 of $22.8 billion. About $8 billion was recouped in taxation of amounts withdrawn, leaving a net cost for these two programs in 1997 of $14.8 billion. The government's own projections indicated the net cost of these programs will be almost $16 billion by 2001.[8] In spite of current high costs, advocates of privatization would like to see even greater tax assistance directed to these third pillar arrangements. They point out that the net cost to the government of such plans will probably decline in future as the baby boom generation moves into retirement and withdrawals from these plans increase—perhaps even exceeding contributions.

Most people do not take full advantage of the tax-assisted voluntary private savings accounts in the third pillar. In 1997, for example, Canadians aged 25 to 64 contributed only 12 percent of the total $185 billion that could have been contributed to RRSPs—generally referred to as "RRSP room." And in the seven-year period from 1991 to 1997, only 14.5 percent of RRSP contributors made contributions each year. Coverage of workplace pension plans has also been declining and only 41 percent of paid workers are now covered by these plans. Income is the biggest factor in private saving for retirement. As income rises, so does the likelihood of having RRSP or RPP savings.[9]

One of the weaknesses of the system of voluntary savings plans in the third pillar is that there is actually no requirement they be used for retirement. Contributors may borrow from their RRSPs, without tax consequences, to finance home purchases and post-secondary education, provided these withdrawals are repaid within a certain period of time. Lump sum withdrawals may be made at any time for any purpose, provided amounts withdrawn are declared as income, which then becomes taxable. In fact, there is evidence individuals cash in their RRSP savings prior to retirement when they face difficult economic circumstances, such as unemployment or financial hardship.

5. Continued Pressure for Privatization

The move to partial funding of the CPP has been welcomed by many as an innovative approach to addressing the concerns generated by pay-as-you-go plans in light of population aging. However, it has not eliminated the pressure for other forms of privatization, although there has been little public support to date for adopting the kind of second pillar arrangements favored by the World Bank which would involve replacing the CPP with a system of individual savings accounts along the lines of the Chilean model.

At the beginning of the 1990s, this approach had been advocated by the official opposition party in the federal parliament, and supported by some research organizations and commentators. More recently, proponents of privatization have advocated that individuals be allowed to opt out of the CPP, which is a defined benefit plan, and have their mandatory contributions directed to private, defined contribution retirement savings arrangements, in much the same way as the system introduced in Britain in the 1980s.

There is no doubt that recent high stock market returns have proved attractive—especially to younger people, who are now particularly susceptible to the argument of the privatization advocates that young people would be "better off" investing for retirement on their own rather than contributing to the CPP. Recent surveys indicate that many Canadians—and particularly younger people—know little about the public pension program and the kind of benefits it provides. Associated with this lack of knowledge is the finding that confidence in the stability of the CPP to be there for individuals' retirement is also very low. Individuals aged 25 to 34 are the most likely age group to believe they will not receive anything from public pensions.[10] In the circumstances, there is fertile ground for anyone trying to make a case for individual accounts and private investment as a replacement for collective responsibility and social insurance.

Notably lacking in the debate so far is any public discussion of the high cost of individual accounts—especially in a decentralized system such as Canada now has, and the very high transition costs of moving from a pay-as-you-go plan to individual savings arrangements—even when those take the form of opting out from the earnings-related pay-as-you-go plan.

According to some researchers, a reduction in the state's involvement in social security by returning social programs to a social assistance function for those most in need, while encouraging market place solutions for income security and maintenance, would likely lead to an increase in rates of poverty and income inequality among future generations of Canadian seniors.[11] Given the acclaimed success of Canada's public pension programs in reducing poverty and inequality among the elderly, it seems unlikely that Canadians would be willing to countenance a reversal in that trend at this point in time.

Notes

1.   The province of Quebec operates its own parallel Quebec Pension Plan, with virtually identical provisions. The two plans are integrated so that individuals with earnings records in both the QPP and CPP receive benefits based on their combined records from both plans. For the sake of convenience, this paper refers to the Canada Pension Plan, although the issues discussed are relevant to both plans.
2.   Organization for Economic Cooperation and Development. 1997. *Aging in OECD Countries.* Paris: OECD.
3.   Myles, John. 2000. *The Maturation of Canada's Retirement Income System: Income Levels, Income Inequality and Low-Income among the Elderly.* Ottawa: Statistics Canada.
4.   Earnscliffe Research & Communications. 1996. *A Report to the Department of Finance Quantitative Research on Pension Issues.* Ottawa: December.
5.   Government of Canada. 1997. *Securing the Canada Pension Plan: An Agreement on proposed Changes to the CPP.* Ottawa: February.
6.   Dollar figures throughout are in Canadian dollars.
7.   MacNaughton, John A. 2000. *Remarks to the Pension Investment Association of Canada Conference,* 4 May, Toronto: Canada Pension Plan Investment Board.
8.   Finance Canada. 1999. *Tax Expenditures 1999.* Ottawa: Department of Finance, Government of Canada.
9.   Statistics Canada. 1999. *Retirement Savings Through RPPs and RRSPs–1991 to 1997.* Ottawa: Statistics Canada.
10.   Human Resources Development Canada. 2000. *Canadian Attitudes Toward the Public Pension Plan and Retirement Planning.* Submitted by Ekos Associates Inc. Ottawa.
11.   Prus, Steven G. 1999. *Income Inequality as a Canadian Cohort Ages: An Analysis of the Later Life Course.* Hamilton, Ontario: McMaster University Program for Research on A Social and Economic Dimensions of an Aging Population. SEDAP Research Paper No. 10.

Bibliography

Government of Canada. 1996. *A Report to the Department of Finance Quantitative Research on Pension Issues.* Ottawa: Submitted by Earnscliffe Research & Communications to the Department of Finance.

—. 1997. *Securing the Canada Pension Plan: An Agreement on Proposed Changes to the CPP*. Ottawa: Department of Finance.

—. 1999. *Tax Expenditures 1999*. Ottawa: Department of Finance.

—. 1999. *Retirement Savings Through RPPs and RRSPs—1991 to 1997*. Ottawa: Statistics Canada.

—. 1999. *Pension Plans in Canada—1 January, 1998*. Ottawa: Statistics Canada.

—. 2000. *Canadian Attitudes Toward the Public Pension Plan and Retirement Planning*. Ottawa: Submitted by Ekos Associates Inc. to Human Resources Development Canada.

MacNaughton, John A. 2000. *Remarks to the Pension Investment Association of Canada Conference*, 4 May. Toronto: Canada Pension Plan Investment Board.

Myles, John. 2000. *The Maturation of Canada's Retirement Income System: Income Levels, Income Inequality and Low-Income among the Elderly*. Ottawa: Statistics Canada.

Organization for Economic Cooperation and Development. 1997. *Aging in OECD Countries*. Paris: OECD.

Prus, Steven G. 1999. *Income Inequality as a Canadian Cohort Ages: An Analysis of the Later Life Course*. Hamilton, Ontario: McMaster University Program for Research on Social and Economic Dimensions of an Aging Population. SEDAP Research Paper No. 10.

Appendix

Sources of Income of Canadians Aged 65+
1981, 1994 and 1997

	1981	1994	1997
Income from public programs			
Earnings-related plans			
CPP/QPP	9.7	20.4	21.4
Unemployment insurance	0.2	0.3	0.1
Total	9.9	20.7	21.5
Income from government sources			
Old Age Security and Guaranteed Income Supplement	34.0	30.2	28.7
Social assistance	1.4	1.0	0.7
Other public programs	1.6	2.7	3.1
Total	37.0	33.9	32.5
Total income from public programs	46.8	54.7	**54.1**
Income from employment or private sources			
Employment income	12.1	7.0	7.6
Investment income	26.9	13.6	11.6
Other money income	1.8	1.8	1.6
Retirement pensions*	12.3	19.1	20.6
RRSPs*	...	3.8	4.6
Total income from employment and private sources	53.1	45.3	46.0
Total**	100.0	100.0	100.0

* Registered Retirement Savings Plans (RRSPs) are voluntary tax-assisted defined contri-
bution savings accounts. Data on RRSPs were included with retirement pensions in 1981.
** Totals may not add because of rounding.
Source: Statistics Canada, Income Statistics Division.

Part 3

Privatization: A Tool for Governance?

7

Germany: Efficiency and Affordability in Social Security through Partial Privatization of Provision for Risks

J. Husmann

1. The Challenges for Social Policy

In many industrialized countries, a paradigm change in social policy can be noted, towards keeping the social security system efficient and affordable over the long term. The goal is an optimal mix of public pay-as-you-go systems on the one hand and private, funded provision for risks on the other. The present dominance of the public collective system cannot go on as it is, primarily for the following two reasons:

Firstly, demographic change, attributable to rising life expectancy and falling birth rates, means that in future a smaller number of people in work will have to support more and more older citizens. This applies not only to pensions, but increasingly to health and dependency insurance as well. For the OECD, the average proportion of those over 65 in the population as a whole will almost double between 1990 and 2030, from 19.3 to 37.7 percent. In the USA and Great Britain this proportion will rise from 19.1 to 36.8 percent and from 24.0 to 38.7 percent respectively. For Germany, an increase from 21.7 to 49.2 percent is forecast. The related burden cannot be borne by the active population and enterprises in the form of even higher taxes and social contributions.

Secondly, payroll costs, especially additional employee costs, which in Germany are fixed at over 60 percent by legislation and state social security, are already a frequent obstacle to investment and new jobs and thus to a reduction in the high level of unemployment which gives such cause for concern in many countries. In Germany, for example, additional employee costs in 1998 were 21.58 marks per hour. On top of that is the excessive tax burden on employees' incomes in countries such as Germany, among others. The tax and social insurance burden on income in some countries is already over 50 percent on average. This leads to a significant disincentive to work.

2. Social Policy Guidelines

The starting point and target scope of social policy can no longer be based on a state pay-as-you-go social system, for which the necessary contributions or taxation to finance it are a kind of balancing figure, without a reduction in demand from the public. Rather, the starting point in all branches of social security will increasingly be a question of what level of services can be delivered for a tolerable burden of taxation. In this connection, the following fundamental principles are of particular importance.

In establishing a compulsory state system to cover life's risks, care must be taken to ensure that it is in harmony with the principle of subsidiarity. Such compulsory systems should not unduly restrict private initiatives and room for maneuver, and should thus be confined to what is absolutely essential, i.e., a basic insurance. Under the principle of subsidiarity, therefore, collective state insurance systems provide a counterpart to private, personal responsibility for risk provision. To help those who cannot provide for themselves or can do so only in part is the task at the origin of social solidarity among those who pay contributions and taxes.

In this sense, social insurance systems are a basic component of a social market economy. On the other hand, it is necessary to limit it to an efficient and affordable size. This is in no way a backward-looking social policy. A basic compulsory state system is instead intended to modernize the social insurance system by concentrating on the essentials and increasing individual freedom of choice. This does not mean achieving equality of outcomes, but equality of opportunity, tempered by a social safety net which adequately provides essential security.

3. The Role of the Economy

A social policy focusing on these basics provides an optimal framework for economic growth and employment, thus ensuring its own financial basis. The central task of a modern, forward-looking social policy is therefore to achieve a significant and lasting reduction in the burden of taxation and contributions on employees and firms through far-reaching and lasting structural reforms in all areas of social security. By this means, in the same way as targeted state incentives, whereby the capacity and willingness of individuals to take out their own supplementary private insurance are strengthened, a better mix of state pay-as-you-go and private-funded risk provision, more advantageous for society as a whole as well as its individual members, is concurrently made attainable. Structuring social insurance systems as mixed systems in this way will in future not only be an essential precondition for improving the economic environment, but also indispensable in avoiding an ever-increasing burden on the state social security system as a result of demographic trends.

Social security systems are factors of production as well as cost factors, and a stable balance must be struck between them in the interests of all concerned. Employers in Germany thus acknowledge their social responsibilities and are in favor of the necessary adequate social insurance for the population. Their participation in social policy, including in the form of joint participation in self-administration of insurance institutions, and their financial share of statutory pensions, health, unemployment, dependency and accident insurance, illustrate their involvement and co-responsibility. This responsibility means seeking new forms of organization of social security systems in the future. Greater individual responsibility through privatization of parts of the previously state-dominated social security system thus assumes particular importance. Without such partial privatization, social security systems will sooner or later become impossible to finance. The transition to a modern mixed system must therefore be tackled in good time, in progressive stages. No one would be served by frictions and sudden changes in the system caused by dammed up pressure for change.

4. Structure of Mixed Systems

A decisive factor in the functioning of a social security system is primarily its structure based on business management methods, ensured quality and a statement of mission. In the case of health insurance, for example, this is highlighted in the World Health Report 2000 of the World Health Organization, published in June 2000, in which the health systems of the 191 WHO Members were evaluated. According to the report, the health system of the USA, first in the world in terms of expenditure, was only 37th in the rankings. With respect to the overstretched social security systems in many industrialized countries, the necessary reforms will have to be carried out on the contributions side. In Germany, social insurance charges currently represent 41.1 percent of wages, compared with 26.5 percent in 1970. Over the next thirty years, other things being equal, a further increase to around 50 percent is forecast.

In the area of statutory pensions insurance it is clear that, in Germany, pensions in future can no longer rise proportionately to trends in net salaries and pay, as they have up to now. Changes are needed to dampen the pace of pensions growth in order to clear the way for achieving the priority goal of stability of contributions. For Germany this means that if contributions are not to rise by over 20 percent in the next thirty years, a gradual reduction in the level of provision from the current 70 percent to 62 percent of relevant income from employment is needed. Statutory pension insurance is no longer in a position to guarantee living standards in old age, so a greater share must be assumed by the other pillars of old-age insurance, such as company pension schemes and private pensions. This should be on a voluntary basis and accompanied by state incentives. In order not to overburden individuals, the state tax burden should be reduced through an appropriate restructuring of tax and social policy. The benefits of such partial privatization are a redistribution of pension insurance amongst the three pillars, giving greater stability and a better economic mix of pay-as-you-go and funding. It also means reducing the state tax burden for individuals and firms to acceptable limits.

Statutory health insurance as well, can and should be retailored on a lasting efficient and affordable basis through partial privatization. Services which lie outside medical need do not belong in a statutory state system, but should be covered by private personal risk insurance. This encourages a cost-effective approach. In addition, fundamental quality assurance measures are needed. For Germany, the resulting potential for rationalization of current services is estimated at 10 percent, which would mean savings of between 25 and 30 billion marks. The average level of contribution for statutory health insurance can thus be considerably reduced. In order to achieve this potential for savings in practice, a return to market economy principles is necessary, i.e., more competition throughout the entire health service. Above all, this means more scope for health insurance funds in contracting with doctors, hospitals, etc., as well as in insurance policies and, accordingly, in services to their insured. Statutory health insurance funds should have the possibility of offering a range of service packages.

There is also a need for action in unemployment and dependency insurance. Direct state and pay-as-you-go financed dependency insurance, introduced in Germany in 1995, are highly dependent on demographic trends. This is because the risk of dependency is primarily a risk of the old and very old, whose number will rise strongly both in absolute and relative terms.

5. New Structure of Social Policy

International experience shows that state social policy up to now is not at all suited to the demands of a modern social system. Only by reverting to the subsidiarity of the state statutory system in insuring life's risks and making social security systems once again a basic insurance system can social and employment policy goals be achieved over the long term. Collective public social insurance systems need to be complemented by private individual provision. Both elements need to be combined in a better mix.

An expansion of services, still occasionally discussed despite the current strained financial situation and especially the future demographically generated financial constraints, cannot, in a country like Germany, be financed without cutbacks in other areas. Instead of increased bureaucracy and interventionism, what is needed is more competition and privatization. Instead of still higher statutory contributions and service levels, efficient and employment friendly social systems are needed. Likewise, social policy must actively pursue the goals of significantly reducing the burden of taxes and contributions, encouraging investment and economic growth, preserving and creating jobs and increasing self-reliance.

8

Privatization: From Panacea to Poison Pill—The Dutch Paradigm

D. Hermans

1. Introduction

Just as in other industrialized Western countries, concern has arisen in the Netherlands during recent decades about the demands being made on the social security system, and how these are to be financed. In addition to intervention in policy relating to conditions, far reaching forms of privatization have also been considered, with a view to achieving a more efficient and effective system.

An initial belief in the miracles of privatization and market forces has, however, recently changed again almost completely; important elements of the administration of the social security regulations will now be more public than ever before.

I will describe this interesting political change of direction and analyze its background.

In the present chapter, I focus mainly on privatization and the introduction of market forces into the administration of collective public regulations. It is important to distinguish between this form of privatization and the privatization of the social regulations as such. The latter has actually already occurred in the Netherlands, for example by the discontinuation of the Sickness Benefit Acts for most insured persons (this act was replaced by a provision whereby the employer is obliged to continue paying the wages of an employee during his/her first year of illness).

2. Background to the Privatization of the Social Security System in the Netherlands

Privatization of the policy area relating to the social security system is not an isolated phenomenon. In the last twenty years a broad trend has prevailed and the spirit of the times in society, certainly in the beginning, has been to expect to find many of the miracles of competition and market forces within nearly all sectors of the social order. The background to all this is a combination of various factors, amongst which increasing international competition, the attendant cutbacks, organizations that are forced to operate more efficiently, as well as changing attitudes towards the distribution of responsibilities between government and social groupings, such as organizations formed by employers and employees, and individuals citizens.

This "new thinking" coincides in the 1990s with an important political turnaround in the Netherlands: the election defeat suffered by the largest sectarian party that had formed part of the government for some seventy years, and the subsequent formation of a first and then a second "purple" cabinet. These cabinets have been headed by the socialist prime minister, Wim Kok, consisting of a hitherto unheard of combination of socialists, liberals and social democrats. When it took office, the first Kok cabinet launched a large political project, focusing on the promotion of market forces, deregulation and the improvement of the quality of legislation. governmental authorities should be confined to their role as a nucleus; if possible, administrative tasks would become ancillary.

The increasing demands being made on the social security system in the Netherlands had been a source of concern to politicians for some time. In addition to the (high) numbers of unemployed,[1] the large and steadily increasing number of invalidity benefit claims[2] gave, and continues to give, particular cause for increased political attention. The latter had given rise to repeated and far-reaching interventions in the policy-related conditions, although usually without achieving any real shifts in the existing trend. On the basis of a parliamentary inquiry at the beginning of the 1990s, with regard to the administration of insurance schemes for employed persons, attention shifted from policy to the quality of the actual administration of the regulations. At the time, the administration of social security schemes, but also of numerous other collective and non-governmental regulations, was the responsibility of administration offices directly managed by the representatives of employer and employee organizations. The administration offices each served one or more specific branches of industry.

On the basis of the findings of the above mentioned inquiry, parliament arrived at a consensus about the next, drastic amendments to be made in administration:

- A distinction had to be made between management *per se* and administration. This entailed requiring the social partners, who up to that point had been directly responsible for the administration of employed persons' insurance schemes, to function within a more distant and formal business relationship, namely as principals of the agencies responsible for benefits (i.e., benefits agencies).

- Administration of the regulations by agencies responsible for private benefits was, in principle, restricted to insurance schemes for publicly employed persons.

- New private sector firms could also set themselves up as agencies responsible for benefits.

- Administration became subject to independent supervision. This is how the Social Security Supervisory Board, an organization that occupies an independent position in the social security sector, came into existence. Supervision had previously also been in the hands of the social partners.

The purple cabinet added three important elements in this context. Firstly, the social partners were shifted an even greater distance away from the actual administration. Where the large sectarian party had always made a case for the community-based organizations and protected the position of employer and employee organizations, its election defeat provided the purple cabinet with an opportunity to review even further the position of the social partners with regard to social security. The employer and employee organizations became completely separate from the benefits agencies and, together with independent members, became part of the (present) tripartite National Institute of Social Insurance, which acts as the sole principal of the current benefits agencies.

Secondly, the cabinet announced that the benefits agencies would, in time, have to compete in an open market. In so doing, the cabinet wished to confer on the administrators a raison d'être that would, via competition on price and quality, make the administration as efficient and effective as possible.

Thirdly, the cabinet announced its wish to engage in a fundamental discussion concerning the basic principles of the social security system.

3. Transitional Phase

At the time of the first Kok cabinet (1994-1998), the laborious task was being undertaken of separating the management of the agencies responsible for benefits (social partners) from the administration, in which process a more client-business type of relationship came into being. In particular, the separation of the administration of the social security regulations, and other duties (commercial collective and/or top-up insurances), required considerable energetic effort. After much insistence from the administration offices, the government finally agreed to the formation of holdings by the newly formed benefits agencies. In the holdings (five in total), these agencies are responsible for the administration of employed persons' insurance schemes and, in other parts of the holdings, commercial insurance policies may be administered. In this way, the government was able to satisfy appeals for keeping these activities together wherever possible, in order to bring one step closer the achievement of efficiency and the reduction of the administrative burden for employers. It was also announced that forms of competition and market forces would be introduced in the near future. The matter became even more complicated when the opportunity was being offered for all sorts of contracting "in" and "out" relationships between the various parts of the holding. The political choices made here were not always accordant or consistent. On the whole, some tasks that had previously been carried out by the agencies responsible for benefits are no longer being dealt with by the holding, such as the regulatory monitoring and counseling of ailing employees.

The above mentioned developments, combined with the "announcement effect" arising from the prospect of competition and market forces, resulted in a number of hazards and bottlenecks:

- Initially, a large part of the legislation necessary for a clearer division between the benefits agency responsible for public duties (hereinafter to be referred to as "the benefits agency") on the one hand, and the other parts of the holding on the other hand, was lacking. This led to a period of trial and error, with all the accompanying (financial) uncertainties and risks.

- Managers within the holding, thus simultaneously managers of the benefits agency, anticipated competition and market forces by fashioning an organizational structure and culture that would make it possible for their organizations to cope with any future competition. In the process, the boundaries of legality were regularly skirted and sometimes breached. To a certain extent, reality was molded by daily practice, and in some cases, a situation clearly existed where the "stable door was locked only after the horse had already bolted."

- Some of the duties formerly carried out by the organizations lapsed, so that large groups of personnel had to be made redundant, resulting in the problem of how to finance (from public or private resources) these redundancies.

- The government wished to achieve a clear distinction among the financial streams within the holding, in order to avoid commercial activities being financed by public funds. The same applied to data management, where it was necessary to prevent data obtained for the administration of public regulations being wrongfully used for commercial purposes. No mean task for the supervisor!

- The quality of the administration deteriorated, partly because of the large-scale reorganization and also because of management's focus on the future instead of ongoing concerns.

4. Coalition Agreement

In the coalition agreement reached by the second Kok cabinet in 1998, it was again explicitly indicated that forms of competition and market forces had to be introduced into the administration of duties with regard to social insurance schemes. In addition, and this will later be shown to be of crucial importance, it was, however, also stated that the legitimacy and the effectiveness of the administration of the system is, and remains, a public responsibility. Following naturally from this, the (first) assessment of the benefit entitlement claim should take place in a public environment, independent of the influences of social partners and commercial interests. In addition to the intended privatization and market forces, a number of other very large-scale changes to the organization and the administration of the system were also announced; I will not touch on these in the present chapter. The government thus wanted to:

- achieve a more active system, focused on increasing the chances of the unemployed returning to the labor market;

- save on the costs of administration by means of the expected improvement in efficiency;

- contribute to the lightening of the administrative obligations imposed on employers.

- In order to prepare for the large-scale change in the organizational structure of the system, a series of (public) consultative documents was published. In this not too distant period, the agencies and parties who had an interest in this huge operation brought considerable pressure to bear on the government and the political parties. Crucial in their lobbying was the positioning of the claim assessment. The holdings tried, with all their might, to substantiate their standpoint that claim assessment had to remain an integral part of the administrative process (to be privatized). And with success; so it seemed.

At the beginning of 1999, the social partners, united in the most important government[3] advisory body, reached an historic agreement, and agreed upon a unanimous recommendation to be addressed to the government about the structure of the system. They were of the opinion that administration should be privatized in its entirety, but that claim assessment should be located in a separate section within the commercial organization. By no means was competition to play a role in claim assessment.

Despite the consensus achieved between employers and employees, the cabinet proposed a plan in which far-reaching privatization and market forces were incorporated, but which proposed that claim assessment be administered by the public sector.[4] However, the cabinet's plan did meet the interested parties halfway. Namely, staff employed by a public benefits agency would be seconded to the commercial benefits agencies to carry out claim assessment there. Because these public officials would not be in the employ of the commercial administrator, sufficient assurance could be given that commercial interests would not be influencing the assessment of a person's right to receive benefits. This proposal (referred to as the "Piloting Model") can be regarded as the search for a compromise between, on the one hand, the wish not to carve up the administrative procedure excessively and, on the other hand, to prevent claim assessment from being influenced by any commercial considerations. The proposal provided for the sale of the existing benefits agencies[5] built up using public funds, with the personnel already employed in the field of claim assessment being seconded as detailed above.

It was in this way that the cabinet wished to accomplish the privatization of the benefit system as far as collection of premiums and payment of benefits were concerned.

It should be noted that, in addition, the implementation of reintegration activities, aimed at helping people to return to work, was to be privatized. To date, these activities are to a large extent carried out by a public organization, run partly by social partners.

Parliament did not grant its full approval to the proposals submitted by the government. Despite the compromise represented by the Piloting Model, the intended sale of the benefits agencies was particularly regarded as too drastic a step to take. Parliament had no objection to the privatization of reintegration, nor to other parts of the far-reaching reorganization proposals.

5. Background to the Political Rejection of the Full Privatization of the Benefits Agencies

In analyzing the debate that took place in parliament, a number of interrelated factors can be distinguished, on which basis the sale of the benefits agencies, which would have been an almost irreversible step, was not considered to be feasible.

- *A market economy is not an end in itself.* Contrarywise to several years ago, belief in the miracles of market forces is now no longer as strong. Nor has privatization always led to the achievement of the results expected in other policy areas. Politicians are critical of the privatization of the regulatory monitoring and counseling of ailing employees during the first year illness and equally, for example, with regard to medical insurance, ambulatory health care and the *Nederlandse Spoorwegen* [Dutch Railways]. Doubts exist within parliament about the freedom of choice that insured persons and employers will have to switch from one agency to another, for example.

- *Privacy.* Banks and commercial insurers were particularly interested in taking over the existing benefits agencies, and had already entered into strategic alliances. According to politicians,
  this interest could be explained by the desire of the above-mentioned parties to use for commercial purposes data that had been
  collected for the carrying out of social security regulations. It was
  feared that misuse would be made particularly of data relating to
  risk selection when offering or admitting persons to certain private insurances. It was not sufficiently clear from the plans drawn
  up by the cabinet how such misuse could be prevented.

- *Complexity.* The total administrative structure proposed is virtually impossible to explain to the individual. When it was being
  designed, too much emphasis was placed on the agencies in place
  (and their interests), so that the result was an administrative procedure which involved too many obligatory steps by the interested
  party. The client would be sent from pillar to post. Each forward-
  ing of a case being handled would also increase the likelihood of
  errors. Responsibilities within the Piloting Model proposed would
  be diffuse, and the risk of disputes over competence and the shifting of responsibility would also arise. Supervision would become
  more difficult; there would be less transparency.

- *Unclearness and uncertainty.* The plan put forward by the cabinet
  did not include a cost benefit analysis. This is significant because
  one of the most important assets of privatization is supposed to be
  the profit in terms of efficiency; no market research was presented.
  It is unclear how a level playing field can exist between the current benefits agencies and any newcomers. Research is still being
  carried out, or is yet to start. Earlier privatization in the social
  security field has not yet been evaluated. In short: it is not at all
  clear what is involved here.

- *Risks for vested interests.* A large-scale reorganization of the benefits agencies would be ushered in by the plans drawn up by the
  government. During public hearings, managers of benefits agencies held up to politicians the prospect of 40 to 50 percent of
  current personnel (approximately 7,000 public officials) having
  to be moved and a part of them seconded. Given the fact that the
  quality of the administration already leaves much to be desired,
  nobody wanted to risk such an exodus. What is more, latent resistance on the part of the management of the benefits agencies had
  been felt, resistance that is not conducive to a successful reorganization.

- *Irregularities.* In the period prior to the discussion of the cabinet's
  plans, a number of irregularities made politicians wary. It became

common knowledge that the salaries of top managers employed by the largest benefits agency, had risen exorbitantly in anticipation of the privatization. It also appeared that, in contradiction to the law, no sanctions had been imposed on employers (the potential future client) for the non-fulfillment of certain legal obligations. As already indicated, the management of some benefits agencies probed the boundaries of the law to the limit, thus presenting the supervisor and the minister with a *fait accompli.*

No objection was made to the privatization of reintegration activities, because:

- the assumption is that the commercial interests of the companies responsible for reintegration are very much in harmony with the aims of the legislature.

- where interests might be minimal, namely for that group of employees difficult to reintegrate, sufficient incentives could be provided by means of bonuses.[6]

- politicians have a negative opinion about the performance of the present, public, reintegration organization as opposed to that of the commercial agencies.[7]

On balance, it is rather striking that it was noted only at the fringes of the political debate that the fundamental discussion of the principles and contents of the social security system, which had initially been announced by the cabinet, had not taken place. In this way, drastic changes were to be made to the administrative structure without any guarantee of a solid basis for the configuration of the collective regulations in the years to come.

6. Change of Course

The cabinet was sent away by parliament with considerable homework to do. The Minister of Social Affairs and Employment promised a further exploration of other options and additional research.

The Department developed five organizational models for the administration of the employed persons' insurance schemes, varying from entirely private (at least within the boundaries of the coalition agreement) to entirely public. The cabinet eventually opted for the latter: organization of the administration of the employed persons' insurance schemes must be completely in the hands of the public sector. The existing benefits agencies must merge into one agency that will be co-ordinated by a management board reporting directly to the minister. Reintegration duties will be completely privatized.

It might be possible to explain this surprising outcome by the following factors:

- The discussion by parliament of the earlier proposal made it quite clear that there was no political room for a far-reaching form of privatization, and thus for the sale of the existing benefits agencies.

- The conclusion was eventually reached that an organizational structure having one voice had to be opted for, whereby the administrative procedure had to be carried out integrally wherever possible: thus by one agency. In this manner, unnecessary cuts in the administrative procedure could be avoided.[8]

- Given the coalition agreement precondition that the claim assessment should be in the public sector, the most logical solution seemed to be to decide to make the administration entirely public.

- Last but not least: the responsible minister and the state secretary, given their experiences with the benefits agencies in previous years, urgently needed to acquire more control of the administration. By making the administration more public than it has ever been before, and by terminating the managerial role of the social partners, stronger governmental control will become possible. To date, co-ordination and accountability occur indirectly, steered by the National Institute for Social Insurance.

7. The Future

Meanwhile, the cabinet has ensured itself of political support for its latest design. Preparations are currently under way for carrying out the huge operation involved in this reorganization. To this end, the minister has appointed a number of experienced managers of change, who are drawing up an implementation plan and will subsequently directly manage the reorganization process. Although the reorganization is accompanied by substantial risks, it is encouraging to note that the minister is aware of the problems involved in implementation, as well as the management experience which will be necessary.

Naturally, the change of course was disappointing for those managing the benefits agencies, who had, for several years, been preparing their organizations for competition and market forces. Given the irregularities already mentioned, and the determination of these managers to hold on to claim assessment, they were to a certain extent also partly responsible for the change of course. In a way, the announcement of privatization worked as a poison pill to the managers of the benefits agencies. Several top managers have already resigned, and some categories of professionals (for example, middle management, doctors, vocational experts and ICT experts) are also leaving. This is not, however, only the result of the altered prospects for the future, but also of the booming economy and the corresponding increased job opportunities. Employees are also aware that the merger of the various benefits agencies into a single agency will entail the loss of a large number of jobs. The risk of an uncontrolled turnover of employees, and with it the likelihood of a shortage of staff in the future organization, is certainly a possibility.

It will come as no surprise that the main resistance to the latest plans proposed by the cabinet originates from the social partners. Their only remaining role is the issuance of orders and the budgeting of reintegration activities. This signals an end to the important role that employer/employee organizations have played for a number of decades now with regard to social security administration in the Netherlands. It is not yet certain what effect the partial loss of the influence of the social partners, and with it, a possible decrease in support for the collective regulations in the business sector, will have.

This period of transition also presents a major challenge to the Social Security Supervisory Board. The supervisor will have to ensure that as few accidents as possible occur in the coming high-risk years. Given the complete reorganization of the system, the position and the organization of the supervision relating to policy and administration will also change. For example, currently under discussion is the independent position of the board in relation to the ministry.

Given the fact that the "shop has to stay open during renovations," the total social security sector will have to give its all to ensure a smoothly running organization, while at the same time maintaining the quality of ongoing operations. Whether the new structure will prove to be sturdy enough for the future remains to be seen. A new swing of the pendulum cannot, however, by any means be excluded.

Notes

1. After that of Luxembourg, the official unemployment percentage in the Netherlands of less than 3 percent, is currently the lowest in Europe by far.
2. Over 900,000 people in the Netherlands receive a disability benefit; more than 12 percent of the national labor force.
3. I am alluding to the Socio-Economic Council, one of the most succinct manifestations of the Dutch "Polder Model."
4. It might be interesting to mention at this point that the former chairman of the Socio-Economic Council, Klaas de Vries, had become Minister of Social Affairs and Employment just a few month earlier and, as such, was responsible for the cabinet proposal which deviated substantially from the recommendation of the council mentioned above.
5. The state can exercise a call option on shares in the benefits agencies.
6. This is an ungrounded and, in my opinion, disputable assumption. It is, in any case, striking that a number of critical remarks, which could also be considered applicable here, have not been put forward in the course of the political debate on the subject of reintegration.
7. The public reintegration organization already lost its monopoly some time ago. Benefits agencies are not themselves permitted to reintegrate, but may contract out part of the reintegration duties to other (commercial) agencies.
8. In this manner, the cabinet was acting in accordance with an important criterion in the recommendation of the Social Security Supervisory Board.

9

Healthy Markets–Sick Patients? Effects of Recent Trends on the Health Care Market

X. Scheil-Adlung

1. Introduction

From the historical point of view, the story of the development of the private health sector is an interesting one. The first hospitals in Europe were founded as a result of the private initiative of the nobility and took in only poor patients, while wealthier persons were cared for at home.[1]

Thus, around 1443, the *Hospice de Beaune "Hôtel-Dieu"* was founded in France as a private hospital to provide health care for a population thoroughly impoverished by the Hundred Years War. Like today's private hospitals, it was richly furnished: world-famous art works, magnificent furniture and colored terracotta tiles made the hospice a "Palace for the Poor" which even today stands as a jewel of medieval architecture.

However, as early as the expansion in 1645 a change could be seen: next to the existing poor ward two additional wards for well-to-do burghers were built on, thus establishing a division between social classes.

Consideration of patients' social standing and purchasing power in health care has, in the course of time, led in many countries to multi-layered health systems, featuring both public and private sectors.[2]

Thus the private sector in most countries today includes:

- service provision in the form of profit-making and charitable enterprises and

- financing, which can be in the form of either complementary, e.g., joint or supplementary insurance, or in full in the form of private insurance.

The importance of the private sector in different health care schemes and regions can, however, vary significantly.

Thus in many *European* countries a private sector has developed which acts as a complement to the public sector. The *private sector* mainly involves supplementary insurance and health care providers. The *more influential public sector* conversely includes health care financed by social insurance or taxation, whereby the state has the duty to ensure public health care and equal access to that health care for the entire population.

The *American model*, on the other hand, relies predominantly on *private insurance and private health care providers* without any significant public sector involvement. Health care is seen as a job for the market. Consequently, tax-financed systems for the poor and the elderly were introduced only in the 1960s,[3] and it has still not proved possible to solve the problem of inadequate health insurance coverage for a major part of the population.[4]

Historically, in most of the *developing countries* of Africa and Asia there was a massive expansion of the tax-financed public sector, which because of financial constraints soon had to be limited, in favor of the *private sector*. Since the 1990s, it has been necessary, however, for governments to intervene to counter undesirable developments.

In many industrialized and developing countries the private health care sector is characterized by commercialization, which, with a few exceptions, pushes the nonprofit private sector[5] into the background.

At the same time there is a growing interrelationship between the private and public sectors. The state itself is increasingly emerging as a player in the market and moving into private capital, e.g., by investing in infrastructure, private providers and private management methods in public health care.

The health care market is thus becoming of central importance for health care provision. This raises the following issues which are considered below:

- which new developments in the health care market should be closely watched, and

- what the consequences are for public health care provision.

2. Health Care Market Trends

Underlying the global growth in health care markets are trends that bring long-term structural changes in health care provision in their wake. In recent years, the following trends could be observed:

- introduction of managed care organizations, disease management, evidence-based medicine and treatment guidelines;

- globalization of the health care market;

- brain drain of highly qualified health professionals.

Introduction of Managed Care Organizations, Disease Management, Evidence-Based Medicine and Treatment Guidelines

The most significant trend in health care provision in recent years is the introduction of managed care organizations, disease management, evidence-based medicine and treatment guidelines. These private business management methods are primarily intended to prevent rising costs and are thus introduced into private insurance, as well as into social insurance and national health systems.

Managed Care Organizations[6] or integrated care systems were originally developed in the United States and can be defined as integrated and coordinated management systems designed to achieve the optimal cost/benefit ratio. Furthermore, cost reductions are achieved by packaging consumer demand by purchasers and lessening the influence of patients and doctors on supply.

Central to this is the idea of de-linking doctor's income from the quantity of services provided. Other characteristics of the networks are:

- existence of a list of service providers, such as doctors, hospitals, pharmacists who make up the network;

- the service provider's consent to lower fees in return for a guaranteed number of patients;

- financial incentives so that insured persons consult the general practitioner as gatekeeper and use the network.

The insured person has the choice of several managed care organizations, types of family doctor, etc., but not a free choice of doctor. The choice of the managed care organization determines also the use of expensive technologies which are limited to the existing medical equipment in the network.

Cost-savings can also be achieved through new forms of doctors' remuneration. Capitation is often introduced to reduce the number of services or fee-per-case and salary for general cost ceilings. This is in contrast to remuneration for fee-for-service, which is an incentive to extend services provided.

Other cost savings can be expected from the introduction of co-payment, insurance excesses and no-claims bonuses, which effectively shift the cost to the insured.[7]

Costs can also be reduced by the use of *"treatment guidelines,"* *"disease* management" and *"evidence-based medicine."* This basically involves minimum standards for cost-effective, standardized basic treatment for typical "cases." It often allows generalists to treat patients previously treated by specialists.

However, these private management methods are often linked to additional costs, because of considerable administrative expenditure due to intensive controlling as regards payment of doctors.

Marketing also involves additional costs. This is where fashions such as fitness and wellness movements or no-tech-medicine, which may sometimes involve the magical and mystical promotion of alternative medicine, are increasingly significant. By this means new services are launched and new customers won in a largely saturated market.

Globalization of the Health Care Market

One of the most significant long-term trends in the health care market is its growing globalization. Globalization trends can be observed in the following areas:

- cross-border supply of services and products, such as telemedicine, biotechnological innovations, pharmaceutical products, medical equipment, etc.;

- cross-border demand for health care services from migrants, tourists, people with specific diseases and students;

- international capital flows, e.g., direct investment in infrastructure such as hospitals;

- worldwide technology transfer, medical advances, training and exchange of experience.

As a result of the important competition due to globalization, strong downward pressure on prices in the health care market can be expected.[8] The potential for lower costs is also envisaged in the area of telemedicine and biotechnological innovations in specific treatments, therapies and medicines.

Other areas, such as high-tech medicine, on the other hand, are likely to lead to rising costs, albeit linked to higher quality in the area of diagnostic and treatment methods.

As a result of the globalization of the health care market, national regulations are increasingly directed towards the international environment. This applies equally to trade in goods and services, protection of intellectual property and international capital flows. In the longer term, deregulation and liberalization can therefore be expected in this area.

Trade liberalization and relaxation of patent protection should, in particular, allow access to new technology in developing countries and thus raise the quality of care.

International capital flows, such as direct investment in infrastructure, lead to the extension of the high-cost segment of health care and in developed health care markets increase the choice of treatment options.

Improved access or quality can also be expected from global technology transfer, medical advances, training and exchange of experience.

Brain Drain of Highly-Qualified Health Professionals

Cross-border training, as well as the globalization of the labor market, lead increasingly to international migration of work forces. This applies particularly to very highly qualified specialists, as well as less well-qualified health professionals. The migration is primarily from southern to northern countries.[9]

Thus, doctors and nurses trained in developing countries emigrate to the industrialized countries or specialists trained in industrialized countries do not go back to their homeland.

The United Nations[10] estimate that between 1960 and 1975, some 27,000 African specialists left the continent, between 1975 and 1984 some 40,000 a year and in 1987, 80,000. Since then, the estimate is around 20,000 persons a year. Thus, there are 21,000 Nigerian doctors working in the United States, while the Nigerian health system is weakened by staff shortages.

Brain drain of labor due to the high salaries and fees paid in the private sector is found not only at the international level but also from the public to the private sector. Movement between these sectors particularly affects highly qualified specialists.

3. Effects of Trends on Health Care Markets

What are the implications of these market trends for health care? Effects which challenge the normative requirements of scope, quality or cover seem to be of some relevance. These effects might include:

- inequalities in health care;

- problems with regard to quality of services;

- unwanted effects on the infrastructure;

- developments in conflict with medical ethics;

- inadequate cover of "unprofitable" markets.

Inequalities in Health Care

Unequal access. Unequal access to health services provided by or insured by the private sector affects people with different income levels. Thus, private insurance polices or private medical services might only be used by the well-off, while other social strata remain excluded.

Irrespective of whether services are delivered by the public or private sector, co-payments or excesses lead to inequalities, as the demand varies in accordance with different income levels.

Differences in education or knowledge also give rise to different opportunities for access to health care. For example, one needs to know about service options in choosing a managed care organization, or in a global market, information about supply of services in other countries.

Unequal treatment. Unequal treatment or social differentiation[11] between patients appear in care networks such as *managed care* organizations. Here the differences in services often occur between

- managed care patients and others.

- patients considered desirable because they can be treated cheaply, and undesirable, because they are atypical cases.

Other inequalities in treatment can be found between the public and private sector. Because of risk selection in the commercial private sector, negative risks remain with the public health system, i.e. the social insurance or national health service. The fragmentation of risk pools leads to shortage of resources and thus declining levels of care, rationing, etc.

The growth of inequalities of treatment between the public and private sector is accentuated by the movement of highly qualified staff from the public to the private sector.

Thus, the commercialization of health care conflicts with equal treatment of

- "rich" and "poor," respectively, patients being treated privately and publicly, and

- patients with similar diseases;

i.e. to horizontal and vertical inequalities.[12] Moreover, there is no equality of treatment within groups of

- privately treated patients;

- publicly treated patients.

Quality of Services. What are the implications of the new market trends for the quality of treatment and services?

As a result of the packaged demand of insurers, managed care organizations, etc. ("purchaser model"), quality standards in the health care market are no longer determined by the standards of the medical profession but by the purchasers' standards. The purchasers' standards can be described by jargon like "treatment guidelines," "disease management" and "evidence-based medicine."

Alongside the reduction in choice of therapy, this often means a reduced choice of treatment and place of treatment. The latest therapies and treatment methods are introduced only after a long delay, even when they show promise of being more effective: a tribute to bureaucratic regulation.

Additional treatments, which the doctor perhaps wishes to provide in the case of atypical cases—estimated at 40 per cent of all cases in HMOs in the United States—are generally not covered. In addition, in managed care organizations, doctors are not encouraged to use or are even discouraged from using non-standard treatments, even when these may be necessary.

With the introduction of new quality standards a decline in specialist and in-patient treatment has been observed.[13] Moreover, there is a shift from short-term hospitalization to a mixture of in-patient and out-patient treatment. This can be attributed to incentives[14] to cost-effectiveness.

In the United States, it was possible to demonstrate that, according to statistics, patients treated in HMOs die significantly earlier than those treated on an individual basis in traditional medical practices.[15] The most affected were lower-middle-class patients, immigrants, self-employed in small and medium-sized enterprises and the elderly. Even if at the same time other factors, such as adverse risk selection, are also critical, the impact of heavily cost-oriented health care remains significant.

Unwanted Impact on the Infrastructure

With respect to the medical infrastructure, there is on the one hand an extension of care through the private sector, along with investments in private hospitals and, on the other, forced closures or amalgamations of hospitals on the grounds that the number of patients is no longer profitable.

Thus in Massachusetts, USA, almost 70 percent of hospitals have been closed or merged since 1980 and only 31 of the 108 hospitals remain unaltered. The resulting restriction of access leads not only to waiting lists, but also to serious regional inequalities in care.[16]

Furthermore the managed care organizations give rise to constraints on surgical operations, e.g., because of concentration of equipment and cost-motivated staff reductions.

Finally, the *brain drain* described above leads in the countries of origin not only to non-viable costs of investment in training and to a loss of development potential, but also endangers the health care infrastructure through lack of specialist staff.

Developments in Conflict with Medical Ethics

The fundamental question is how the scarcity of financial resources in the public and private sector can be reconciled with the ethical aspects. The ethical question has been made more acute with the introduction of private business management methods. Thus, major ethical decisions are affected by the inclusion or exclusion of doctors in managed care organizations, medicines and therapies, restrictions on access, waiting lists or delays in treatment. In the end, it comes down to deciding about,

- the monetary value of human life, thus who lives or survives;

- the degree of pain and discomfort in which people live, and

- who dies.[17]

Also problematic from an ethical standpoint is the exclusion of cost-intensive or terminal diseases in the private sector. Thus, private insurance policies frequently set ceilings on insurance cover or exclude certain diseases from cover. In particular, insured persons with preexisting conditions, incurable diseases and the dying are excluded from sickness insurance coverage.

Even if this seems acceptable to the client when the contract is signed, the fact is that such rationing in the private sector leads to medically unethical decisions.[18]

Inadequate Cover of "Unprofitable" Markets

The profit motive prevailing in the private sector puts profitable (in-patient) services at the forefront, which therefore leads to gaps in primary health care of the population. Because of the residual risk structure and financial state of the public sector, these gaps are difficult to fill.

The flaws in profit-based markets also result in under-provision in

- countries and regions, whose health care markets are not very developed;

- diseases which affect people with little purchasing power or concern small numbers of people, because product development is adapted to potential markets.

4. Conclusions

There is no doubt that the introduction of the private sector and private business working methods has major positive effects on health care provision for the public. This also applies to the more recent market trends, where cost efficiency means

- better quality of profitable treatments;

- extension of services, products and infrastructure;

- innovations in diagnostic and treatment methods;

and thus relieves the burden on public funds.

Although the health sector of the economy is expanding, equal access to health care and the quality of health care globally is an enormous challenge. The negative consequences of the new market trends which have been observed mainly stem from

- economic considerations, which are given precedence over health policy and medical considerations;

- flawed development of the health market, where, unlike with other markets, it is not the customer, i.e., the patient, at the center, but the product, i.e., services;

- a shift in power to the private sector, which is increasingly taking over public sector functions and is thus subject to stricter regulation.

Clearly the potential of the state and market, i.e., market regulation, audit, controls and private business management methods are not enough in themselves to achieve equality and improved quality and avoid medically unethical developments.

As well as the necessary market efficiency and the essential control function of the state, stronger involvement of

- medical professionalism, and

- the legitimate interests of the patient

could correct the state and market system and most probably lead to a balance between market dominance and over-regulation of the health care schemes.

A new balance of forces could be sought, in which the role of medical specialists in diagnosis and treatment is strengthened. At the same time, the market and state regulation should still be used to achieve cost savings and exercise control.

There also seems to be a need to define the role of patients as more than just the silent sick who "lie around cluttering up the system,"[19] and take account of their legitimate interests in the quality of treatment and access. Thus, patients' rights, such as the right of litigation, compensation, arbitration tribunals in the case of incorrect treatment, etc., could be reinforced, in order to overcome the defects in the existing health care schemes.

Notes

1. See Richmond, C. 1996. "NHS waiting lists have been a boon for private medicine in the UK," in *Canadian Medical Association Journal*, No. 154, pp. 378-381.
2. See on this subject: Salmond, G. "Integrated Care–The Ethical Debate," in *Healthcare Review online*, http://www.enig.nzma.co.
3. See Varvasovszky, Z. 1999. "The private role in health care," unpublished paper, September.
4. See Navarro, V. 1999. "The political economy of the welfare state in developed capitalist countries," in *International Journal of Health Services*, Vol. 29, pp. 1-50.
5. The following paper does not consider further the private nonprofit sector, such as mutual benefit societies, church agencies etc. See on this subject, Carrin, G.; Jancloes, M. and Perrot, J. 1998. "Towards new partnerships for health development in developing countries: the contractual approach as a policy tool," in *Tropical Medicine and International Health*, No. 3, pp. 512-4.
6. See, in particular, Greber, P.-Y., Rilliet Howald, A., and Kahil-Wolf, B. 1998. "Who gets what? New policies on access to health care and meeting needs," in *International Social Security Association, Developments and Trends in Social Security, 1996-1998, Social security at the turn of the 20th century: current issues and new challenges*. Marrakech, October.
7. See Scheil-Adlung, X. 1998. "Kostensteuerung durch Verhaltensanreize?" in *Zeitschrift der Betrieblichen Krankenversicherung*, Vol. 86, No. 4.
8. See Bettcher, D., Yach, D., and Guindon, G. 2000. "Global trade and health: key linkages and future challenges," in *Bulletin of the World Health Organization*, Vol. 78, No. 4, pp. 521-531.
9. See Buse, K., and Walt, G. 2000. "Global public-private partnerships," in *Bulletin of the World Health Organization*, Vol. 78, No. 4, pp. 549-561.
10. See Johnson, D. 1999. "Africa's Brain Drain Slows Development," in *www.africana.com*.
11. See Scheil-Adlung, X. 1999. International Health Reform: Trends and Innovations, lecture to the GKV Specialist Symposium, Munich. October, unpublished paper.
12. See Musgrove, P. 1999. "Public spending on health care: how are different criteria related?" in *Health Policy*, Vol. 47, pp. 207-223.
13. See Greber, P.-Y., *op.cit.*

14. See Scheil-Adlung, X. 1998. "Steering the health care ship: Effects of market incentives to control costs in selected OECD countries," in *International Social Security Review*, Vol. 51, No. 1.

15. See on this point, Findlay, S., and Miller, J. 1999. "Down a dangerous path: The erosion of health insurance in the United States," in *National Coalition on Health Care*, May.

16. See Greber, P.-Y., *op.cit.*

17. See Maynard, A. 1998. "Making difficult choices in health care," in *Summit of International Managed Care Trends*, Delegate Handbook, Informational Resource Kit. Miami Beach, 9-12 December.

18. See on this point, Byrne, M., and Thompson, P. 2000. "Death and dignity: Terminal illness and the market for non-treatment," in *Journal of Public Economics*, No. 76, pp. 263-294.

19. See Stein, R. 1999. "Der unmündige Kranke," in *Frankfurter Allgemeine Zeitung*, 15.12.

10

Social Health Insurance Development in Low-Income Developing Countries: New Roles for Government and Nonprofit Health Insurance Organizations in Africa and Asia

G. Carrin, M. Desmet, and R. Basaza

1. Introduction

Scarce economic resources, low or modest economic growth, constraints on the public sector and low institutional and organizational capacity explain why design of adequate health financing systems in low-income developing countries[1] remains cumbersome and the subject of significant debate. Cost-recovery health financing systems involving payment for health care via user fees were established in many developing countries usually as a response to severe constraints on government finance. Most studies alert decision-makers to the negative effects of user fees on the demand for care, especially that of the poorest.[2]

Alternative conceptual and operational frameworks for health financing exist, de-linking utilization from direct payment, and thereby protecting the most vulnerable groups from having to resort to various coping mechanisms.[3] These are systems that are funded via general taxation revenues and/or via health insurance contributions, that pool risks and are, in principle, apt to provide health services according to need. What immediately hampers general taxation-driven health financing in low-income countries is the sheer lack of a robust tax base, due to a small formal sector, the low institutional capacity to collect taxes and weak tax compliance. It is suggested that health insurance schemes, whether they are part of a social security framework or are established on a voluntary basis or at community level, have less difficulty in identifying their members and to collect contributions.[4] Benefits are perhaps more visible and seen to be linked to the contributions that are paid in.

In this chapter, we address the perspectives for an adapted application of the social health insurance concept in low-income developing countries. Specifically, it will be studied how government and non-government institutions could co-operate in order to attain the objective of full population coverage. In section 2, we return to the concept of social health insurance, implementation issues and the possibility of involving nonprofit health insurance organizations which may operate at the level of enterprises, trade unions or communities. In the third section, we review the pros and cons of these organizations and focus thereby on selected schemes in Bangladesh, the Democratic Republic of Congo and Uganda. Proposals for new roles of the nonprofit health insurance organizations and government are discussed in the fourth and fifth sections, respectively. We return to the selected schemes in section 6 to discuss some prospects for their future development. We conclude in section 7.

2. Social Health Insurance: From Concept to Implementation

The Concept

Social health insurance (SHI) can be described as a method for financing and managing care that is based on pooling of members' health risks, on the one hand, and pooling of contributions of enterprises, households and government, on the other hand.[5] Generally, social health insurance schemes define the health risks that will be covered. Covered risks should include at the minimum those risks that, in the absence of insurance, would entail a financial burden on households as a result of the cost of treatment.

Contributions are set in such a way that predefined entitlements to health services (or health insurance benefits) are guaranteed to those who need care, irrespective of their individual health risk or socioeconomic status. Contributions are collected by one or several health funds that have the potential to purchase the health services for their members according to priority needs and other criteria such as cost-effectiveness. These health funds generally have some degree of autonomy but operate within a framework of government regulation.

The concept of social health insurance is generally associated with compulsory membership involving basically all of the population. In doing so, social health insurance steers clear of the pitfalls of health insurance on a voluntary basis. It avoids the chance that certain population groups, such as the poorest and most vulnerable, become excluded. Exclusion can arise in a voluntary scheme because there may be a sheer lack of political interest in including the vulnerable and/or because the poorest do not have the capacity or willingness to pay the premiums[6] on a regular basis. Compulsory insurance by its vary nature also inhibits adverse selection. The latter occurs when health insurance tends to attract the "bad" health risks instead of a mixture of good and bad health risks. In a voluntary framework, adverse selection and its impact on costs and premiums may even lead to the discontinuation of insurance: premiums may become so high that the offered health insurance package stops to attract potential members.

Difficulties in Implementation

Social health insurance is recognized to be a very powerful method to grant access to health services to the population in an equitable way. Indeed, it implies that beneficiaries pay according to their means while receiving the right to health services according to need. So why is it that most developing countries have so far not introduced SHI on a large scale? Four main reasons may be invoked. *First*, it may be particularly difficult to arrive at a nation-wide consensus between various partners to accept the basic rule of SHI, that is to stay, guaranteeing similar health service benefits to those with similar health care needs, regardless of the level of contributions that were made. In fact, this problem may be very acute when countries prove to have a significant inequality of incomes and assets. Should SHI seek a contribution as a percentage of income, contributions per household will then differ substantially across households. In countries, for example, where the highest and medium income is a ten-fold and five-fold of the lowest income, respectively, the former income groups pay ten and five times as much as the low-income households. This may be too much to ask of the middle and higher income households. In other words, policy-makers may be compelled to take account of some limit in society on the solidarity across socioeconomic population groups. In such settings, a rather slow SHI process is likely to evolve.

Secondly, SHI schemes would have to ensure their members that they will effectively receive the health insurance benefits. The health services infrastructure, the human health resources and the other necessary components of health services, such as drugs and laboratory examinations, need to exist and should be combined to produce adequate health services. If promised benefits can not be delivered, it makes little sense to start a SHI scheme. If a government still goes ahead with such a scheme, it will quickly find out that trust of the population disappears leading to non-compliance behavior such as a refusal to pay regular contributions.

Thirdly, governments may not yet have the necessary managerial apparatus to organize a nationwide insurance system. Often this problem is compounded by communication problems, such as lack of adequate roads, telecommunications and banking facilities, that inhibit a potential SHI scheme to collect contributions and organize reimbursements, to manage revenues and assets and to monitor the necessary health and financial information.

Fourthly, there is the factor of poor political stability, usually linked to economic insecurity that interferes with a steady development of social health insurance.[7] Indeed, implementation of a social health insurance policy will be prohibited or severely delayed if there is no strong and steady political support. As a result, the population's trust in government, which is crucial for social health insurance implementation, may dwindle.

Despite the impediments to social health insurance on a national scale, we do see a number of government initiatives targeting civil servants, workers in the formal sectors, and their families. This does not mean that the active population in the agricultural sector or in the informal sector (such as in urban areas) would be totally devoid of health insurance. One does observe voluntary health insurance schemes, frequently organized by nonprofit institutions with an important degree of autonomy vis-à-vis government. Such schemes are labeled in various ways, including community health insurance,[8] mutual health organizations or associations[9] and medical aid societies[10] or medical aid schemes.[11] The common characteristics, however, are that they are run on a nonprofit basis and they apply health insurance principles. In this chapter, we put them under a common denominator as nonprofit health insurance schemes (NPHIS). In addition, private for-profit health insurance is increasingly offered in developing countries, targeted mainly at high income population groups that reject membership in a voluntary social health insurance scheme, or that want to improve upon their insurance coverage when an existing compulsory scheme only offers substandard protection.

Summarized, it is not uncommon for many developing countries, even low-income countries, to have a limited social health insurance scheme, a number of nonprofit health insurance organizations and sometimes a few private health insurance companies. The key question is whether we have to expect a deadlock in this situation, or whether there might be a way forward? In section 4, we hypothesize that there is probably scope for strengthening the role of insurance schemes of nonprofit organizations in areas that are not yet reached by government-regulated social health insurance. However, before turning to this hypothesis, and to be aware of strengths and weaknesses of NPHIS, we will briefly review the international literature on their performance. We also look closer at the experiences of selected NPHIS in Africa and Asia.

3. Current Performance of Nonprofit Health Insurance Schemes

Selected Findings from the International Literature

Bennett et al. (1998) made an extensive review and analysis concerning 82 nonprofit health insurance schemes for people outside formal sector employment in developing countries. They observed, among others, that very few of these schemes covered large populations or did not even cover high proportions of the eligible population. From a subset of 44 of the schemes, the median value of the percentage of the eligible population covered was 24.9 percent; 13 schemes had a coverage rate below 15 percent whereas only 8 had a coverage rate above 70 percent. On the whole, schemes suffered from considerable adverse selection, which made them vulnerable to financial risk.

Another conclusion was that very few schemes reached the vulnerable population groups that in principle should be able to benefit significantly from health insurance. The authors recognize, though, that such schemes could offer a far greater protection for more families or individuals, and could play a suitable role within the broader health care system. It will be an important ask for government to develop a suitable policy towards such schemes, facilitating their creation, yet steering them towards an adequate health insurance design via regulation.

The authors also note that there may be intra-scheme inequities (as a result of de facto exclusion of the poor) as well as inter-scheme inequities, which the government could help offset through subsidies from general tax revenue. In addition, they recommend that more attention should be paid to the integration of local insurance initiatives into a risk-pooling function for the health system as a whole. Finally, in establishing the respective roles of local-level schemes and national government, account should be taken of the local context and community preferences.[12]

The issue of health insurance as a tool for promoting better and equitable health services provision through health insurance was also addressed at an international conference in Antwerp, Belgium, in 1997.[13] One general conclusion from the discussions around the experience in some sixteen low- and middle-income developing countries was that universal coverage, involving risk sharing between all population groups in a community or a nation, is the ultimate goal. Extension of coverage, including for the poorest population groups, should therefore be high on the agenda of NPHIS as many of them currently show limited coverage. This extension could be facilitated via financial involvement from government. It is realized that time and tedious discussions may be needed before reaching overall population coverage. However, schemes should not invoke this argument to justify standing still, but should take well-planned steps towards an equitable health insurance structure. One example of a scheme that made improvements over time, especially in terms of coverage, is the Bwamanda hospital insurance scheme in the Democratic Republic of Congo, with a membership rising from 27.5 percent in 1986 to 60-65 percent in 1997.[14]

It was also observed that, when schemes are the result of local initiatives, unequal insurance coverage may arise among populations of different districts or regions, as some are protected by health insurance and others do not. Here is again a role for government to facilitate both the establishment of well-designed schemes, and to stimulate networks among them so as to bring them closer together for the sake of risk pooling.

Another finding was that some schemes were closely intertwined with local initiatives in socioeconomic development, such as cooperatives[15] and credit schemes. Members of a cooperative might be enrolled more easily when a new voluntary health insurance is established. One can hypothesize that if a cooperative manages to bring greater income security to its members, willingness to pay for health insurance might be enhanced. Some credit schemes[16] appeared to show interest in promoting health insurance, among others, to reduce default in credit reimbursement; the reasoning was that insured credit scheme members would be protected from major financial loss due to illness, so that they would be able to respect credit reimbursement schedules.

Finally, although universal coverage with risk-pooling on a population-wide basis is the ultimate objective, a unique blueprint of health insurance design is hardly feasible since countries or communities are at different stages of economic, social and political development.[17] Therefore, different speeds at reaching this objective are likely to be seen in practice.

In a recent book, van Ginneken (1999) addresses health insurance for those who are currently excluded from statutory social security protection. A majority of the people in developing countries is covered neither by social insurance nor by tax-financed social assistance. He notes that people do increasingly pay out-of-of pocket for health services. Access to health care becomes an important concern, and one of the responses has been self-financed social insurance. Applied to health, this means that peoples' needs for protection against the costs of illness are met through mutual support schemes by communities or groups, or by non-governmental organizations and voluntary agencies.

As far as informal sector workers are concerned, van Ginneken (1999) writes that their schemes are frequently organized on an occupational or sectoral basis.[18] The latter generally constitute a good basis for building trust among members, which is part of the foundations of any social insurance initiative. One important conclusion from his study is that, when such schemes prove to be small-scale, and many of them are, they need an umbrella organization that can provide administrative and technical support. As an example he refers to the UMASIDA[19] health insurance scheme in Tanzania that was the result of a regrouping of five informal sector associations. Such an organization could more easily assume the responsibility of extending and replicating the health insurance schemes. A scheme like UMASIDA also better meets the vital criterion of pooling of risk among larger groups of people.

The importance of the role of government is also underlined by the same author. The government is advised to assume the role of regulator of the design and implementation of schemes. It can also establish the legislative framework for the efficiency and transparency of schemes' operations. government is also in the best position to guarantee the replication of different experiences across areas, sectors or occupations.[20]

It is interesting to note a convergence in two key conclusions from the above mentioned studies. First, insurance coverage of all of the eligible population is an accepted objective. Secondly, the role of government in promoting, regulating and co-financing of NPHIS is also recognized. One key challenge, expressed commonly as well, is the establishment of an inter-connection between the NPHIS themselves as well as between the NPHIS and a country's formal social health insurance system.

Findings from Selected Schemes in Bangladesh, Democratic Republic of Congo and Uganda

Issues of Coverage. The key characteristics of the voluntary schemes selected[21] for further study are presented in Table 10.1. All schemes are providing health insurance on a family basis.

We observe that the population coverage rates vary: the schemes in Uganda have very low rates, those in Bangladesh are around the median mentioned in Bennett et al. (1998), whereas only the Bwamanda Health Plan can boast a rate of 60-65 percent. Reported reasons for these disparities include, *firstly*, the way in which the premiums are collected (linked to economic factors, such as the purchase of cash crops, or to benefiting from micro-credit); *secondly,* the strength of the interaction between health care providers and communities they serve; *thirdly*, the existence of entry points in the community, such as family groups of borrowers of micro-credit, burial societies and savings groups, or other social groups and associations.

Most schemes try to link the time of payment of the premium with a suitable event in the community. For instance, burial societies in Uganda (the so-called *engozi* societies) use their monthly meetings for the collection of premiums, either for first-time members or for those who renew their membership. In Bwamanda, the nurse of the community-based health centers collects the annual premium at the time when the Centre de Développement Intégré (CDI) purchases cash crops. The latter runs both the health care system (hospital and community-based health centers) and the health insurance scheme. In the GK scheme (GK: Gonoshashthya Kendra), a similar situation is observed as premiums are paid to the community nurse during home-visits. Also note that GK runs both the health care system and the health insurance scheme. Notable differences between the Bwamanda and GK schemes, however, are that (i) in Bwamanda, the CDI health care system has a virtual monopoly, while in the GK catchment area other providers (outpatient as well as in-patient facilities) are competing with GK; and (ii) that the premiums and co-payments are flat in Bwamanda but graduated in GK according to the socioeconomic level of household members. In the Grameen Health Plan, the premium is paid from the accounts that members have in the Grameen micro-credit scheme (Grameen Bank members represent more than 98 percent of the subscribers of the Grameen Health Plan). In the Bwamanda Health Plan as well as in the GK scheme and Grameen Health Plan, the permanent intense interaction with the eligible population appears to be a key factor in explaining the level of population coverage. In contrast, in the Ugandan schemes, which suffer from a lack of such active and sustained links, first-time membership and subsequent renewal are very low.

Insurance coverage rates by socioeconomic group show mixed results for those schemes where data are available. In Bwamanda, they are relatively lower in the poorest and richest socioeconomic groups. In the GK scheme, insurance cover is higher in the two lowest socioeconomic groups. The preferential scales for premiums and co-payments in favor of these particular groups can explain the latter. While one can anticipate adverse selection in this case, it has been the explicit objective of GK to especially protect the poorer households.

As membership is voluntary, members can withdraw from the schemes. In all of the schemes discussed, the dropout of insured members has been attributed to their perception that they did not benefit in case of non-use of insured health services. In the Ugandan schemes, the use of a flat premium was seen as a deterrent for the poor households. Other reasons for discontinuing membership have been (i) refusal of preferential treatment when it was expected; (ii) the long distance from the health facilities; (iii) lack of transport to the health facilities in case of need for care; and (iv) the high level of premiums and co-payments. Adverse selection materializes when the members that drop out are associated with the lower health risks, leaving behind the people with higher risks. To avoid such adverse selection, the Ugandan schemes initiated a rule demanding Ugandan *engozi* societies that at least 60 percent of the families renew their membership. Only through intensive contacts between the schemes and the *engozi* societies could this target be achieved.

The likely trade-off that exists in schemes between the level of premiums and co-payments, on the one hand, and population coverage on the other, implies that there are constraints on the so-called cost-recovery. While there is evidence that at the level of community-based health facilities,[22] modest premiums and co-payments may cover the majority of costs,[23] this is not all so at first and higher referral levels. The latter assessment is relevant for four out of the five schemes discussed. Only in the Bwamanda Health Plan are about 67.4 percent of the running cost of the hospital covered through health insurance.[24] Given limits on the population's capacity to pay, it is clear that other sources of financing may be needed, especially at referral level hospitals.

Factors for Continuous Development. Several lessons can be drawn from the experiences in the Bwamanda and GK schemes, as these have shown a continuous development. The factors that have permitted these schemes to establish and develop themselves relate to several issues within a broader policy context, to the social and economic environment, to the schemes' functioning and management and to the benefit packages they offered.[25]

Table 10.1
Key Characteristics of Selected Nonprofit Health Insurance Schemes

Countries	Bangladesh (1995)		D. R. Congo (1990)	Uganda (1999-2000)		
Scheme	GK[1]	Grameen Health Plan	Bwamanda Health Plan	Kisizi	Mutolere	Nyakibale
Starting date of the scheme	1975-1976	1993	1986	1998-1999	1998-1999	1998-1999
Eligible population (number of households)	37,200	37,500	19,400	19,900	11,500	23,500
Population coverage rate[2] (per cent)	27.5	41.0	60.0-65.0	6.1	2.0	1.4
Insured services	Community-based facility and hospital level OP and IP[3]	Community-based facility level OP	Hospital-level IP	Hospital-level OP and IP	Hospital-level OP and IP	Hospital-level OP and IP

Notes:
[1] GK=Gonoshashthya Kendra.
[2] Population coverage rate = ratio of insured population to eligible population.
[3] OP and IP stand for outpatient care and inpatient care, respectively.

First, the national policy setting. Relevant policy issues included the establishment of a National Health Policy on health care provision in the Democratic Republic of Congo in the beginning of the 1980s,[26] aiming at the delivery of Primary Health Care based on a coherent set of objectives[27] through a systemic approach.[28] The policy design benefited from long-term action-research projects in health care organization,[29] which were already being replicated within and outside Congo. Such policy guaranteed a more rational approach to health care delivery. Another policy issue in the Democratic Republic of Congo was the decentralization of health care delivery and financing. Based on the National Health Policy, the country was subdivided in "health zones," and the management and financing of health services was decentralized to these zones. It should be said that direct government financing decreased substantially. However, health zones could experiment with various forms of community financing. The community's contributions would usually complement those from bilateral development partners and non-government organizations. Together, the policies towards rational health care delivery and community financing have constituted prerequisites to the development of the Bwamanda Health Plan.

In Bangladesh, a special agreement with the government in the mid-1970s allowed GK to operate a health care system as a demonstration project situated in a geographical area at 50 km from the capital Dhaka. Although the GK project contributed to the formulation of official guidelines on selected health care delivery mechanisms (e.g., on the role and functions of female community health workers), a fully fledged national health policy has so far not been developed.

Second, the socioeconomic setting. Initiated by the Catholic mission in Bwamanda, the CDI in Bwamanda started as an integrated development project at the end of the 1960s. Primary and secondary schools, which were already run by the same mission, were integrated in the CDI project. The CDI gradually improved agricultural activities in the area: it introduced soya as a new crop aside from existing cash crops, such as coffee, and organized the purchase of produce at guaranteed prices. This resulted in fairly stable economic conditions in the Bwamanda region throughout the 1970s and 1980s which has enhanced the capacity and willingness of the population to enroll in the Bwamanda Health Plan initiated by the CDI.

In the case of GK, its initiators soon realized that a comprehensive approach to development and uplift of the rural population, and particularly of girls and women, was the only sustainable way to improve the health situation in the region. Several socioeconomic activities were gradually developed and female education and employment was promoted wherever possible, through micro-credit and through employment in traditionally male occupations such as carpentry, welding, crafts, and printing.

It should thus be highlighted that the health insurance schemes in Bwamanda and GK were fully embedded into broader development projects. CDI Bwamanda and the GK overall project have gradually developed and continuously supported economic activities and social activities in the education and health sectors. They both took responsibility from the start for a population (in both the cases, more than 100,000 population) which also constituted the population of a defined catchment area for health care delivery. They are highly committed and their involvement is long-term and sincere.

Third, functioning and management of the two NPHIS has benefited substantially from action-research; initial plans were adjusted based on empirical research findings. Furthermore, a monitoring system, more developed though in Bwamanda than in the GK scheme, guided the implementation of the scheme. Both have developed appreciable project management capacities. The CDI Bwamanda and the GK overall project were financial guarantors for proper funding in the case of any financial shortfall. In Bwamanda, the CDI also developed several value-maintaining mechanisms for the funds collected by the scheme, including investment in foreign currency and advance purchase of medicine.

Finally, in both the cases, the health insurance benefit package included hospital care. The GK scheme has added community-based health services to the benefit package as well. The health services provided by the respective projects received high quality ratings from the population. The schemes were known for their capacity to run the services as efficiently as possible. In fact, in both schemes, but particularly in Bwamanda, cost containment through rational health care delivery was an important objective.

The relationship developed over the years between both the projects and their respective populations became characterized by trust of the communities in the managerial capacities of the project leadership. The development of the health insurance schemes could build upon this high level of credibility of the overall projects in general, and of the health services in particular.

4. Towards a New Role for Nonprofit Health Insurance Schemes

The experiences reviewed above are hopeful. Yet, the schemes' achievements are limited, and would need substantial development before achieving universal coverage among the targeted population. Still, they operate in environments where either government intervention in health is absent or weak. These schemes also constitute institutions that benefit from some degree of trust by the population. We hypothesize therefore that the NPHIS could further contribute to filling the gap in insurance coverage. Of course, they would have to work so as to avoid the problems associated with government's weaknesses discussed earlier in section 2. *First*, they would need to ensure a consensus across the eligible population group and among the partners involved in the scheme. Should there exist basic social solidarity[30] and limited inequality among the population, it may be easier to fulfil the requirement of pooling. However, if a population group should be segmented into subgroups like landowners and land-less, insurance may be hard to establish.[31]

Secondly, a NPHIS should in principle allow for greater mutual control of activities between partners. Reaction by members when promised benefits are not delivered is expected to be quicker and more forceful. In view of the more limited scale of a NPHIS, non-compliance and moral hazard among members should also be easier to control in principle.

Thirdly, given the smaller target population and a smaller number of concerned health service providers, a NPHIS can usually respond more easily to the managerial requirements. In addition, communication problems within one defined local catchment area can be better overcome.

One important issue immediately arises. Obviously, because a NPHIS lacks the legal right to coerce people into subscribing to health insurance, it will not capture all of the target population. What to say then when certain population groups, for instance the poorest, would be left out? The answer depends upon how strong society's feelings are with respect to differences in well being across individuals and families. In any case, the objective of universal coverage in social health insurance leads to the necessity of including the poor. The NPHIS should therefore be stimulated to expand coverage to the poor as well. The latter may require extra financial resources as well as support related to the design of the schemes. In section 5, we discuss what government could do to facilitate this expansion.

5. Connecting the Nonprofit Health Insurance Schemes to Government

Towards a New Role for Government

The experiences discussed above clearly show that health insurance as organized by NPHIS is feasible even among low-income populations. But how does this fit into a national health insurance policy?

Social health insurance concerns the whole nation, and society would have to pronounce its choice and consensus, usually through parliamentary consultations and/or constitutional provisions. Once a social health insurance accord is obtained, a national health insurance policy needs to be detailed. As coverage of the national population is the final objective, connecting the activities of NPHIS and their associations to government becomes obvious. Indeed, without some real perspective of nationwide replication, NPHIS may well remain associated with the welfare of particular groups in society only. Thus, the need for government as a chief designer of health insurance policy is warranted. We agree here with Criel and Van Dormael (1999) who write that if NPHIS "are to significantly contribute to an increase in solidarity and a reduction of social exclusion, the support of a public authority will eventually be needed," and that they will "thus, sooner or later, be confronted with the problem of the role and the performance of the state."[32] Also already some twenty-five years ago, Aubry et al. (1974) argued that small-scale mutual benefit societies could be instrumental in establishing more extensive schemes, but that government assistance was needed, among others, to define and monitor the functions of these schemes.[33] The latter was also a key message in the earlier cited work of van Ginneken (1999).

We reiterate that government needs to shape the policies relevant to the establishment and expansion of social health insurance. It would have to show stewardship,[34] giving direction in health financing policy, addressing methods of revenue collection, pooling arrangements, the definition of health insurance benefit packages, and the purchasing of health services.[35] However, policy concerning the health care service organization is equally relevant. It will have to address, among others, issues of rational health care, quality of and access to care, proper utilization of care and patient flow, and cost-containment, which are crucial to social health insurance development.

The role of the NPHIS is likely to be addressed in both of the above-mentioned policies. In this chapter, however, we focus on the possibility of expanding their role as health insurers. Government will be prompted to further define its interrelation with them. We would propose four basic functions for government: that of promoter of health insurance, monitor of NPHIS activities, trainer, and that of co-financier. Related to the promotion of health insurance, government should be seen to steer NPHIS in the direction of social health insurance. A *first* problem to address is that of incomplete and asymmetric information.[36] The population may know more about its own health risks than the NPHIS. As the latter have imperfect knowledge about the health risks of different population groups, they are likely to define health insurance premiums on the basis of "average" health risks. In a voluntary setting, members of the healthier population groups may judge that the contribution is too high compared to their risk, so that they may reject the NPHIS offer. This will leave the NPHIS with a disproportionate fraction of the population with high health risks, which forces it to increase the contribution. The process of healthier people withdrawing from the scheme may continue, leading to enrollment of the people with bad risks only. As we know from section 2, this process is called adverse selection.[37] In its extreme form, there is no longer risk pooling and cost sharing between the healthy and the sick. If bad risks are associated with a low-income level, such a situation would also imply absence of any solidarity between the higher income and lower income population groups.

Government could help reduce the problem of adverse selection, by introducing simple rules. It could recommend to start up a NPHIS only when a minimum percentage of the target population could be enrolled, say 50 percent. Waiting periods could also be recommended, so as to refrain people from signing up with a scheme only when they are ill. Government could also strongly recommend not to enroll on individual basis but rather on a family basis. Apart from the percentage enrollment, the size of a NPHIS is an equally important concern. Excessively small schemes, for instance with only a few hundred members, do not constitute a solid risk pool capable of insuring its members adequately. Larger risk pools could thus be advised, for instance via the establishment of an alliance of NPHIS.[38] In general, government could advise the NPHIS to develop a health insurance development plan that would aim at increasing population coverage and greater risk pooling over a certain period of time.

Secondly, government could formulate recommendations on the composition of alternative health insurance benefit packages. These packages would have to reflect the health care needs of the population, and be designed in a cost-effective way, for instance through standard treatment protocols. For the sake of cost-effectiveness, they would also have to integrate regulations as to a rational health care delivery system. From a pure insurance point of view, insurance against the costs of inpatient care would be of prime benefit to the insured, because the relatively high financial consequences of such events would be avoided. However, the costs of outpatient care for the chronically ill, and the treatment cost of ambulatory care for certain communicable diseases like tuberculosis, also entail risks worth insuring. Because of its aim to decrease disease incidence, preventive care, such as immunization, antenatal care and under-five growth monitoring, and promotive care, such as health education, should also be included. For similar public health reasons, basic outpatient care could be insured as well. Indeed, insurance of certain types of outpatient care, such as treatment of malaria and other parasitic diseases, helps prevent transmission of disease. In welfare economics language, we say that it reduces the negative externalities from communicable diseases. There may also be economic and financial reasons for insuring outpatient care. Certain infections when untreated may result in a greater amount of workdays lost. With health insurance enabling members to receive adequate treatment, this economic loss could be averted. Financial losses can also be avoided when, in the case of non-treatment (provoked by absence of health insurance for outpatient care), patients would turn sicker and in the end need hospitalization, which would be far costlier to the NPHIS.

Thirdly, government could assist NPHIS in establishing a management information system (MIS) whenever this is deemed feasible in view of the size of the membership and the scheme's administrative capacity. This MIS could be simple at first, focusing on recording membership and basic characteristics of members (e.g., age, occupation, size of household to which they belong), insured members' contributions, demand for health care (inpatient admissions, attendance for curative, preventive and promotive activities), costs of health care delivery, etc. Such a system can be very helpful in establishing and/or adjusting the health insurance contributions so as to ensure a scheme's financial equilibrium. It can also be helpful in spotting elements of adverse selection and tracking progress towards an expanded population coverage. A simple MIS could also be the precursor of an information network linking the various NPHIS to government.

Next to the tasks of promotion, government can offer to monitor the basic performance of each NPHIS, track progress across the different schemes through time, and perform comparative analysis. Monitoring should not be understood as passive, but as enabling government to stimulate the establishment of NPHIS, to signal problems to existing NPHIS and to offer practical advice concerning these problems. An important recommendation is for government to develop a standardized monitoring protocol which could be applied by all NPHIS, and which could facilitate comparative analysis. Note that at the level of the NPHIS, complying with such a protocol could be facilitated through a proper MIS as discussed above.

The results from monitoring and the promotion activities also provide a natural input into training activities that government could offer. The scope of these training activities can cover the entire range of issues that concern the establishment and adjustment of health insurance, i.e., determination of the benefit package and of the contributions, collection of the contributions, issues of delay in payment of contributions and non-compliance, management information systems and the establishment of health insurance development plans.

Related to co-financing, government can play a substantial role in enabling access of the low-income groups to health insurance.[39] *First*, at the level of a NPHIS itself, government could subsidize, partially or fully, the health insurance contributions of the poorest.[40] These subsidies would be financed out of general taxation revenues. Government could also come to an agreement with donors, however, allowing them to reallocate part of their funds as subsidies. *Secondly*, government could enact an inter-NPHIS solidarity rule, whereby some percentage share of contributions is siphoned off into a Solidarity Fund that would be used, for instance, to finance unexpected expenditure (such as in the case of local epidemics) or to pay for deficits of the least well-off NPHIS in the country. In this respect, we refer to van den Heever (1998) who studied employer-based health insurance schemes[41] in South Africa. He notices that, since the late eighties, new employer-based medical benefit schemes for low-income and largely black workers have been established, and that these are largely separated from the funding of medical benefits for high-income workers. In other words, virtually no cross-subsidy seems to exist, so that the health insurance benefits of the former schemes are relatively limited. Policy proposals were therefore made to establish an equalization mechanism across medical schemes, probably through a parastatal, in order to offer a similar basic package of health insurance benefits.

A further argument for government to be involved as financing partner is to counteract, to some extent, the regressive character of flat contributions by households in many NPHIS. Of course the latter presupposes that the taxation system itself is progressive, which is not necessarily guaranteed. Finally, note that in quite a number of cases, government (co-) finances capital costs of health facilities as well as important proportions of recurrent costs such as salaries. In the short run, government should in principle continue to co-finance those budget items. It is only at a much later stage that new ways of cost sharing could be explored. In general, government's co-financing also foreshadows that it would preserve a role as a contributor in a nationwide social health insurance scheme, such as can be observed in many mature social health insurance schemes in the world.[42]

It should be understood that we do not think of government to have a role in the day-to-day management of NPHIS. Rather, government should assume a role as prime facilitator with the objective to widen the population's access to health insurance. Besides, one can learn here from the experience with micro-finance projects. Morduch (1999) writes that when they were operated directly by governments, borrowers defaulted more rapidly on the loans. Governments are also likely to better tolerate such non-compliance, for political reasons.[43]

Further Concerns

The Need for Enhanced Capacity in Government. One may rightfully ask which capacity is needed before government undertakes its new role. A team composed of staff with skills in law, public health and medicine, actuarial science, applied economics and financial management, and computer information systems will be necessary. This team could be set up as a quasi-autonomous government agency. It could, however, also be connected to a government Health Insurance Agency already established to develop health insurance in the formal sector. In whichever institutional framework the team will function, it is of overriding importance to maintain close professional links with the managers of the NPHIS. This agency could use the best performing NPHIS as models to gradually develop the technical instruments for the establishment of new NPHIS, such as benefit packages, contribution levels, avoidance of adverse selection, non-compliance and moral hazard in both the formal and informal sector, standardized monitoring protocols, district-based social health insurance development plans, etc. Seeking the technical support and know-how of managers of some of the best performing NPHIS, or of an association of NPHIS, is also likely to be a good strategy,[44] as it may enhance the agency's credibility.

This new government agency would also have to develop the overall legal framework for the cooperation with NPHIS and for the accreditation of new schemes. One important way whereby government can steer and regulate the establishment of NPHIS is through contractual relationships. By way of legal contract,[45] government can give a licence to a specific NPHIS to operate at district level,[46] provided a number of minimum conditions are satisfied. As an example, these conditions could include insurance on family basis and the use of a minimum benefit package, including both hospital- and community-based care. The conditions could also include the definition of a schedule of family contributions, respecting certain ranges, and the acceptance of a maximum co-payment rate. The contract could also define, for instance, that the poorest families need to be accepted as full members. A health insurance development plan stipulating an increased population coverage could also be required. Provided all these conditions are satisfied, government can grant subsidies for the poorest families, as well as conditional grants upon fulfilling the required population coverage targets. In this case, government can award an official label to the contracted NPHIS.[47] The latter has the additional advantage that potential members' asymmetry of information regarding the quality and seriousness of the NPHIS is reduced if not eliminated.

This new governmental capacity should be made available on a continuous basis, however. Any interruption as a result of political instability or maladministration is likely to reduce the trust of the general population[48] and the associated NPHIS, which, in turn, may jeopardize the continuation of the new arrangement.

The Issue of Timing. It is clear from experience that attaining universal compulsory coverage takes time.[49] How exactly and in how many years countries will reach this endpoint depends on a set of factors, including social and economic development and political consensus. What matters most is that countries engage in a process of social health insurance development. This process will be somewhat different if countries already started compulsory health insurance for the formal sector. If they did, the NPHIS would mostly have to target the population in the agricultural and non-formal sectors. Such is the case of Ghana where the government now explicitly promotes mutual health organizations in rural districts.[50] If they didn't, the NPHIS could in principle be asked to take on board all population groups.

Government could engage in the following process. It could stimulate extension of coverage in *existing* NPHIS. Simultaneously, they could foster the establishment of *new* NPHIS. The latter two-track scenario would be relevant, whether compulsory insurance already exists for the formal sector or not. Again, this may take time, although we anticipate that a first phase whereby the government agency establishes the necessary technical tools and the legislative framework should not take more than three years. It is imprudent to predict, however, how much time it will take to the endpoint of full coverage (and therefore compulsory membership). Adequate risk pooling is a central concern during this transition. Along the way, alliances of NPHIS could be stimulated. In addition, at some time during the process, greater cooperation or even mergers with existing compulsory insurance pools for formal sector workers may well become opportune.

Note that during this whole process, certain regions or districts may well remain without NPHIS for some period of time. Meanwhile, it is imperative that the government maintains at the least its classical budgetary allocations to these areas.

6. The New Roles and the Selected Schemes: Some Perspectives

The experiences of GK and Bwamanda show that formulating and implementing policies on overall health financing and its links to health care delivery are the primary steps before any meaningful start of NPHIS. As discussed above, this role can clearly be assigned to the government. A properly defined policy on health care delivery and the targeted beneficiaries is evidence-based, and in line with societal choices. Such a policy more specifically should protect sound health care practice within a well-organized and integrated health care system. This policy will thereby facilitate the determination of the type and content of benefit packages that can be offered. The specific responsibility of providers is to ensure technical quality in service delivery that is accepted by the population. They will also have to engage in sound practice through the use of protocols for diagnosis and treatment in curative, preventive and promotive care. An overall health financing policy should indicate what each financing source is supposed to contribute and at which level of the health care system. It must explicitly contain the readiness of the sources other than the NPHIS to contribute to the overall financing of the system.

Related to the function of promotion of health insurance, the available evidence and how-know in existing and successful NPHIS should enable the governments in the respective countries to properly understand their dynamics and achievements. Such schemes can cooperate with government to address technical issues relating to the functioning and management of NPHIS, such as identification of health risks, setting of premium and co-payment levels, ways to avoid adverse selection, definition of benefit packages and protocols for curative, preventive and promotive activities, the establishment of health service contracts and a proper management information system.

Similarly, existing monitoring protocols used by well-functioning NPHIS could assist government to develop standardized protocols that could become applicable nationwide. Training of associations and organizations interested in social health insurance is another government task for which such well-performing NPHIS could be of assistance.

In many countries, non-government health care providers, although they may be important actors in the health sector, face dwindling donations from abroad. For four of the NPHIS presented in section 3, this has been the prime reason to experiment with health insurance. Apart from GK with its intended concentration on the poor, they initially saw health insurance as a means of collecting more funds (instead of user fees) to cover (increasing) health care costs. However, some governments are already stepping in to assist nonprofit health institutions. For instance, although the Ugandan schemes may still be small and fragile, the Ugandan government is increasingly subsidizing them through official aid. As soon as more NPHIS exist and more data about their performance become available, other types of government financing, such as through equalization mechanisms, should be considered.

Finally, virtually no NPHIS in the respective countries is currently linking up with services provided by government health facilities. If this has not happened so far, it is because these facilities are too often associated with a poor track record of quality of health care delivery, and with instability due to changing political realities. At least two recommendations should be considered in this respect. *First*, that interested nonprofit organizations should be encouraged to take up management of health insurance, when government cannot do so alone properly. However, the nonprofit organizations that currently provide health services should also be considered as full partners in the implementation of national health policies: to fill gaps in health care service delivery, or even to take over, where possible, the management of government health facilities. The latter could be implemented via contracting arrangements. *Secondly*, that there are few arguments to promote NPHIS, if they cannot provide health services that are well organized and accepted and trusted by the communities intended to be covered by these NPHIS. Hence the new guiding role of government, discussed earlier, to ensure that "good" health services get provided as an important prerequisite for successful expansion of NPHIS.

7. Conclusion

This chapter contains a set of recommendations meant for use at the onset of a process of social health insurance development that includes nonprofit health insurance organizations. We basically welcome such organizations, as they can contribute to filling a gap in insurance coverage. At the same time, they are not to work independently. Government has the task to define their place within the context of a national health financing policy. The latter policy should steer these organizations in such a way that they contribute to reaching the goal of universal coverage. In this respect, we propose that government, by way of a special agency, assumes four basic functions: (i) that of promoter of nonprofit health insurance but with the definite aims of adequate protection included for the poorest; (ii) that of monitor of the organizations' activities, so as to be able to adjust their performance; (iii) that of trainer of interested nonprofit groups wishing to establish nonprofit health insurance; and (iv) that of co-financier of health insurance operations. Related to co-financing, Government is especially invited to contribute significantly to the financing of the premiums that cover the insurance of the poorest.

The above mentioned process can only work when certain preconditions are met, however. A country would need to have a minimum amount of well-functioning nonprofit organizations for it to go the proposed route in a meaningful way. In addition, in several countries, these organizations currently receive considerable donor support. Should this support diminish, their survival will be at stake, and government would then need to be ready to take over with the necessary financial resources. Another prerequisite is the entente between government and the nonprofit organizations: a balance will have to be struck between the often-desired self-reliance of nonprofit organizations and the need for overall guidance by government. Last but not least, the newly proposed set-up will only function if the concerned parties show credibility so as to satisfy the population's demand for trust, if a properly organized health care delivery system is operating that enjoys the same level of trust, and if a minimum political and economic stability is attained.

Notes

1. Low-income developing countries are defined as having a Gross National Product per capita of $760 or less.
2. McPake (1993).
3. Sauerborn et al. (1996).
4. WHO (2000, pp. 97-98).
5. See further, Normand and Weber (1994, Ch. 2) and ILO (1997, Module 1). Note that social health insurance is usually part of a social security system, and is therefore different from a system financed directly via general taxes.
6. In this chapter, "premium" and "health insurance contribution" paid by an individual or family will be used interchangeably.
7. Sanguan, Nitayarumphong (1998).
8. Ron (1999).
9. Criel and van Dormael (1999) and Atim (1999, p. 883). Note that a mutual health insurance scheme could be managed at the level of a community, an enterprise, a trade union, etc.
10. Atim (1999, p. 883).
11. van den Heever (1997, p. 162).
12. Bennett et al. (1998, p. 62).
13. Carrin et al. (1999).
14. Criel et al. (1999) and Moens (1990).
15. Ron (1999).
16. Desmet et al. (1999).
17. Carrin et al. (1999, p. 864).
18. van Ginneken (1999, p. 182).
19. UMASIDA is the acronym for Mutual Society for Health Care in the Informal Sector. See Kiwara (1999) for a detailed analysis.
20. van Ginneken (1999, p. 186).
21. For the schemes in Uganda, see Noble (1999) and Review Team UCHFP (2000). For those in Bangladesh and Bwamanda, see Desmet et al. (1999) and Criel (1998),

respectively.
22. These facilities are typically staffed by one nurse and one or two nursing assistants-clerks, provide comprehensive curative, preventive and promotive care, and take care of 80 to 90 percent of the health problems in the community for which the facility has an explicit responsibility.
23. Desmet et al. (1999).
24. The other internal sources of financing include user fees from the non-insured, and external aid.
25. For discussions on this topic, see also Criel (1998), op.cit., Bennett et al. (1998), op.cit., and Kutzin (1997).
26. Ministry of Health, Zaire (1983).
27. These objectives include equity; aspects of health care organization, such as integration, comprehensiveness, and continuity of care delivery; and aspects of the role of communities to take care of their health problems and to manage and (co-) finance health services. See Van Balen (1989) and Chabot et al. (1995).
28. A "systemic" approach views health care delivery through functional tiers within a "district-based" health care system. In this district level, there are two tiers, a community-based one (a "Health Center") and a referral tier (a General Hospital staffed by general practitioners; this tier is the first one of the referral levels). Both have specific and mutually exclusive roles and responsibilities. There are clearly defined referral and counter-referral principles.
29. See, for instance, The Kasongo Project Team (1982).
30. Musgrove (1996, p. 52) draws attention to the factor of social solidarity or equity that was behind the expansion of social health insurance in many OECD countries.
31. Note that Ray (1998, pp. 393-394 and pp. 601-602) explains that this unwillingness to insure is due to a restricted flow of information between such sub-groups. For mutual social support to succeed, information flows should be intense.
32. Criel and Van Dormael (1999, p. 159). More general support for this statement is from Mills et al. (1997, p. 309) who write that "While government weaknesses may bolster arguments for relying less on the state, there is sufficient evidence of the dangers of unregulated health markets to suggest that the state cannot simply withdraw."
33. Cited in Midgley (1984, p. 209) who provides a general discussion of the role of mutual benefit and cooperative societies. The latter collected regular contributions from (voluntary) members in order to assist them in the case of sickness, in the payment of the cost of funerals, in providing income support for widows etc.; see Midgley (1984, p. 95).
34. WHO (2000, Ch. 6).
35. WHO (2000, Ch. 5, pp. 95-97).
36. Musgrove (1996, p. 21). Pindyck and Rubinfield (1992, Ch. 17).
37. See, for instance, Supakankunti (2000) for a discussion of adverse selection in the voluntary Health Card Program in Thailand.
38. See Mills (1998, p. 298). Dror and Jacquier (1999) also refer to the possibility of reinsurance in the event of small schemes.
39. This is also a role for government highlighted by Mesa-Lago (2000, p. 44) in his recent study on social security reform in Latin America.
40. Burgess and Stern (1991, p. 73) also point at the greater potential of central government to deal with redistribution in favor of the indigent.
41. Called "medical benefit schemes" in South Africa.
42. See Preker (1998, p. 119).

43. Morduch (1999, p. 201).
44. That it is not unusual for NGOs to receive an advisory role in government policy was mentioned by Walt (1994, p. 118). For instance, since 1987, Save the Children acted as advisor on legislation concerning children to the Ugandan Ministry responsible for social welfare.
45. For a discussion of the contractual approach in the framework of health service delivery, see Perrot and Adams (2000).
    We can reinterpret contracts as a response to a principal-agent problem. The agent is the actor who acts on behalf of the principal. In this case, the principal and the agent are the government and the NPHIS, respectively. While the government may have social health insurance objectives, the NPHIS may initially have different objectives. In concluding a contract, the principal can ensure that its objectives are met, building in the right incentives in the contract. See Pindyck and Rubinfield, op.cit. and Scott Bierman and Fernandez (1993, Ch. 7).
46. See section 3.
47. This is akin to a franchise system with the government (franchiser) giving the right to a NPHIS (franchisee) to use know-how and technical assistance of the franchiser; see Perrot et al. (1997).
48. That population preferences matter has been demonstrated in the more general context of health reform by Soeters (1997, Ch. 8).
49. An often cited example from developing countries is the Republic of Korea that took twenty-six years to develop universal coverage since the inception of its first statutory health insurance law: a period between 1963 and 1977 during which health insurance was developed on a voluntary basis, and a period between 1977 and 1989 during which compulsory insurance was established. It is recognized that economic development as well as urbanization were fundamental factors in this relatively rapid development. See Moon (1998).
50. Atim (1998, pp. 62-64).

Bibliography

Atim, C. 1998. *Contribution of mutual health organizations to financing, delivery, and access to health care*, Maryland: Abt Associates, Partnerships for health reform, Technical report No.18.

—. 1999. "Social movements and health insurance: a critical evaluation of voluntary, non-profit insurance schemes with case studies from Ghana and Cameroon," *Social Science and Medicine*, Vol. 48, pp. 881-86.

Aubry, P. et al. 1974. *The Achievements of Mutual Benefit Societies in Developing Countries*, Geneva: International Social Security Association.

Bennett, S., Creese, A., and Monasch, R. 1998. *Health Insurance Schemes for People Outside Formal Sector employment*, Geneva: World Health Organization, WHO/ARA/CC/98.1.

Burgess, R., and Stern, N. 1991. "Social Security in Developing Countries," Ch. 2 of Ahmad, E., Drèze, J., Hills, J., and Sen, A. (eds.), *Social Security in Developing Countries*, Oxford: Clarendon Press.

Carrin, G., De Graeve, D., and Devillé, L. 1999. "Introduction to Special Issue on the Economics of Health Insurance in Low and Middle-Income Countries," *Social Science and Medicine*, Vol. 48, pp. 859-864.

Chabot, J., Harnmeijer, J.W., and Streefland, P.H. 1995. *African Primary Health Care in times of economic turbulence*, Amsterdam: Royal Tropical Institute.

Criel, B. 1998. "District-based Health Insurance in sub-Saharan Africa," *Studies in Health Services Organization and Policy*, Nos. 9 and 10, Antwerp: Institute of Tropical Medicine.

Criel, B., Van der Stuyft, P., and Van Lerberghe, W. 1999. "The Bwamanda hospital insurance scheme: effective for whom? A study of its impact on hospital utilization patterns," *Social Science and Medicine*, Vol. 48, pp. 897-911.

Criel, B., and Van Dormael, M. 1999. "Mutual Health Organizations in Africa," *Tropical Medicine and International Health*, Vol. 4, No. 3, pp. 155-159.

Desmet, M., Chowdury, A.Q., and Islam, Md.K. 1999. "The potential for social mobilization in Bangladesh: the organization and functioning of two health insurance schemes," *Social Science and Medicine*, Vol. 48, pp. 925-938.

Dror, D.M., and Jacquier, Chr. 1999. "Micro-insurance: extending health insurance to the excluded. *International Social Security Review*, Vol. 52, No. 1, pp. 71-97.

Ginneken, van W. (ed.). 1999. *Social Security for the Excluded Majority-Case studies of developing countries*, Geneva: International Labour Office.

Giusti, D. 1999. *The effects of user fees on utilization. A case study of 4 Not-for-Profit Hospitals in Uganda*, Paper presented at the National Workshop on Cost-sharing, May, Ministry of Health, Uganda.

Heever, van den A. 1997. "Regulating the funding of private health care: the South African experience," Ch. 10 of Bennett, S., McPake, B., and Mills, A. (eds.), *Private health providers in developing countries*, London: Zed books.

ILO. 1997. *Social Health Insurance*. Geneva: ILO and ISSA.

Kasongo Project Team. 1982. *The Kasongo Project: Lessons from an experiment in the organization of a system of primary health care*, Brussels: Goemaere publishers.

Kiwara, Angwara Denis. 1999. "Health Insurance for the Informal Sector in the United Republic of Tanzania," Ch. 5 of van Ginneken (1999).

Kutzin, J. 1997. "Health insurance for the formal sector in Africa: 'Yes, but...'," *Current Concerns paper*, No. 14, Geneva: World Health Organization.

McPake, B. 1993. "User charges for health services in developing countries," *Social Science and Medecine*, Vol. 36, No. 11, pp. 1397-1405.

Mesa-Lago, C. 2000. "Desarrollo social, reforma del Estado y de la seguridad social, al umbral del siglo XXI," *Serie Políticas sociales*, No. 36, Santiago de Chile: CEPAL, Naciones Unidas.

Midgley, J. 1984. *Social Security, Inequality, and the Third World*, New York: John Wiley & Sons.

Mills, A., Bennet, S., and McPake, B. 1997. "Future research directions," Ch. 18 of Bennett S.; McPake, B. and Mills, A. (eds.), *Private health providers in developing countries*, London: Zed books.

Mills, A. 1998. "The Route to Universal Coverage," Ch. 11 of Sanguan,

Nityarumphong and Mills, Anne (eds.),*Achieving Universal Coverage of Health Care*, Nontaburi, Thailand: Office of Health Care Reform, Ministry of Public Health.

Ministry of Health, Zaire. 1983. *Stratégie Nationale des Soins de Santé Primaires*, Democratic Republic of Congo.

Moens, F. 1990. "Design, implementation, and evaluation of a community financing scheme for hospital care in developing countries: a prepaid health plan in the Bwamanda Health Zone, Zaire," *Social Science and Medicine*, Vol. 30, pp. 1319-1327.

Moon, Ok Ruyen. 1998. "The Korean Health Insurance Progamme," Ch.8 of Sanguan, Nityarumphong and Mills, Anne (eds.). *Achieving Universal Coverage of Health Care*, Nontaburi, Thailand: Office of Health Care Reform, Ministry of Public Health.

Murdoch, J. 1999. "Between the State and the Market: Can Informal Insurance Patch the Safety Net?," *The World Bank Research Observer*, Vol. 14, No. 2, pp. 187-207.

Musgrove, Ph. 1996. "Public and Private Roles in Health—Theory and Financing Patterns," *World Bank Discussion paper*, No. 339.

Noble, G. 1999. *Progress Report on Community Health Studies Financing Project*, Kampala: Uganda Community Based Health Financing Association.

Normand, C. and Weber, A. 1994 . *Social Health Insurance. A Guidebook for Planning*, Geneva: WHO and ILO.

Perrot, J. and Adams, O. 2000. *Applying the contractual approach to health service delivery in developing countries*, Geneva: WHO, Department of the Organization of Health Services Delivery, discussion paper.

Perrot, J.; Carrin, G. and Sergent, F. 1997. "The contractual approach: new partnerships for health in developing countries,"*Macroeconomics, Health and Development Series*, No. 24, Geneva: WHO.

Pindyck, R.S. and Rubinfield, D.L. 1992.*Microeconomics*. New York: Macmillan Publishing Company.

Preker, A.S. 1998. "The introduction of universal access to health care in the OECD: Lessons for Developing Countries," Ch. 3 of Sanguan, Nityarumphong and Mills, Anne (eds.), *Achieving Universal Coverage of Health Care*, Nontaburi, Thailand: Office of Health Care Reform, Ministry of Public Health.

Rawls, J. 1971. *A Theory of Justice*. Cambridge, MA: Harvard University Press.

Ray, D. 1998. *Development Economics*, Princeton: Princeton University Press.

Review Team UCHFP. 2000. *Uganda Community Health Financing Project— Output to Purpose Review*. Kampala: Ministry of Health, Department of International Health. Draft report.

Ron, A. 1999. "NGOs in community health insurance schemes: examples from Guatemala and the Philippines," *Social Science and Medicine*, Vol. 48, No. 7, pp. 939-950.

Sanguan, Nityarumphong. 1998. "Universal coverage of health care: Challenges for the Developing Countries," Ch.1 of Sanguan, Nityarumphong and Mills, Anne (eds.), *Achieving Universal Coverage of Health Care*,

Nontaburi, Thailand: Office of Health Care Reform, Ministry of Public Health.

Sauerborn, R.; Adams, A. and Hien, M. 1996. "Household strategies to cope with the economic costs of illness," *Social Science and Medicine*, Vol. 43, No. 11, pp. 291-301.

Scott Bierman, H. and Fernandez, L. 1993. *Game Theory with economic applications*, New York: Addison-Wesley Publishing Company, Inc.

Soeters, R. 1997. *Rapid Assessment of Health Reforms in Africa: the case of Zambia*. Ph.D thesis, University of Amterdam (Faculty of Medicine).

Supakankunti, Siripen. 2000. "Future prospects of voluntary health insurance in Thailand," *Health Policy and Planning*, Vol. 15, No. 1, pp. 85-94.

Van Balen, H. 1989. "Le financement extérieur des services de santé," *ITG Health and Community Working Paper*, No. 15, pp. 1-9, Antwerp: Institute of Tropical Medecine.

Walt, G. 1994. *Health Policy. An introduction to process and power*, London: Zed Books.

WHO. 2000. *Health Systems: Improving Performance*, The World Health Report 2000. Geneva: WHO.

Part 4

The Empirical Framework:
National Experiences of Privatization
in Various Branches of Social Security

11

The Privatization of Pensions in Latin America and Its Impacts on the Insured, the Economy and Old-Age People

C. Mesa-Lago

Latin America has been at the vanguard of pension "privatization" in the world: by mid-2000, half of the twenty countries in the region had introduced structural reforms that are having and will have significant social and economic effects. Such reforms, in turn, have influenced others in various regions of the world (e.g., Eastern Europe) and are the subject of international study and debate. This chapter is divided in two parts: (1) a summary of the models and characteristics of the pension reforms in the region; and (2) an evaluation of their impact on the insured, the economy, and old-age people.

1. Summary of the Models and Characteristics of Structural Pension Reforms

Ten countries have introduced social security pension reforms in Latin America following three general models. This part focuses on structural reforms, i.e., those that significantly transform a "public" system by introducing a "private" system in divergent degrees; nonstructural reforms improve a "public" system without changing its nature and will not be discussed herein. A "public" system is characterized by: non-defined contributions, defined benefits, financing method of pay-as-you-go (PAYGO) or partly funded collective (PFC), and administration by social insurance. A "private" system is characterized by: defined contributions, non-defined benefits, fully-funded-individual (FFI) financing method, and management by private or multiple types of administrators.

General Models

There are three general models of pension reform: (1) *substitutive*: the public system is closed (new affiliations are not permitted) and replaced by a private system; it was first implemented by Chile (1981) and followed by variants in Bolivia and Mexico (1997), El Salvador (1998), and Nicaragua (2000); (2) *parallel*: the public system is not closed but reformed (totally or partially) and an alternative competitive private system is introduced; it was initiated by Peru (1993) and modified by Colombia (1994); and (3) *mixed*: the public system is not closed albeit reformed, and becomes the basic component of an integrated new system which also has a supplementary private component; its prototype was set up in Argentina (1994) and followed by variations in Uruguay (1996) and Costa Rica (2000). The reforms of Costa Rica and Nicaragua have just been enacted and we lack data on them, hence this paper will concentrate on the remaining eight countries.

Characteristics. Although there are three general models, the eight reforms have significantly different characteristics which are summarized below.

Contributions. In the substitutive model, contributions are defined (fixed indefinitely), but in the parallel model this is true only of the private system not the public which has non-defined contributions (they tend to increase in the long run); in the mixed model the basic component has non-defined while the supplementary component has defined. Only in two countries the contributions of the insured and employer were unchanged (Argentina and Mexico); three countries eliminated the employers' contribution (Chile, Bolivia and Peru), one reduced it (Uruguay) and one raised it (Colombia); but in six countries the insured contribution was raised.

Benefits. In the substitutive model, the pension amount is uncertain because it will be based on the amount accumulated in the insured individual account, which in turn will depend on wage contributions, capital returns, macroeconomic performance, etc. In the parallel model, the same is true of the private system but the public system has defined benefits, i.e., the law regulates the formula for calculating the pension, sets minimum and maximum pensions, etc. In the mixed model, benefits are defined in the public component and non-defined in the private component. However, in all private systems there is a minimum pension guaranteed, except in Bolivia and Peru (established in the law but not regulated yet). In Mexico, those who were insured when the reform was enacted have the right to choose between the higher pension resulting from either the rules of the closed public system (defined benefit) or the amount accumulated in the individual account (non-defined).

Financing Method. In the substitutive model, as well as in the private system in the parallel model and the supplementary component in the mixed model, the financing system is FFI. In the public system of the parallel model in Peru, as well as in the basic component of the mixed model, it is PAYGO. In Colombia's public system it is PFC.

Administration. In the substitute model (and Peru's private system within the parallel model) the administration is done by private-for-profit corporations of exclusive dedication (they can only manage social security pension funds), except for Mexico where the administration can be of multiple nature (private, public or mixed). The public systems in Colombia and Peru, as well as the basic components in Argentina and Uruguay, continue to be managed by the social insurance institute; the administration of the supplementary component in the mixed model is multiple.

Implicit Pension Debt. The present value of all long-run pension obligations (current and future) or implicit pension debt (IPD) is made totally evident ("explicit") in the substitutive model (except in Mexico because of the option granted to the insured). In the private system of the parallel model and the supplementary component in the mixed model, the IPD is also made explicit, but the IPD of the corresponding public system/component is postponed.

2. Evaluation of the Impacts of the Pension Reform

The effects of the pension reform will be evaluated on: (1) the insured (freedom of choice, coverage, compliance, financial burden—contributions and commissions, and entitlement conditions), (2) the economy (competition and cost reduction, capital accumulation, investment yield, portfolio diversification, and national savings and fiscal costs), and (3) old-age people (long-run impacts of the previous effects, trade off between fiscal costs and benefits).

The Insured

Freedom of Choice. Within the substitutive model, in Chile all the insured at the time of the reform were granted the option for six months to stay in the old public system or move to the new private system, but all new entrants into the insured labor force must join the private. Conversely, in Bolivia and Mexico all the insured had to move from the old to the new system. In El Salvador there was a cut by age: the majority of insured, who are young, had to move to the private system, as well as all new entrants in the insured labor force, a minority of old insured had to remain in the public system, and only a small fraction of insured where given the option. Within the parallel model, in Colombia the insured (current and future) can select between the public and the private system and change every three years; in Peru it is possible to change from the old to the new but not the opposite. Within the mixed model, in Argentina the insured (current and future) can select between the public and the mixed system, but in Uruguay those insured when the reform was enacted were divided by age and income and only part of them was given that option, while new entrants must join the mixed system. Concerning the freedom to change administrators within the private system/component: there is no legal limit in Chile and Peru, one change per year is allowed in Mexico, and two in Argentina, Colombia, El Salvador and Uruguay. No changes were permitted in Bolivia in 1997-2000.

Coverage. Coverage is measured as the total number of affiliates and active contributors as percentages of the labor force in 1998. Chile had 109 percent based on affiliates (which excludes 23 percent of the labor force who was either insured in the old system and the armed forces or uninsured), versus 59 percent based on active contributors. Corresponding percentages in the other seven countries were: 72 percent and 66 percent in Uruguay; 63 percent and 30 percent in Argentina; 51 percent and 41 percent in Colombia; 36 percent and 23 percent in Mexico; 26 percent and 13 percent in Peru; 29 percent and 20 percent in El Salvador; and 13 percent in Bolivia (no data are available on active contributors). Reasons for the significant difference between the two sets of estimates, as well as the 109 percent in Chile, are: unemployment, slow transfer of accounts when the insured changes administrator (thus being counted twice), employers' delay in transfer of contributions, temporary work, permanent exit from the labor force, and moral hazard. Excluding Chile, a comparison of affiliate coverage prior to the reform indicates a decline with the possible exception of Colombia. A comparison of coverage prior to and after the reform, based on active contributors is not feasible, due to lack of data, but their percentages are all much lower than those based on affiliates. These figures refer to salaried workers but coverage among the self-employed is considerably lower (e.g., 10 percent and 3.8 percent in Chile) and, in some Latin American countries the majority or a very large percentage of the labor force is made up by these workers; in Argentina and Uruguay such coverage is mandatory while in the remaining countries it is voluntary.

Compliance. The degree of compliance (measured as the percentage of affiliates who are active contributors) in the private system is low: 62-65 percent in Mexico, El Salvador and Uruguay; 51-52 percent in Colombia and Chile; and 44-45 percent in Peru and Argentina. The average in the seven countries for which we have data is about half. Compliance in Chile declined from 76 percent to 52 percent in 1983-99.

Contributions and Commissions. With few exceptions, the burden of the reform has been mainly placed on the insured. It was noted above that the insured contribution has been raised in six countries: Bolivia, Colombia, El Salvador, Peru and Uruguay (in El Salvador the contribution will increase almost five times by 2002). In addition, the insured are responsible for paying commissions for the administration of the old-age program and a premium for disability and survivor's insurance. The sum of the contribution and the commissions results in the following percentages deducted from the insured wage in 1999: 15 percent in Uruguay, 12.67 percent in Chile, 12.5 percent in Bolivia, 11.8 percent in Peru, 11 percent in Argentina, 6 percent in El Salvador, 3.785 percent in Mexico and 3.5 percent in Colombia. The percentage increase of that total over the contribution paid prior to the reform was: 10 percent to 100 percent in Chile (due to multiple contributions), 15 percent in Uruguay, 26 percent in Colombia, 50 percent in Bolivia, 78 percent in Mexico, 166 percent in Peru, and 300 percent in El Salvador (there was no change in Argentina). The increment in the financial burden on the insured is a disincentive to join the system, stimulates noncompliance, and has a negative effect on coverage; the high commission reduces the amount deposited in the individual account.

Entitlement Conditions. In most countries, the reform has tightened entitlement conditions for the old-age pension. For instance, the age of retirement was augmented from: 50/55 (women/men) to 65 (both sexes) in Bolivia; 55/60 to 65 in Peru; 55/60 to 60/65 in Argentina; 55/60 to 57/62 in Colombia (public system); and 55/60 to 60 in Uruguay (no change in Mexico, and impossible to summarize in Chile due to the diversity of programs prior to the reform). The years of contribution were raised from 10 to 25 in El Salvador; 13-15 to 20 in Peru; 10 to 20 in Colombia; and 30 to 35 in Argentina. The increase in contributions and tightening of entitlement conditions have helped to financially reinforce the public system in Colombia and the basic component in Uruguay, and are expected to increase the pensions paid by the private system/component.

The Economy

Competition and Cost Reduction. Effective competition is an outcome of the number of pension administrators, available information of their performance, education and freedom of choice of the insured, etc. The number of administrators increases with the size of the insured population and vice versa: in 1999 Mexico had 14.6 million insured and 14 administrators; Argentina 8 million and 13; Chile 6 million and 8; Colombia 3 million and 8 (but multiple administrators which facilitates entry); Peru 2 million and 5; El Salvador 655,000 and 4; and Bolivia 356,000 and 2. In the latter the small number of insured forced the government to authorize only two administrators and the insured were assigned to them based on their domicile; furthermore no changes were authorized until 2000, hence, there is no competition but a duopoly. An important lesson of this is that small countries should be careful to implement this type of reform, unless they allow multiple administrators and do not require exclusive dedication. Even in those countries that have a good number of administrators there is a significant degree of concentration of affiliates in the largest three, for instance, 79 percent in Chile (steadily raising from 59 percent in 1983). Mexico has the lowest concentration (45 percent) because the law established a limit of 17 percent of the total for each administrator. Concentration in the rest was: 100 percent in Bolivia; 75 percent in Peru; 69 percent in Uruguay; 60 percent in Colombia; and 54 percent in Argentina. One could argue that concentration is not bad if the largest administrators have the best performance; but in Chile the biggest three have not systematically in the tewnty years charged the lowest commissions and paid the highest investment yields; the most important factors in the selection of those three seem to be advertising and salespersons. Advertising does not provide essential information to the insured to make a good selection, but emphasizes security in old age. Salespersons are paid a commission by the administrator for each affiliate that is transferred; in 1998 there was a salesperson per 160 active contributors in Chile, and 1 per 180 in Peru. Because of poor competition, administrative costs have not been significantly reduced: the commission for managing the old-age program—which is the largest component—has oscillated but been either stagnant or declined very little in the long run; conversely, the disability-survivor premium (the smallest component) has exhibited a decreasing trend except in Colombia and Mexico where it is still managed by social insurance.

Capital Accumulation. Results are positive in this indicator although the accumulation in the pension funds varies among countries according to the size and performance of their economies, the time period that their systems have been in operation, and their investment yields. Having the oldest system (20 years), a middle size economy with excellent performance and the second-best investment yield, Chile showed the highest accumulation in 1998 in millions US dollars: 33,246; accumulation declined to 15,241 in Argentina and 8,300 in Mexico (both larger economies than Chile but with newer systems), about 2,300 in Colombia and Peru, about 450 in Bolivia and Uruguay, and 118 in El Salvador (the smallest economy and the newest system). As a percentage of GDP, the accumulated pension fund was 40 percent in Chile; 5 percent in Argentina; 2.5 percent in Mexico, Colombia and Peru; 1 percent in Uruguay; and 0.4 percent in El Salvador.

Real Investment Yield (RIY). There is a positive performance in this indicator also, but with fluctuations caused by economic cycles. The annual average of the RIY from the inception of the system to the end of 1998 or mid-1999 was: 12.4 percent in Argentina; 11.3

percent in Chile; 10.1 percent in Colombia; 8 percent in Mexico; and 7.4 percent in Bolivia, Mexico and Uruguay. The economic recessions of 1995 and 1997-98, however, generated a negative RIY in those years, reduced the annual average in 1995-99, and pulled down the total period annual average. For instance, in Chile the RIY was -2.5 percent in 1995 and -1.1 percent in 1998, the annual average was 2.6 percent in 1995-99 versus 13.8 percent in 1981-94, and the entire period average was 11.3 percent in 1981-99. The fluctuations in the RIY are logical in the long-run but risky for the insured, as they can significantly affect the fund accumulated in the individual account and, hence, the amount of the future pension. If retirement takes place at the peak of a boom the pension will benefit, but if it occurs at the trough of a recession the pension will be harmed. The insured could wait until a recession passes but nobody knows how long it would last. Furthermore, the RIY of Chile in the last five years was less than one-fifth the average in the first fourteen years, therefore, the individual account of those who recently joined the system has grown considerably less than the older accounts. Such risk diminishes in a mixed model because it combines a guaranteed defined benefit and a non-defined benefit submitted to market fluctuations.

Portfolio Diversification. A diversified pension fund portfolio helps to compensate risks because some instruments may decline in value while others increase, thus attenuating the problem noted in the previous section but also generating substantial growth in the long run. Although some diversification has taken place, concentration is still quite significant, for instance, from 64 percent to 97 percent of the fund is invested in public securities in Mexico, El Salvador, Bolivia and Uruguay (51 percent in Argentina). Usually, this type of investment is relatively safe; furthermore, the state has paid a high interest in order to promote a high RIY also, but this is costly for the economy and might not be sustainable for a very long period of time. Conversely, stocks which usually generate a higher dividend than public securities in the long run (but are more volatile in the short run) and contribute to the expansion and diversification of the capital market, have a small share in the pension fund portfolio in three countries: 37 percent in Peru, 17 percent in Argentina and 13 percent in Chile (virtually zero in the rest). Finally with relatively few opportunities for investment in the domestic market, foreign investment could be an alternative but seldom is: 25 percent in Peru and 12 percent in Chile (negligible or prohibited in the rest).

National Savings and Fiscal Costs. Some countries have undertaken the pension reform in order to increase national savings, and capital accumulation has indeed been impressive particularly in Chile whose system is the longest in operation. But the measure of such impact should be done, on an annual basis, subtracting fiscal costs from capital accumulation. Fiscal costs result from the state paying three types of expenditures during the transition period of the reform (35 to 65 years depending on the country): (i) the deficit generated in the closed public system which is left either with no contributors or a declining minority (because all or the majority of insured moved to the private system), but with all the pensions; (ii) the so-called recognition bond which is the value of all the contributions paid to the public system by the insured who moved to the private system (in most countries such value is annually adjusted to inflation, and two—Chile and Colombia—pay an annual interest of 3-4 percent also); and (iii) a guaranteed minimum pension to all insured in the private system (both old and new entrants), when their amount in the individual account is insufficient to finance such pension (the state pays the difference). In addition, a few countries (Argentina, Chile and Uruguay) grant social assistance pensions to the uninsured who are poor, and provide other guarantees such as a minimum investment yield and payment of pensions in case of bankruptcy of administrators and insurance companies. Substitutive models (especially those that forced all the insured to move from the public to the private system) result in immediate and high fiscal costs (the IPD is made explicit), while parallel and mixed models lead to lower fiscal costs in the short and medium terms but not in the long run (the IPD is postponed). Two studies conducted on Chile show that the net outcome of the reform has been negative on national savings during its first 15 years (fiscal costs were higher than capital accumulation) averaging -2.6 percent of GDP annually.

Old-Age People

Long-Run Impacts of Previous Effects. If low/declining coverage and compliance continue in the future, there will be an increase in the number of elderly people without social insurance pensions and mounting pressure on the state to provide social assistance pensions.

The rise in contributions and tightening of entitlement conditions would have opposite effects; on the one hand they should strengthen the finances of public and private systems/components and improve pensions, on the other hand the first measure may aggravate the problems of coverage/compliance. High commissions reduce the amount of the wage contribution that might be deposited in the individual account and so the pension. Fluctuations in the RIY may cause also risks (a high versus a low pension), particularly, in substitutive models.

Trade Offs between Fiscal Costs and Benefits. The reduction of fiscal cost of the transition involves a sacrifice in the beneficiary's welfare, i.e., a lower pension. Chile has the most generous regulations concerning the transition but also the highest fiscal costs; subsequent reforms tried to reduce such largess to save in expenditures. For instance, not granting the recognition bond or restricting it (not adjusting it to inflation, not paying interest, placing a ceiling, requiring a number of previous years of contribution), or not guaranteeing the minimum pension or restricting it. Bolivia and Peru are the two countries that have the lowest fiscal costs but restricted mostly the benefits and, hence, harmed the pension of future beneficiaries.

Bibliography

Asociación Internacional de Organismos de Supervisión de Fondos de Pensiones (AIOS). 1999. *Boletín Estadístico* 2do. Semestre, Buenos Aires.

Barrientos, Armando. 1998. *Pension Reform in Latin America*, Aldershot, Ashgate.

Bonilla García, Alejandro and Conte-Grand, Alfredo H. (eds.). 1998. *Pensiones en América Latina: Dos Décadas de Reforma*, Geneva, International Labour Office.

Cruz-Saco, María Amparo and Mesa-Lago, Carmelo (eds.). *Do Options Exist? The Reform of Pension and Health Care Systems in Latin America*, Pittsburgh, University of Pittsburgh Press.

Gillion, Colin (ed.). 2000. *Social Security Pensions: Development and Reform*, Geneva, ILO.

International Social Security Association. 2000. *Reforma de los Sistemas de Pensiones en América Latina*, Buenos Aires, AISS-Oficina Regional para las Américas. See also several articles published in *Estudios de la Seguridad Social*, 1997-1999.

Mesa-Lago, Carmelo. 1998. "La Reforma Estructural de Pensiones en América Latina: Tipología, Comprobación de Presupuestos y Enseñanzas," *Pensiones en América Latina*, Bonilla and Conte-Grand (eds.), pp. 77-164.

—. 2000a. *Estudio Comparativo de los Costos Fiscales en la Transición de Ocho Reformas de Pensiones en América Latina*, Santiago, CEPAL.

—. 2000b. "Social Assistance on Pensions and Health Care in Latin America and the Caribbean," *Shielding the Poor: Social Protection in the Developing World*, Nora Lustig (ed.), Washington D.C., Brookings Institution and Inter-American Development Bank.

Queisser, Monika. 1998. *The Second-Generation Pension Reforms in Latin America*, Paris, OECD Development Centre Studies, Working Paper AWP 5.4.

12

First Experiences with the Privatization of the Polish Pension Scheme: A Status Report

E. Borowczyk

Introduction

A radical old-age pension reform, implemented since 1 January 1999, was one of the more significant symptoms of structural transformation during the recent decade in Poland. It was linked with the adoption of completely new principles and a new philosophy for the system as well as with a considerable number of quality changes.

A new philosophy for the system became part of the transformations connected with the transition from a centrally planned to a market economy: an old-age pension is an individually earned benefit with its amount being closely related to the total number of contributions accumulated over a professional career, which means that it is a function of individual entrepreneurship, resources, earning capacities and the longest employment possible.

The quality changes in the new pension system consist of:

- a close relationship between the pension and the contributions paid;

- conversion of the defined benefit scheme into a defined contribution scheme;

- elimination of early entitlement to pension;

- creation of incentives for late retirement;

- elimination of pension privileges for certain social and professional groups.

In the Polish context, "privatization in pension security" means a three pillar system, including two compulsory pillars which form a part of the social security system covered by state guarantees. The third pillar is composed of voluntary life insurance and voluntary occupational pension programs.

2. Basic Principles of the Compulsory Pension System

The 1 January 1999 reform introduced two separate sources of old-age incomes:

- the first pillar pension, based upon the pay-as-you-go principle, albeit having the nature of a defined contribution system, with the following formula for benefit calculation:

$$\text{Pension} = \frac{\text{Sum of collected and indexed contributions and of the initial capital}^1}{\text{Average life expectancy beyond the age equivalent to the retirement age, expressed in months}}$$

- the second pillar pension, of a funded nature.

The rate of the old-age pension insurance contribution is 19.52 percent, of which 11.22 percent is transferred to the first pillar, 7.30 percent to the second pillar and 1 percent to a Demographic Reserve Fund.

The reform has been introduced without any supplementary contribution to the compulsory funded pension system. However, a part of the contribution, which had earlier been transferred to the one-pillar pay-as-you-go system, is now transferred to open pension funds.

3. "Privatization" Elements of the Compulsory Pension System

Poland is one of the few European countries which (since 1 January 1999) have introduced, as a compulsory second pillar, a funded pension system in the form of open pension funds. Twenty-one open pension funds function presently. They have registered a total of 10.2 million members.

Open Pension Fund (OPF) invests contributions, which are collected for and transmitted to them by the Social Insurance Institution

(ZUS). In this way ZUS, being a public institution having legal status, plays the role of a transferring agent for OPFs.

Shifting part of the contributions to the second pillar resulted in the so-called structural deficit in the first pillar, amounting to ca. 15 percent of the Social Insurance Fund's revenue. It is assumed that the deficit will be compensated for by the state budget subsidy and, to be more precise—by the revenue that the state budget receives via the economic privatization process.

However, even in the first pay-as-you-go pillar, the formula for pension calculation includes some elements that are identifiable as an incentive for individual entrepreneurship: highest possible earnings and the longest possible employment period are the only factors shaping the benefit amount. Social elements, such as non-contributory periods, permanent pension element, guaranteed to every person insured (in the old system—24 percent of the so called basic amount), are non-existent in the new system. In this respect, we may speak of specific privatization of the old-age risk in the first pillar as well.

4. "Privatization" in Social Security— Current Fashion or Permanent Change in the Way of Thinking about Social Insurance?

If we accept that the pension system is closely related to the economic system of a given country, it is difficult to consider that the pension security privatization process initiated is a passing fancy.

However, preparations for the new pension system in Poland resembled an advertising campaign for a fashionable new product— pension system—which would be fair, because "everyone pays contributions to his own pension," which would ensure high pensions (pension funds advertised their services by showing pensioners holidaying in tropical countries) and which would relieve the state budget of an excessive burden.

Taking into account the so far very advantageous legal regulation of open pension funds and the difficulties that would be involved in introducing any changes that would infringe upon OPFs' interests, which afford them the position of the biggest financial institutions in the country, one may assume that the direction of the reform initiated in Poland in 1999 will continue.

Economic reasons—capital market development, reform as an impulse for privatization—as well as the psychological aspect, i.e., specifically forcing every individual to provide for his/her old-age income, thanks to a sense of individual responsibility, are mentioned by the proponents of the reform as elements strongly supporting it.

After almost two years of implementation of the reform, it is under criticism because:

- it is already known that total benefits under pillars I and II will be no higher than those received under the old one-pillar system;

- the outflow of a contribution to pillar II resulted in a gap in pillar I; its compensation is a growing challenge for the state budget, particularly in view of planned cuts in social expenditures;

- the reform has been introduced hastily, without sufficient time for technical and administrative preparation, and for this reason it has threatened the stability of ZUS, depriving it of its earlier reputation as a reliable institution having never failed;

- at the start, the irresponsibility of some OPF agents, who enrolled ineligible or non-existent persons in the funds, disturbed their reliability. At a peak canvassing period, 450,000 pension agents functioned in Poland and 176,000 agents have so far been deleted from the list for various reasons.

The forthcoming years will allow for more precise balance in the pension system privatization process, in the spheres both of macroeconomic and social effects. It will be a constant challenge to reconcile the discrepancies among the formulated objectives of the reform: of a social, financial and economic as well as political character. The discrepancies are to be noted not only between different groups of objectives, but also within the same group of objectives. For example, the social objective—aiming at the maintenance or even growth in the achieved level of pension benefits—is opposed to the aim of growth of expenditures on education and health protection—at the expense of pension expenditures.

The financial and economic objective—limitation of the state budget subsidy—is contradictory to the declared objective of limiting employer-paid contributions.

The political and economic objectives of the reform—limitation of the role of the state and the development of private pension funds, increased support for privatization processes through the utilization of assets left to privatization for the purposes of pension reform, stimulation of capital market development through the development of pension funds and stimulating future economic growth by increasing savings on pension funds—appear under Polish conditions to be a permanent trend to the extent that the direction of the country's economic development is permanent and stable.

Note

1.   Initial capital is a new element of the Polish pension system. It is, in fact, the calculation of the hypothetical pension to which those persons who did not reach 50 years until 1 January 1999 would be entitled on 31 December 1998. This hypothetical amount is multiplied by the estimated average number of monthly pensions for a person at the age of 62. The outcome is equal to the initial capital, which is registered, along with contributions being currently paid and indexed, on the account of the insured person as of 1 January 1999.

13

Austria's Discussion on Social Security Privatization: Some Notes Focusing on Old-Age Insurance

W. Geppert

Throughout the world, in developed and a few developing countries, social security systems are under discussion and a subject of reflection. The starting point is the supposed inability to finance social security. From an economic viewpoint especially, doubts are expressed as to whether pay-as-you-go systems will be able to meet future demands in a changing world. Foremost among these are demographic changes—low birth rates and rising life expectancy—which, in fact, are a measure of the success of the social security system. The demographic problem is aggravated further by changes in the economic environment due to globalization. The increase in international competition, and the related pressure to adapt, have led to labor market problems in many countries, which makes the financing of social security systems more difficult. The answer to the question whether social security is thus a motor of economic development, or a brake, may well depend on whether the country concerned is an industrialized country, a so-called developing country or one in transition to a market economy. As experience shows, it is primarily economically successful countries which have a high level of social protection. Any good and effective social security system frees people from the worry of providing for something which, in financial terms, they themselves are hardly able to afford. It allows people to apply their skills, capacities and resources to other socially important matters, from which society as a whole ultimately benefits in the country concerned.

1. An Overview of the Austrian Old-Age Insurance Scheme

In most industrialized countries, pay-as-you-go public (state) old-age insurance schemes are the predominant source of income for people in retirement. The Austrian old-age insurance scheme is not the result of a single "giant push." Old-age insurance has existed for white-collar workers since 1909, for blue-collar workers since 1939 and for the self-employed and farmers since 1958. In mid-2000 (July) almost 3.3 million people were covered by old-age insurance. Most of them are in paid employment (some 2.8 million blue and white-collar workers). Their pension entitlements depend on the length of insurance, the calculation base and also, in the case of old-age pensions, on age. More than 1.9 million pensions are paid each month. Some 55 percent of these are old-age pensions. At present, women can retire at 60 and men at 65. As far back as 1992, a law was passed (and confirmed as constitutional) to gradually raise the legal retirement age of women up to that of men starting in 2019. It rises by six months a year. From 2034, the normal pensionable age for both sexes will be 65 years.

The basis of the Austrian old-age insurance scheme consists of statutory old-age insurance. It is earnings-based and financed on a contributory pay-as-you-go basis. Those who earn more than the maximum contributory ceiling (2000: 43,200 ATS) can opt for voluntary old-age insurance. Some firms see them as non-compulsory occupational pensions. Occasionally, there are also compulsory collective contribution agreements (concluded between the trade unions and employers, associations). One can thus divide the Austrian old-age insurance system into three parts: the first "pillar," statutory old-age insurance, and two supplementary options, company and personal private old-age provision (pillars two and three). However, it is comparable with the Swiss "three-pillar system" only to a limited extent. In Austria, maintenance living standards are built into the statutory old-age insurance and not, as in Switzerland, the statutory occupational pension scheme, where the first "pillar" provides only a very low level of basic pension. Most of the financial resources required by the Austrian old-age insurance system come from employees' and employers' contributions. These are supplemented by contributions from the federal budget (general taxation), mostly for non-contributory benefits. It is estimated that 20 to 30 percent of pension payments relate to non-contributory "substitute periods," e.g., attendance, childcare and unemployment allowances.

2. The 1997 and 2000 Reforms

At the forefront of the 1997 pensions reform was the commissioning by the federal government of a report by Professor B. Rürup (Darmstadt, Germany) on the future viability of the Austrian old-age insurance scheme up to the year 2030. One of his central messages was the finding that the statutory old-age insurance scheme in Austria was generally adequate in its current form and that it was appropriately financed on a contributory pay-as-you-go basis. It was a clear rejection of the World Bank's 1994 pension reform proposals. A warning which in Austria is also supported by the trade unions and also appears in the "Pensions 2000 Plan," put forward by the government of the day. An evolving system is thus the preferred way.

According to Rürup, Austria's old-age insurance scheme, with its high level of benefits, is among the best in the world. He particularly highlighted the strong social element. As a prime example, he pointed to the maintenance of living standards linked to the best fifteen years' earnings and the supplements designed to avoid poverty in old age. Action is of course still needed in some areas. The target must be improving justice as between individuals and generations and the elimination of internal errors. In this connection Rürup also suggested aligning the various pension models historically structured along occupational lines, which was taken up in Austrian policy.

In 1997 under new rules on extended insurance coverage (to so-called "atypical" occupational patterns) to stem "early retirement" by those insured who retire before the statutory retirement age (60 for women, 65 for men) a 2 percent reduction (malus) per year was introduced with effect from 1 January 2003. In addition (with effect from 1 January 2002) the calculation period was extended from 15 to 18 years. At the same time, the percentage increase for each year of insurance was standardized at 2 percent, in order to remove any incentive to take early retirement. A year earlier (1996) the qualifying period of insurance for early retirement was extended from 35 to 37.5 years. In 2000 came further changes, primarily affecting so-called "early retirees," without however waiting for an evaluation of the 1997 pension reform. The policy was intended (in a budget-setting context) to reduce the federal contribution and prescribed, among other things, a progressive rise from 1 October 2000 in actual retirement ages of 1.5 years, which raised constitutional issues (primarily breach of the fiduciary principle which prohibits abrupt changes in the law), so that in Austria the Constitutional Court must consider the matter. In the legislative process, this law also in fact sought to reverse the low actual retirement age. In Austria it has fallen since 1970 by almost four years from just under 62 to around 58 years. There is no agreement on the reasons for this trend.

3. Old-Age Pensions, a Responsibility of the State?

Under Article 22 of the Universal Declaration of Human Rights adopted in 1948 by the United Nations General Assembly, everyone has the right to social security. Article 25 provides for protection in old age. The Universal Declaration is addressed to the family of nations, i.e., the parliaments and governments of the Member States of the United Nations. They must therefore provide the necessary framework for the implementation of human rights to social security. This is more than just a moral obligation. The United Nations International Covenant on Economic, Social and Cultural Rights of 1966 also applies. By ratifying it (see Article 9), the States Parties recognized the right of every individual to social security. The 1961 European Social Charter on the same subject makes it even clearer that (respective national) social security systems must be maintained at a satisfactory level, at least consistent with the minimum required by the ratification of the ILO Social Security (Minimum Standards) Convention (No.102), which Austria ratified in 1970. A strong mandatory pillar with guaranteed benefits is required, on a pay-as-you-go basis. If circumstances allow, a full commitment to pension income of up to 70 percent of the average occupational income is expected by the ILO. The European Parliament in Strasbourg and Economic and Social Commissions of the EU are also in favor of the preservation of contributory pay-as-you-go as the basis of statutory pensions insurance.

4. The World Bank Old-Age Pensions Model: Pros and Cons

In Madrid in 1994, in its report on "Averting the Old-Age Crisis," the World Bank proposed a "multi-pillar" system as an alternative to the traditional publicly managed (mostly by social insurance institutions) old-age insurance schemes, with the emphasis on privately managed models. Drawing on the system introduced in Chile in 1981 (under Pinochet), they recommended (as a "second" pillar) a fully funded system with defined contributions, that should be operated, for example, by special funds or insurance companies. According to this model, insurance contributions should be saved and the capital invested domestically and abroad. According to the World Bank, this would not only bring advantages to the pensioner, but would also lead to a rise in savings activities, thus stimulating demand for capital growth i.e., economic development. Unlike the ILO, however, the World Bank, believes that a compulsory social protection of perhaps 20 to 30 percent of the average income from employment is sufficient, but in some countries this was below the poverty line and the minimum income level for those in active employment. Although the World Bank approach was concerned with pensions policy in developing countries only, it also contains recommendations for reform of the old-age insurance schemes in industrialized countries with demographic and labor market-related problems, which led to fierce criticism by many in those countries.

The reaction to the World Bank report was highly varied. Essentially, to put it simply, there are two opposite camps: the economy and the social security institutions. The fact that the issue was recognized was mainly due to the opposing viewpoints of the World Bank, OECD, IMF and the ILO and ISSA, albeit that the debate has since lost its edge somewhat. Nevertheless, underlying all of this are stand two rival values. If at the beginning of the 1970s the emphasis was on collective insurance, in subsequent years, in keeping with the spirit of the age, individual responsibility based on the market gradually came to the forefront. Since then, old-age insurance schemes have frequently been discussed in conjunction with the financial sector and especially with measures for development of the capital markets, which naturally aroused the interest of the World Bank and the IMF. Herein lies one of the points of criticism of the ILO and ISSA. One should not, as they have rightly pointed out, make social insurance systems the instruments of capital market development. In the opinion of their experts, the strategies recommended by the World Bank involve unacceptably high risks for employees and old-age pensioners. Not only, in their view, would the cost of pensions be considerably higher, but the present generation of employees would bear a heavy financial burden during the transition from one system to another. The reform process should, in any case, reduce the inherent weaknesses and disadvantages of the existing system and as far as possible correct them.

5. Funded Pension Schemes: Pros and Cons

The main argument for giving consideration to funded schemes is the level of interest on capital. It is fundamentally higher than earnings growth. It is of course an open question whether this bonus return will actually materialize in the long term. High yields are primarily achievable through shareholdings and other forms of participation. Little attention is paid to the higher risks generally related to them. It is also kept mum that extreme price falls could occur when (future) pensioners want to sell their securities or indeed are forced to. The result: the pension benefits promised have to be reduced. According to a report by the EU Commission, Japanese pension funds achieved an average return of 6.5 percent between 1984 and 1993. But if the period is extended to 1996, the average return falls to zero percent!

Those who believe that funded schemes are vastly overrated, and have functions and potential that they are unlikely to deliver, are not entirely wrong. Certainly, the widespread assertion that funded old-age insurance schemes would be immune from demographic changes is false. They too must adjust their pension conditions to a rise in life expectancy, as can be seen in practice (see tables on changes in mortality). Equally doubtful is the view that only pay-as-you-go and not funded schemes are subject to political risks. One has only to think of the changes in taxation. In a democracy, moreover, the increasing concentration of economic power in a few private hands due to the extension of investment by old-age insurance schemes seems politically questionable.

The main argument against full funding is increasingly the availability of the necessary capital stock in the country concerned. According to prudent estimates, a multiple of GDP (in 1997 over 2,500 billion ATS) would be necessary, many times more, of course, than the amount saved in private savings deposits (1997: 1,267 billion ATS). Capital of this order is also impossible to place in one's own country, so one is driven to invest in other countries. Secure and profitable investment opportunities are needed. Foreign commitments are not particularly suitable. One thinks of foreign exchange risk and crises in the financial markets in Asia, in whose "Tiger economies," not so long ago, the OECD recommended that pension funds should invest their accumulated capital. The so-called Mexico crisis in 1994 should really be seen as a crisis of the American pension funds, which had invested heavily in Mexico and had to absorb heavy losses there.

There is thus a high risk related to foreign capital investment that must be weighed in the balance in deciding between pay-as-you-go and funded schemes.

6. Funded Schemes: An Alternative?

In the opinion of many economists, funded schemes make a contribution to old-age pension schemes only as long as they are marginal in macroeconomic terms. Contributory pay-as-you-go schemes, on the other hand, offer a high level of security, but cannot guarantee a given level of pension. In addition, they work only when they reach a sufficient size and are not able to escape their responsibilities. An erosion through insurance-free employment, apparent independence and the like should not be allowed to happen. Contributory pay-as-you-go schemes are not, therefore, threatened only by demographic processes. The legislator must react as quickly as possible to changes in patterns of employment due to new information technologies, as occurred in Austria in 1997 with the new rules on insurance coverage and the introduction of a range of new employment forms (in the jargon: atypical working practices).

From a social policy point of view, the objections to a change of system (from pay-as-you-go to funded scheme) are primarily on employment and policy grounds. There is particular concern about old-age insurance schemes being given a stronger role in serving economic policy. There is a suggestion, for example, that greater capital formation and thus stronger economic growth can be achieved through funded pension schemes. However, as the example of the USA shows (a country with a strongly funded old-age insurance scheme), the savings rate there is not very high. Moreover, as past experience shows, labor market problems cannot be solved over the long term by old-age insurance, because, sooner or later, problems will surface in the old-age insurance scheme itself.

It must first be evaluated as a matter of priority to what extent old-age insurance schemes fulfil their insurance function. Only pay-as-you-go schemes allow the spread of risk across socially representative generations. In addition, the negative choices, which are usual in private insurance, disappear. It is generally asserted repeatedly that the "generational contract" has proved itself extremely well up to now and also offers the assurance of a relatively high level of welfare state services in times of economic crisis and social upheaval. Furthermore, living standards in old age do not depend only on demographic changes, but also on a country's labor market and economic strength.

Every country must seek and find solutions to problems appropriate to itself and its people. In this respect, as experience shows, in addition to the cultural heritage, economic and social patterns in particular must also be taken into account. The theory, correct in principle, that all social expenditure must be resourced from the current domestic product can be and often is complemented by the idea that the consent of all those who generate that social product is needed. In 1997, those consulted in a representative survey in Austria described the old-age insurance scheme of that time as very good. In the longer term, the majority of them thought that statutory pay-as-you-go pensions insurance was safer. The point was frequently emphasized that the state stands as guarantor of the statutory pension scheme. Private (funded) old-age pension provision was regarded in Austria as having only a supplementary function in relation to the statutory old-age insurance scheme. The number of people who already used such schemes was around 20 to 25 percent. In general, they affect only people who earn more than the maximum contributory income. In Austria, that means some 10 to 15 percent of employees.

7. Reform Proposals for Pay-as-You-Go Systems

It is unrealistic to think that any single pension reform could overcome all the decades of problems in this important area. The discussion about adapting the (in Austria statutory) old-age insurance scheme to socioeconomic changes will continue for decades to come. Reforms in the area of old-age insurance must therefore constantly be monitored, discussed and, when necessary and possible, introduced as policy. That cannot be done overnight, since, in Austria especially, the generally accepted fundamental fiduciary principle applies, that clearly prohibits sudden legal measures. All the reform options currently under discussion must be continuously analyzed and discussed under the headings of fair distribution, medium and long-term affordability of the pensions system, fiduciary safeguards and public acceptance. One must also strike a balance, make judgments, that are mutually feasible and compatible. The social elements should not be overlooked. Women's policy aspects should also be taken into account. The goal is clear: finding an effective, socially balanced reform without abandoning the basics generally supported by the public. In Austria, these are the principle of social solidarity, the pay-as-you-go system and management of social insurance by the social partners (jargon: self-administration).

The structure of national old-age pension schemes is very heavily dependent on country-specific conditions. Pension reforms, if they are to take hold, cannot, however, in countries, like Austria, which have an occupationally based pension system, be confined to the pension system alone, but must involve the social sphere as a whole. The social framework for more employment, in particular, must be improved. The more employed people there are, the more provision for old-age pensions is secured by their contributions paid under the pay-as-you-go system. In Austria, however, the number of people who have to take early retirement on medically certified health grounds is fairly high. The majority of the employees concerned must give up work because of motor and bone disorders. There is also a large number of mental disorders, especially among women, which is more a result of their being overburdened and of role-sharing between the sexes. The conclusion is that work must be matched to age. This of course applies to everyone and not just to older workers. An improvement in working conditions and the development of preventive programs focusing on free time in moderation could certainly relieve the financial strain on the old-age pension system.

14

The Evolution of Public and Private
Insurance in Sweden during the 1990s

E. Palmer

1. Introduction

From the latter half of the 1980s major changes have occurred in pension insurance in Sweden. The trend has been from defined benefit (DB) constructions in public, occupational and private schemes towards defined contribution (DC). Notional defined accounts (NDC) have been introduced in the public pay-as-you-go (PAYGO) system together with a mandatory financial account scheme, with major "quasi-mandatory" labor-management negotiated group occupational schemes following suit. Much of the development regarding the introduction of DC financial accounts in both the public and quasi-mandatory schemes has piggybacked the development in the 1990s of the investment side of the private insurance market. This, in turn, followed the international trend of deregulation of financial markets and the rapid growth of domestic and international stock markets beginning in the 1980s. This study explains how and why the trend in pension insurance in Sweden since the mid-1980s has gone in the direction of defined contribution schemes in both public and private insurance.

2. The Era Preceding Public System Reform
and Financial Market Development of the 1990s

Sweden has had a universal old-age social security benefit, formulated as a *defined benefit*, since 1913, with the first major change coming in 1960, with the introduction of the earnings-related ATP scheme. Prior to the war, in the 1930s, the state provided a benefit consisting of a flat-rate benefit supplemented by a small contribution-related component. Persons with very limited means could also qualify for extra assistance based on the regional cost of living. For the average beneficiary, the flat rate benefit was 80 percent of the total state benefit and these benefits together provided only very rudimentary poverty relief.

Following a decade of deliberation, three official commission reports, and public debate and stormy discussions in Parliament, a new pension system was legislated and implemented in 1960. This consisted of the existing flat-rate *folkpension*, supplemented with a new earnings-related scheme, ATP. The full benefit age was set at 67, and the benefit was to be based on an average of the 15 best years of earnings, with 30 years of acquired rights needed for the full benefit. Transition rules meant that the first cohort that could receive an ATP benefit had a right to three-twentieths of a full benefit in 1963, and that a full benefit could not be received by anyone until 1980.[1]

The fact that benefits were low helps to explain why a large percentage of men worked past the age of 65. In fact in 1963, before the ATP reform could have a significant influence on the outcome, 43 percent of all men 65 to 74 years old were still in the work force. With the ATP reform of 1960, more generous rules for earnings replacement for disability were also introduced, and as time progressed qualification rules for disability for persons 60 and over were relaxed. By 1975 only about 20 percent of men age 65 to 74 were working, and since the mid-1980s only a small percentage of persons over 64 are in the work force.

Private insurance covering both occupational groups and individuals began to develop by the 1930s. The first legislation regulating the private insurance market was introduced in 1904, and with this the first insurance supervisory board was established, and it can be said that private insurance has existed in Sweden at least this long. By 1957, when the first major post-war reform of the public system was being formulated, 8 to 9 percent of the privately employed work force were covered by some form of private pension plan.[2] This was changed, however, with the introduction of the new public ATP scheme in 1960 when most of these plans were converted into the first quasi-mandatory occupational benefits in Sweden.

With the implementation of the mandatory and universal earnings-related ATP system in 1960, quasi-mandatory[3] occupational schemes were also introduced for various groups. As a consequence of the ATP reform, in 1960 existing private insurance arrangements for white-collar workers were converted into a single group scheme. By 1976, the number of white-collar workers covered by the 1960 agreement constituted 21-22 percent of the work force. With an agreement reached in 1973 for blue-collar workers (about 33 percent of the work force in the first half of the 1970s), practically all private employees (around 55 percent of the work force) were covered by these quasi-mandatory agreements. Agreements developed also for employees of the public sector, separately for municipal and state employees.

By the mid-1970s, labor-management agreements covered over 90 percent of the labor force. These precluded employment past the age of 65 (with limited exceptions upon mutual agreement). In 1976 the full-benefit pension age in the public system was reduced from 67 to 65. After 1976, it was still possible to work past the age of 64 according to the public system rules, but this possibility was strongly restricted by the quasi-mandatory agreements.

The replacement rate from the mandatory public and quasi-mandatory occupational schemes together were claimed to provide 65 to 75 percent replacement of final earnings. This replacement rate was illusory in two respects, however. First, the earnings-related ATP benefit was based on the average of the worker's best 15 years. With real earnings growth through retirement, the average of the best 15 years *occurs eight years prior to retirement.* This means that the replacement rate from ATP *at retirement* was necessarily lower than the 60 percent of average earnings specified in the formula. For example, with 2 percent real growth, the replacement rate from the whole public system was in fact around 56 percent of final earnings—not 65 percent. Consequently, for blue-collar workers, what on paper was advertised as a 75 percent replacement rate, including the quasi-mandatory supplement, was closer to 65 percent in an environment with real earnings growth.

Secondly, benefits were price-indexed, not wage-indexed. Consequently, with economy-wide real growth in individual earnings, the relative value of a pensioner's benefit to a contemporary worker's earnings declined. This meant that the ratio of an average (full) benefit of a pensioner to an average wage of a contemporary worker was closer to 48 percent from the public system—giving around 58 percent when topped up by a quasi-mandatory benefit. Due to the transition rule in the new public system, it was not possible to receive a full benefit from ATP until 1980. In addition, many older women among generations born before 1920 had no or only a short workforce record, and were only entitled to a small flat rate benefit and after the death of a spouse a survivor's benefit. As a result, with many low-income elderly women and others not fully covered by ATP (or entitled to a full benefit), as recently as 1985 the ratio of an average benefit in Sweden to an average wage was around 35 percent. This changed radically in the following decade and a half, however, as welfare was transferred dramatically to households with pensioners.[4]

With the implementation of the ATP reform in 1960, and the development of the quasi-mandatory, occupation-related schemes there was little room left for private insurance. On the other hand, there might have been a greater demand if there had been better knowledge about the long-term outcomes of the public mandatory and quasi-mandatory systems. At the same time, traditional insurance has always had to compete with other forms of household saving for the business of individuals. Investments in private homes, stocks and bonds have always provided a more liquid alternative and frequently more lucrative form of saving, as we will discuss in greater detail below. Reforms of the public old-age and survivor's schemes, beginning with widow's benefits in 1989 and continuing with the reform of the main earnings-related scheme, may change this, however, by creating a greater demand for insurance not provided by the mandatory and quasi-mandatory schemes. At the same time the insurance industry is now offering more attractive and competitive investment products, as we will discuss below.

3. Reform of the Public and Quasi-Mandatory Schemes in the 1990s

As time progressed, more and more people qualified for full benefits and at a lower full benefit age—65—than the age of 67 originally intended in 1960. Presently, most workers leave the workforce at latest at age 65, but many leave earlier with disability or occupational early retirement. By 1997 only 34 percent of men and 27 percent of women actually had work at age 64 before retiring at age 65.[5] Running against the trend from 1960 towards earlier exit, the average life expectancy of men and women together increased by about a year for every ten years that passed from 1960 to 2000. Similar increases are expected for several decades to come.

Together, shorter working careers and more years in retirement create financial stress on a DB PAYGO scheme that does not relate benefit entitlements proportionately to lifetime earnings and life expectancy. The Swedish ATP system implemented in 1960 with only 30 years of acquired rights needed to qualify for a full benefit and no dependency on life expectancy was a good example of this. In addition, DB systems can embody unfair and arbitrary redistributional characteristics—in the sense that the redistribution created may not go from the rich to the poor. For example, anything short of a lifetime earnings rule is always unfair to those who work and contribute longer than what is required for a full benefit, and still provides an incentive to leave the workforce once the rule is fulfilled. Seniority rules that allow early retirement after fulfilling the number of years required for a full benefit, implying a longer payout period for a given sum of contributions, are also unfair in the same sense—somebody else has to pay for this favoritism. For these reasons DC systems are fairer, in addition to providing an apparatus for creating financial stability. These are also primary reasons why schemes at all levels have moved in the direction of DC.

Two central features of DC schemes are that all contributions from earnings provide rights and that annuities are calculated taking some estimate of life expectancy into account. Traditionally, scholars and practitioners have associated DC with full advance funding—and some have gone so far as to link DC schemes with private with private management. However, it is possible to construct a PAYGO system using all the ideas of the advance-funded framework, but with only demographic funding. Sweden moved in this direction during the 1990s.

In 1992, the Swedish Working Group on Pensions presented the idea of NDC PAYGO in a document outlining the framework for the coming Swedish pension reform. A more detailed proposal was presented in the beginning of 1994, and in June 1994 the Parliament passed the first legislation on the way to implementation of the new pension reform. The reform itself has been implemented in stages, beginning with the setting off of funds for the mandatory financial account component already in 1995, and will be fully implemented in 2003.

The new system consists of *two* earnings-related components: An NDC PAYGO component based on a contribution rate on earnings of 16 percent and a component consisting of advance-fund individual financial accounts with a contribution rate of 2.5 percent.[6] In the financial account system, individuals themselves choose from among a large number of registered funds during the investment phase. A choice of variable or fixed rate annuities, including the possibility of a joint-life product, is provided by a state monopoly.

A major milestone was reached in early 1999 for the public system, when all accounts were converted into NDC and financial accounts and the first account statements were sent out to the entire insured population. Individual fund choices in the financial account system begin in the fall of 2000. By 2000 around 500 market funds had registered to participate in the system, some of which are those

---

Box 14.1
An Overview of Swedish Pension and Saving Arrangements for Retirement

- Social insurance

- NDC PAYGO (16 percent contribution rate)

- DC financial accounts (2.5 percent contribution rate)

- Quasi-mandatory occupation-related schemes

- Blue-collar workers in the private sector: DC 3 percent from year 2000 (2 percent in 1998-1999)

- White-collar workers in the private sector: DC 2 percent from year 1993

- Employees of local government: DC 3.4-4.5 percent from year 2000

- Private insurance (premium payments are tax deductible up to a ceiling)

- Individual retirement saving accounts (available since 1994, with tax deductible payments up to the same ceiling as for private insurance)

- Private saving of all other forms

already associated with unit-link private insurance (to be discussed in greater detail below).

The quasi-mandatory schemes for private blue- and white-collar workers and for local government employees all changed in the 1990s. Beginning in 1993, private white-collar workers could choose their own funds for administration of a 2 percent contribution rate on earnings. Beginning in 1998, blue-collar workers were given a similar arrangement also with a 2 percent contribution rate, which was later increased to 3 percent from year 2000. Blue-collar workers can choose their own insurance company from among about a dozen, with a choice of traditional or unit-link investments, and an optional survivor benefit. Beginning in 2000 also local government employees have converted to DC, with a contribution rate of 3.4-4.5 percent, depending on employment category. The employee must by agreement be given the opportunity to choose the investment form for 1 percent, but the employer can also let the employee invest the whole sum. If the employer keeps his portion of the contribution for investment, then the lowest return allowed is a government bond rate.

Box 14.1 summarizes Swedish pension and saving arrangements for retirement after the reform of the public system and changes in the quasi-mandatory systems in the 1990s.

In sum, there was a clear exchange in ideas between developments in the private insurance market and the evolution of the public mandatory and quasi-mandatory occupation-related schemes in the 1990s, with the introduction of unit-link insurance in 1993 serving to lead the way. Especially important was the idea of separating the investment phase from the annuity phase, and providing a choice between different funds in the investment phase. The new financial account system in the mandatory public system is built up around the idea of separation of the investment from the annuity phase, and the same idea was instrumental in the reengineering of the quasi-mandatory schemes during the 1990s.

4. Private Pension and Life Insurance

Until the 1980s little happened on either the product or investment side of private insurance. Portfolio composition was strongly regulated as a part of an overall government strategy to regulate the financial market. The prevailing idea was that supply-side restrictions could be used to regulate the phase in the business cycle with strong demand by putting a ceiling on the lending of financial institutions.

During the 1960s and into the 1970s, the government of Sweden undertook to build a large number of housing units in the major cities, creating an accompanying need for mortgage-backed financing. Capital market players, that is, the large public pension fund, insurance companies and banks, were required to hold a specified percentage of their portfolios in government or mortgage-backed bonds, with artificially low yields determined by the interest-setting policy of the Central Bank.[7] With tight restrictions on foreign investments and the domestic capital and loan markets, including placement ratios for banks, it was possible for the state to dictate portfolio holdings of government and mortgage-backed bonds and the rate of return offered. By the mid-1980s, most of these restrictions had been lifted, however, creating space for freer portfolio choice, the development of financial institutions and the introduction of new financial instruments. For a discussion of regulations and an analysis of their effects see Gottfries, Persson and Palmer.[8]

During the period 1963-1982, private insurance offered the best after-tax return of all financial "assets" households could hold, because insurance premium payments up to ceiling[9] were tax deductible during a period when marginal direct tax rates on earnings could be as high as 70 percent. From 1963 through 1981, the after-tax return on all other major financial assets was negative.[10] In those days, the best financial transaction an average household could undertake was to *borrow* money and purchase a home. Inflation increased the market price of real estate investments while, to the extent that individual wages followed inflation—which by and large they did—the real cost of servicing borrowed money fell over time. With high rates of inflation, this process was very advantageous for many years. Following the change to open financial markets, the government and the Swedish Central Bank focused on holding the rate of inflation to a low target level.

In spite of the favorable after-tax return on money invested in private pension products, relatively few people saved in this form in the 1960s and 1970s. By 1980, only 4 percent of persons age 18-64 utilized a tax deduction[11] for private insurance, in spite of the fact that for at least two decades this was the most lucrative financial "asset" to hold. There are several reasons why private pension policies were not more popular.

One reason why so few people purchased private insurance was that most workers did not have earnings over the ceiling for the public system, and that the earnings of those who did (frequently white-collar workers in the private sector) were covered by the quasi-mandatory schemes. As late as 1985, only about 9 percent of all male earners and 1 percent of all female earners—or around 5 percent or all earners—had total earnings that surpassed the ceiling for the public pension system (ATP). For people with total earnings below the ceiling, the combination of the mandatory ATP benefit and the quasi-mandatory supplement may have seemed sufficient. In addition, until 1989 the public system offered a fairly generous widow's benefit. What remained was a life insurance market for high-income earners who were not satisfied with the coverage of the mandatory and quasi-mandatory schemes.

Also, by definition a private pension policy is illiquid, making it less attractive in general compared to other saving alternatives. In Sweden, policies can not be liquidated until the holder reaches the age of 55, and then the withdrawal must be phased over at least five years. As we have already noted, by far the best form of saving into the 1980s was ownership of a private home.

Around the mid-1980s the picture changed. Beginning then, four factors combined to increase interest in private pension and life in-

---

Box 14.2
Some Facts about Private Pension Insurance in Sweden

- Individual annuities can be claimed from age 55 with a minimum phased withdrawal of 5 years for annuities financed by tax-deductible premiums.

- Individual annuities can be combined with survivor products.

- The cap on the tax deduction was ca. US$8,500 before 1995, and US$4,250 from 1995 (using an exchange rate of SKr8 per US$).

- Benefits are taxed with the same tax rate that applies to earnings and other non-capital income.

surance, although the impact was gradual. First, as the 1980s progressed, the earnings of more people began to approach the earnings ceiling for the public pension system. In addition, younger people were becoming more skeptical about the their own future prospects in the public system with repeated news about the coming burden of financing the baby-boomers. Younger workers were beginning to wonder whether there would be "anything left" for them when it was time for them to retire—it was well known that the baby-boomers would use up the large social insurance fund.

In 1989, a much more concrete event occurred in the public system: The widow's benefit was abolished for women born 1945 and later. This clearly put increased focus on both the option for men of purchasing life insurance or for women of purchasing some form of pension insurance. This change in the rules of the public system explains why annual premiums paid to insurance companies increased by almost 50 percent from 1988 to 1990. (See Figure 14.1.)

A second important factor was the rapid development of Swedish financial market institutions and instruments from the mid-1980s. As the 1980s progressed, financial markets became deregulated in both Sweden and abroad. With deregulation, the Swedish stock market began to grow and develop. Banks are generally conservative lenders, and prefer established, larger business or household mortgage-backed borrowers. Bank loans were never really good substitutes for stock issues anyway, and certainly not a substitute for venture capital.

With the growth and development of the stock market came also general public interest in investing in stocks, and large gains in returns on stocks were beginning to outstrip inflation by far, bringing large capital gains and fueling even more general public interest. This had two effects. The first was that the interest of savers was now focused on the stock market with its high returns, rather than the insurance market, with its more conservative investment policies and illiquid saving form. The second was that the development of the domestic and international stock markets prepared the ground for the introduction of unit-link insurance.

Following a trend increase from 1983, growth in the insurance market more or less stagnated as the recession of the early 1990s tightened its grip. In 1993, when the country was still in deep recession, the third major event occurred: Unit-link funds were introduced into private insurance. This meant that insurance customers were given much greater latitude in determining how their funds were to be invested, including investments abroad. An insurance company could now offer a range of funds for customer choice, with the insuree's future annuity linked to the long-run performance of his/her fund(s). Since 1993, an increasing share of growth in the market has also come through unit-link contracts (Figure 14.1).

Finally, a fourth event undoubtedly affected the demand for private insurance. This was the reform of the public pension system, first with the presentation of the framework in 1992 and the ensuing discussion, and then with the presentation of the actual proposal in the winter of 1994, passed by Parliament in June of 1994. To begin with, the discussion and debate surrounding the reform proposal definitely served to focus people's interest on their own retirement income perspectives.

In part, the reform itself had piggybacked on the ideas of unit-link insurance, as we have seen above, a part of everyone's mandatory contributions would provide a financial account to be invested as in unit-link insurance. This in itself focused the spotlight even more intensely on financial accounts with individual fund choice in insurance. In addition, however, the reform meant that all but the oldest workers would have to save more or work longer to maintain the replacement rates advertised by the previous system. Without a survivor benefit, especially persons with higher earnings were given even greater incentive to purchase insurance products that combined individual pensions with a survivor's annuity.

A final factor influencing the development of private insurance was the introduction of individual retirement saving accounts in 1994. These are tax deductible under the same (gross) rule as premiums paid for private insurance. As with private insurance, accounts must be held to age 55, and withdrawals must be made over a period of five years. Banks and investment funds provide the account services, and the typical saver can usually choose among a number of alternative funds. Individual retirement accounts are not a perfect substitute for insurance, but nevertheless have become an attractive saving form that competes with private insurance.

So, who uses deductions for individual pension saving? The most recent information available, from 1997[12] shows that since 1991 more women than men use deductions for private pension premium pay-

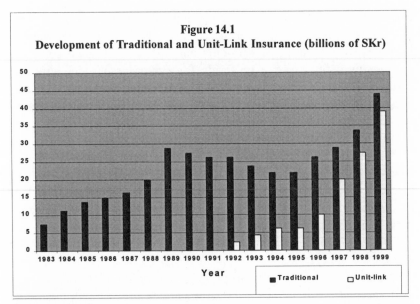

Figure 14.1
Development of Traditional and Unit-Link Insurance (billions of SKr)

Source: Berg, 2000.

ments, and that the gap is increasing. An effect of the reform of the public system appears to have been to create a perceived need to save for retirement on the part of women. In 1997, about 33 percent of women and 25 percent of men had some tax deferred payments, either for pension premiums or individual retirement accounts. (The source of data for this does not allow us to distinguish between these two forms.)

The same study also shows that the older one is the more likely it is that he/ she will utilize a deduction. Better-paid white-collar workers are more likely to utilize a deduction, but the difference between other categories of workers is not great. Since 1994, a tax deduction can even be claimed for saving in individual retirement saving accounts, and this has become an increasingly popular form of saving.

The market offers a large choice of insurance providers. In 1999, there were 129 nationwide insurance companies of which 6 administer the quasi-mandatory schemes described above.[13] Of the remainder, 12 companies provide unit-link products, and 24 traditional life insurance. The remaining 87 provide non-life (pension) insurance. There are also 22 foreign companies in the Swedish market and 322 smaller local (non-life) companies.

Box 14.3
Who Uses Tax Deductions?

- People 18-64 utilizing deductions have increased from 4 percent in 1980, to 17.5 percent in 1990 to 29 percent in 1997.

- In 1997, about 33 percent of women 18-64 and 25 percent of men utilized a deduction.

- The average amount of a deduction has decreased from ca. US$1,250 in 1990 to US$750 in 1997 (with an exchange rate of SKr8 per US$), following the 50 percent cut in the allowable deduction in 1995.

- The size of the deduction utilized increases with age.

Source: Johannisson, 2000.

Total assets of all insurance companies amounted to Skr1,700 billion in 1999. A little less than half (SKr810 billion) were in traditional life and unit-link insurance companies. A large portion of the remaining assets (SKr774 billion) were held by the insurance companies responsible for the assets of the quasi-mandatory schemes. Assets of non-life insurance companies accounted for SKr160 billion. The total assets of life insurance companies and insurance companies managing the portfolios of the quasi-mandatory schemes

Box 14.4
Assets of Traditional Life and Unit-Link Insurance Companies, 1999

	Total		of which foreign assets	
	MSKr	% of total	MSKr	% of category Total
Bonds	276	34.1	73	26.5
Shares	453	56.0	145	31.9
Real estate	41	5.0	1	3.2
Other	40	4.9	3	6.7
Total	810	100	212	27.4

Source: Swedish Insurance Federation. Swedish Private Insurance in Figures, 1999.

amount together to about 85 percent of GDP, which is a large percentage by European standards.[14]

Box 14.4 shows the distribution of asset holdings in traditional life and unit-link companies together. Shares in the stock market are the major form of holding, with bonds being the second most important. Real estate holdings are relatively small. Over a quarter of bonds held and around a third of shares were of foreign origin.

5. Summary

Public, mandatory, quasi-mandatory occupation-related schemes and private insurance have all undergone radical change since the late 1980s. Deregulation of the financial market in the early 1980s was probably the first stimulus to development. Growth of the stock market from the mid-1980s led to a popularization of this saving form among individual savers, and set the stage for the introduction of unit-link funds, which in turn became a part of the evolution of the public mandatory and major quasi-mandatory occupational schemes during the 1990s.

The general trend in public, quasi-mandatory and private insurance has gone from defined benefit to defined contribution systems. These changes were driven by two major forces: First, the financial burden of unfunded liabilities and the unfairness of DB rules in the old system forced Sweden to reform the old earnings-related public DB systems, replacing them with NDC PAYGO and DC financial accounts. Second, the growth and popularization of investment funds and the development of new financial instruments in the 1990s enabled the public system to take advantage of developments in the financial market.

Most important were the ideas introduced with unit-link insurance in the private insurance market in Sweden 1993. Especially important was the idea of separating the investment phase from the annuity phase, and providing a choice between different funds in the investment phase. These ideas also underlie changes in the component of the new public system with individual financial accounts, and have played a major role in the reconstruction of the quasi-mandatory schemes during the 1990s. Individual interest in pension saving has increased dramatically, with a major jump towards the end of the 1980s when the widow's benefit was abolished in the public system.

Since its introduction in 1993, unit-link insurance has dominated insurance market growth and even established laid the ground for the mandatory public financial account scheme and the major quasi-mandatory occupation-related schemes. In fact, innovations in both private and public insurance have served to reinforce the development of one another. Finally, a general outcome of the reform of the public system in the 1990s has been to increase awareness about pension rights in the public and quasi-mandatory systems about individual responsibility in saving for old age.

Notes

1.   Although 30 years were required to qualify for a full benefit, persons born 1896-1913 could only receive a partial benefit based on 20 years of acquired rights from 1960, with the first benefit being 3/20 of a full benefit and granted to a 67 year old in 1963. Thereafter, coming age cohorts were required to have 21, 22 years of acquired rights for a full benefit until 30 was reached.

2.   See Markowski, A. and Palmer, E. 1979. "Social Insurance and Saving in Sweden," *Social Security versus Private Saving*, von Furstenberg, George (ed.), Cambridge, MA: Ballinger.

3.   The term quasi-mandatory means that everyone employed in the occupations covered by an agreement are also covered by the insurance, regardless of whether they themselves are members of the union in question, and that their employers are required by the agreement to cover the costs.

4.   See Gustafsson, B., and Palmer, E. 2000. "Was the Burden of the Deep Swedish Recession Equally Shared?" Mimeograph. Stockholm: National Social Insurance Board.

5.   See Palme, M., and Svensson, I. 2000. "Micro-Modeling of Retirement in Sweden," Mimeograph, Stockholm: Stockholm School of Economics.

6.   There is a guarantee minimum amount, too, and the difference between what people have earned and what the guarantee entitles them to is financed by general revenues from the state budget. There are also transfers into the NDC and financial account systems covering insured periods of sickness, unemployment and disability and to cover child-care rights and other social transfers that may be seen as desirable by politicians.

      See Palmer (2000) or *www.pension.gov.se* for a lengthier presentation of the Swedish reform.

7.   It is generally maintained in the Swedish financial literature that the yield was held down by at least an average of one percentage point over the whole period of regulation.

8.   See Gottfries, N., Persson, T., and Palmer, E. 1989. Regulation, "Financial Buffer Stocks, and Short-run Adjustment," *European Economic Review,* No. 33, pp. 1545-1565.

9.   The ceiling follows inflation, but not real earnings growth. For this reason, it is difficult to state its relative value over time. In 1994, before it was decreased in 1995, was somewhere around 40 percent of an average wage in that year. With the dollar-crown exchange rate in that year, the nominal value of the maximum deduction was very roughly US$11,000. (With the change in the dollar value of the crown from 6

crowns per dollar to 9 crowns per dollar, between 1995 and 2000, the dollar value of an unchanged deduction in crowns fell dramatically.)

10. See Palmer, Edward. 1985. "Household Saving in Sweden and Its Composition," *National Institute of Economic Research*, Occasional Paper, No. 14, Stockholm: Almqvist and Wicksell International.

11. See Johannisson, Inger. 2000. "Tax-deferred Pension Saving in Sweden," Mimeograph, Gothenburg: Department of Economics, Gothenburg University.

12. See Johannisson, Inger. 2000. "Tax-deferred Pension Saving in Sweden," Mimeograph, Gothenburg: Department of Economics, Gothenburg University.

13. All statistics presented here on the composition and assets of the private insurance market are taken from information published by the Swedish Insurance Federation.

14. Adding the assets of the public social insurance funds brings the total of assets in private, quasi-mandatory and mandatory insurance up to about 120 percent of GDP.

Bibliography

Berg, Lennart. 2000. *Sparandets guldålder*, Stockholm: Merita-Nordbanken.

Gottfries, N., Persson, T., and Palmer, E. 1989. Regulation, "Financial Buffer Stocks, and Short-run Adjustment," *European Economic Review*, No. 33, pp. 1545-1565.

Gustafsson, B., and Palmer, E. 2000. "Was the Burden of the Deep Swedish Recession Equally Shared?," Mimeograph. Stockholm: National Social Insurance Board.

Johannisson, Inger. 2000. "Tax-deferred Pension Saving in Sweden," Mimeograph, Gothenburg: Department of Economics, Gothenburg University.

Markowski, A., and Palmer, E. 1979. "Social Insurance and Saving in Sweden," *Social Security versus Private Saving*, von Furstenberg, George (ed.), Cambridge, MA: Ballinger.

Palme, M., and Svensson, I. 2000. "Micro-Modeling of Retirement in Sweden," Mimeograph, Stockholm: Stockholm School of Economics.

Palmer, Edward. 1985. "Household Saving in Sweden and Its Composition," *National Institute of Economic Research*, Occasional Paper, No. 14, Stockholm: Almqvist and Wicksell International.

Reformerat pensionssystem. Kostnader and idivideffekter. 1994. Bilaga A. *Betänkande av Pensionsarbetsgruppen*. SOU, No. 21, Stockholm: Fritzes.

15

Tunisian Health Insurance: Towards Complementarity of Public and Private Sector

M.R. Kechrid

The initiation of research on the introduction of a new health insurance scheme lies within the framework of the implementation of the objectives of the 9th Plan of Economic and Social Development (1997-2001).

This reform project follows the implementation in 1992 of an earlier reform aimed at reorganizing the national health system and modernizing the administrative methods of the public health structures by making them responsible for developing their own administrative policy and for ensuring their own financial equilibrium.

1. Description of the Current System

The main characteristics of the current Tunisian health insurance system are the multiplicity of actors involved and the diversity of the cover schemes available, i.e.,

1. The state provides health cover for lower-income groups; an estimated 130,000 beneficiaries were provided with totally free cover in 1999, and 7,600,000 beneficiaries were covered at reduced rates.

2. Two social security funds provide health cover for their members:

- The National Social Security Fund (NSSF) for workers in the private sector, with a membership of 1,282,807 actively employed workers and 271,440 pensioners in 1999;

- the National Pension and Social Insurance Fund (NPSIF) for state employees and employees of certain public enterprises. This fund covered 518,134 actively employed workers and 148,285 pensioners in 1999.

The schemes managed by these funds are different:

(a)   The NSSF provides a uniform system of health care for all its members whatever their socio-professional group, which comprises:

- The provision of direct benefits in health structures administered by the Ministry of Public Health. Access to all available benefits is provided in return for the payment by the NSSF of a lump sum to the state, and co-payment on the part of the user.

In this context, it is worth noting that a system of invoicing was introduced in 1998 as part of the reorganization of the national health system. Under this new system, the social security funds cover the cost of the health care provided for their members based on partial invoicing carried out by the public health structures within an agreed package. This new system is intended to replace the flat rate payments which have been in existence since the introduction of the social security schemes.

- Six polyclinics, located in towns where there is a high density of beneficiaries, provide the members of the NSSF and their dependants with a very wide range of out-patient care in return for co-payment.

- At the same time, health coverage has been developed to complement the care provided under the first two schemes, usually to cover costly benefits such as: care provided abroad, cardio-vascular treatment, organ transplants, kidney dialysis, lithotrity and the provision of various medial appliances.

(b)   The NPSIF administers a mandatory health insurance scheme which provides a choice between:

- Reimbursement of costs in the event of long-term illness or surgical operations.

The members of the reimbursement scheme have the option of supplementary coverage for ordinary illness within the framework of the optional health insurance scheme.

- The provision of care in Ministry of Public Health structures under the same conditions as those provided for members of the NSSF.

Members of the NPSIF thus have the option of supplementary health coverage identical to that developed by the NSSF.

Other forms of cover have developed alongside the health benefits provided by the Ministry of Public Health for lower-income groups and by the social security funds for their members:

3.   Group insurance offered by private insurance companies. This optional cover, introduced as a result of the dissatisfaction of those insured under the mandatory scheme and thanks to national collective agreements, covered 183,000 members working in the formal sector in 1999;

4.   Mutual funds cover certain groups of state employees (teachers, public health, Ministry of the Interior ...);

5.   Medico-social services developed by certain public enterprises.

2. The Achievements of the Current Health Insurance System

The structure of the system of health protection as described above presents a number of advantages, in particular:

● exhaustive health cover for all social groups;

● guaranteed access to health care thanks to the existence of social security schemes and free medical assistance.

As the demographic, economic and social indicators show, these advantages have produced a situation which is satisfactory (see statistical appendix).

As regards the hospital infrastructure, 18,085 beds were available in the public sector in 1999 compared with a figure of 6,075 on the eve of independence, and the number of primary health centers rose from 979 in 1984 to 1,951 in 1999, i.e., one center per 5,000 inhabitants. The number of doctors employed in the public sector was 3,775 in 1998 (compared with a national total of 666 in 1966).

Side by side with the progress made in the public sector, the private health sector has grown in both size and strength. As a result, 3,044 doctors were employed in the private sector health in 1998, i.e., 45 per cent of the total number of doctors working within the national territory, and there were 156 medical analysis laboratories, 81 haemo-dialysis centers, 95 radiology centers and 65 polyclinics with a total capacity of 1,944 beds.

3. The Motives behind the Search for a More Efficient System

The nationwide efforts to organize health care, combined with the multiplicity of different schemes has led to:

- an annual average growth rate in national health expenditure higher than that of GDP based on current prices, i.e., 11.6 per cent compared with 9.9 per cent between 1987 and 1999;

- a proliferation of types of cover with no coordination or harmony;

- inequalities in the distribution of the costs and benefits of health care;

- no freedom of choice of medical practitioners;

- general dissatisfaction on the part of all parties involved, whether beneficiaries, providers of public and private health benefits or finance organisms;

- a mismatch between the uncontrolled rates charged by private health care dispensers and reimbursement rates, particularly those provided for their users by the social security funds.

These considerations led to a general acceptance of the need to reform a system of health coverage which had become out of date and which had been overtaken by a general evolution of both attitudes and health structures, public as well as private.

4. The Main Thrusts of the Reform

The basic principles behind the reform are as follows:

- the unification of the current schemes administered by the social security funds to create a single basic scheme covering all those insured;

- provision by the basic scheme of all care affecting the health of the individual, whether long-term sickness, surgery or common diseases;

- separation of the organizations for the provision of health benefits and the financing organisms;

- recourse to optional complementary schemes to supplement basic cover, either in terms of care not included or of the level of reimbursement, independent of the basic scheme: the management of these supplementary schemes will be the joint responsibility of the social security organisms and private insurance companies;

- the introduction of agreed rates of responsibility to be observed by the contracting parties, which would serve as a basis for the coverage of health care expenditure by the social security funds, in accordance with specifications;

- establishment of specifications to define the conditions and protocols for the provision of benefits to users and fix the rates of responsibility that the health insurance organisms and the practitioners agree to observe.

This new system must specify the rights and obligations of health professionals and provide a legal framework for the provision of health insurance.

5. Towards Improved Integration between the Public and Private Sectors

The introduction of a system of agreed tariffs will constitute above all an instrument to provide almost automatic access for those insured to the health care market and to health professionals, whether public or private. It will also constitute a tool to control spending on the part of the health insurance system. In addition it will serve as the vector which will enable the private health care sector to integrate the national health insurance system in a coherent and organized way.

The introduction of a system of agreed tariffs will present the following advantages:

- the introduction of a spirit of competition between the various providers thus encouraging improvement in the quality of the care provided;

- the reinforcement of the role of the private sector in satisfying the needs of beneficiaries, within the framework of a coherent national health system;

- control of health expenditure thanks to the introduction of agreed tariffs subject to revision;

- the institution of a new type of relationship between private medical practice and the social security organisms.

The new health insurance system will allow wide scope for controlling the cost of health care whether in the provision of care, as described above, in the prescription of medication and the method of payment which may vary according to therapeutic usefulness (vital, essential or "comfort" medication), or in terms of investment policy which must take into account the health chart of the epidemiological needs of the population in the creation or extension of health structures.

At the same time, the development of the infrastructure must be based on complementarity and competition between the different public and private health structures in order to ensure optimal cover of the different regions of the country.

As regards the nature of the benefits dispensed by the public and private sectors, apart from sensitive fields requiring the intervention of public authorities for their implementation such as preventive medicine and primary health care of a kind essential and vital for the individual, other health measures could clearly be provided by private health structures within the framework of the system of agreed tariffs already discussed.

The involvement of private insurance companies in the administration of the supplementary sickness insurance alongside the social security funds is such as to encourage them, above all the former, to innovate in the administration of the schemes and to optimize their services. This behavior, which will be encouraged by the spirit of competition between the social security funds, nonprofit-making public organisms and private insurance organisms on the one hand and between the private insurance companies on the other, will enable the insured to benefit from a higher quality of health insurance services at lower cost.

This new approach to health organization, in which the private sector will be a health care provider of the same importance, or almost, as the public sector, will necessitate the creation within the finance organisms, social security funds and private insurance companies, of medical control structures with personnel who have the special training required to enable them to carry out their role effectively, a role which will be above all to control the quality of the services provided, to assess the degree of efficiency of the system of benefits to be implemented and to ensure proper respect of the agreements and of the health criteria to be defined.

Appendix

Economic and Social Indicators on Tunisia

	1999
Area:	
	162,155 km2
Population:	9,442,900 inhabitants
Active population (for the year 1997):	2,503,000
GNP per capita:	D2,641
Total health expenditure (as a % of GNP):	5.6
Exchange rate US$1 =	D1,1374

Social security

Listed members of the NSSF:	1,282,807
Rate of coverage of NSSF schemes:	78.71 %
Listed members of the NIPSF:	518,134
Rate of coverage of NIPSF schemes:	100 %
National rate of coverage:	83.86 %

Health

General practitioners (year 1988):	3,520
Medical specialists (year 1998):	3,299
Population per doctor:	1,259

Demographic factors

Life expectancy at birth:	72.4
• Men:	70.6
• Women:	74.2
Gross birth rate (%o):	17.3
Gross death rate (%o):	5.4
Infant mortality rate (%o):	24.7

16

Impact of Private Sector Involvement in Health Insurance in Uruguay: A Status Report

J. Pilón

1. Background

Health insurance is the area of social security introduced most recently by the Government of Uruguay.

Until 1970, social security was in fact concerned with retirement and old-age pensions, unemployment insurance, but not health.

Mutual nonprofit organizations have been operating in Uruguay since the mid-nineteenth century.

At the beginning of the twentieth century, social security began to provide for retirement and old-age pensions without, as already mentioned, addressing the health sector.

Consequently, the mutualist organizations took responsibility for this area, as the one not covered by social security. As they developed, the mutualist organizations had to cope with the fierce rise in costs resulting from the formation of oligopolies of service providers. It led the mutualist organizations to establish their own health centers, where the medical staff became part of the salaried establishment.

Starting in 1935, doctors who did not work for mutualist organizations began to form professional cooperatives, modeled on the relationship between mutual benefit societies and their members (comprehensive care in return for a flat rate contribution), by offering a service comparable in nature to that provided by mutualist bodies and with similar contributions.

Until the late 1950s, people joined a mutual benefit society or cooperative, on a voluntary basis, and paid the relevant contributions. Among those who did not belong to any of these institutions, the well-off were treated privately, while those on lower incomes were treated in state hospitals.

Gradually, the trade unions began to organize funds by branch of activity which, by means of a levy from the worker and the employer, respectively, and a joint employee/employer administration, undertook to pay contributions to mutualist or cooperative associations on behalf of workers and, in some cases, their immediate families.

As of 1970, the Social Security Administration assumed responsibility for the collection of contributions, administration of the funds and payment of contributions to mutualist and cooperative associations.

This brings us to the current situation, where the Social Security Administration collects and pays over contributions for all workers in the commercial, industrial and agricultural sectors. It does not assume any responsibility for state employees, who, with the exception of the police and the military which have a special regime, have attained various insurance systems under specific agreements in each state entity.

In the last few years, the Social Security Administration has also assumed responsibility for retirement pension contributions for lower paid workers in commerce, industry and agriculture.

The insurance system covers only active and retired workers, but not their immediate families.

2. Current Overview

In recent times, governments in many countries, especially in Latin America, have been trying to limit the cost of social security.

This is a common feature of almost all pension scheme reforms. Governments want to balance their budgets and, consequently, seek means permitting them to limit expenditures in the social sector.

As soon as an attempt is made to apply this to the health sector, difficulties immediately arise.

Until now, there is no known formula for providing comprehensive health care to the whole population of a country within a limited budget.

This raises a number of questions, the following in particular:

- Is the possibility for a country's people to have access to different levels of health care, according to their purchasing power acceptable?

- What might be reasonable limits in setting limits of access?

- What might be the limits?

All these questions, and many others, are difficult to answer, given that the society in question aspires to a comprehensive level of health for all its people.

Some countries have transferred the payment of contributions and care of the population to the private sector (insurance companies).

What happens is that an insurance company, as a profit-making enterprise, will establish a system of premiums and benefits based on the relevant actuarial calculations. In consequence, people most at risk are faced with higher and higher premiums. When it comes to the point where someone can no longer pay the premium, he is no longer covered and must rely on state assistance.

In this way, the government in question will find that the savings it made by shifting responsibility for all its population's health care are cancelled out as soon as people with the greatest morbidity drop out of the private system and the state must look after them or leave them to die in the street.

In Uruguay, there exists a strong tradition among the public that the state is not a good provider of health services and that nonprofit private institutions (mutual and cooperative associations) are the most reliable and responsible entities for achieving lifelong comprehensive care through the payment of a fair flat rate contribution.

Aware of this, the Social Security Administration has sought to fulfil its obligation to provide health care to active and retired workers through agreements (reinsurance) with the mutualist and cooperative associations which form the nonprofit system that provides health care to over half the population of the country.

3. The State and Institutions Providing Health Service

Current Situation

The medical care system provided by nonprofit institutions is subject to significant control by the authorities: fixing of benefits, contribution rates, the price differential paid from the social budget, prohibition for mutual and cooperative associations to obtain income from other sources.

Parallel to this, insurance companies are beginning to emerge offering partial or comprehensive coverage to the public as private profit-making companies. These companies are not regulated or controlled by the state. This situation leads to differential treatment by the different types of institution. It would seem reasonable to have regulations for all the different activities or no regulations for any of them.

This last option may seem the more attractive nowadays. The state should confine itself to requiring each institution wishing to operate in the sector to provide clear information about the services it offers and to controlling the proper delivery of these services.

Under equal conditions, no company can exist that is capable of offering comparable services at a lower cost than a mutualist type of institution.

This must be true, given that, where both organizations have a finely tuned administration, the costs must be similar. The profit-making institution must necessarily remunerate the capital invested, since it is a profit-making enterprise. The profit which it must generate is the differential favoring nonprofit mutualist institutions.

As a conclusion of the foregoing, it can be assumed that in any country where there are well organized and administered mutualist associations, leaving aside market distortions that may be caused by unequal government regulations, the private profit-making sector has little chance of operating successfully to the detriment of the mutual sector.

Future Trends

The state's role must be to act as a regulatory body which lays down the rights and obligations of each type of institution operating in the market, while requiring a clear definition of the consumer's obligations and rights.

A clear distinction must be drawn between insurance institutions that also provide medical care, as in the case of Uruguay, and those that merely act as insurance companies, contracting services with third parties.

The former are care providers, while the latter are merely insurance companies. This distinction can be very important in establishing the rights and obligations of different types of institution. The state may indirectly subsidize nonprofit institutions through tax exemptions, while profit-making institutions must cover all their obligations, including taxation, applicable to insurance companies.

If these distinctions are not clearly established, the market will not be able to act as a regulator, since it will not have the necessary transparency, which is a basic requirement for the market to fulfil its regulatory function.

If these basic differences are not taken into account and precise regulations are not established which clearly define the different situations, private profit-making companies may create great difficulties for nonprofit institutions. In a first stage, they can offer services at low prices through annual contracts which do not clearly inform the public of their rights and obligations. This results in a shift of sections of the population with greater purchasing power from nonprofit institutions to the insurance companies. This in turn can lead to a gradual deterioration of nonprofit institutions due to inadequate financing caused by the loss of a significant part of their members.

Obviously, if nonprofit institutions disappear, the result will be a section of the population without medical care which will have to be looked after by the state, at a higher cost than that achieved by nonprofit institutions.

Outlook for the Future

The Uruguayan mutual benefit societies, the leader in the development of private nonprofit health insurance, is faced with a situation which will require an enormous effort if it is to continue to provide services, by being a model in terms of costs and quality of services, by seeking rules for competition and, consequently, cohabitation with the profit-making private sector. It is an exciting challenge. Can a private, mutualist nonprofit system cohabit with a pure capitalist system?

In tribute to the endeavors of those who strove so hard in the past to develop the mutualist idea, there is no question that today's leaders must be capable of rising to this challenge.

17

China: From Public Health Insurance to a Multi-Tiered Structure

A. Hu

The attempt to restructure China's former Health Insurance (HI) for urban workforces in line with the updated requirements of the general reform of the economic system began as early as the late 1980s. Decree No. 44 (1998) of the State Council set out principles and policy guidelines for the establishment of a new HI system and, since then, HI restructuring has entered an essential stage. Although the formulation of the new HI is still at the beginning of its long reform process, and many of its aspects have not yet been clearly defined, the trend of converting the single-tiered HI for urban workers into a multi-tiered system with increasing roles for non-governmental stakeholders, and of providing for supplementary HI programs, has been fully confirmed both in theory and in practice. Consequently, as in the field of old-age insurance, multiple players and multiple financing resources have been emerging in the domain of health protection, both inside and outside the public HI system—the Basic Health Insurance System for Urban Working Population (BHISFUWP).

Thus, insured persons are obliged not simply to seek financing for health protection from the public BHISFUWP, but also from all kinds of complementary HI programs if any, and not to rely only on the financial support of the state and their employers. They and their families also have to assume financing responsibilities necessary for health protection.

1. Provisions of the Public HI System

Whatever the reorientation, the BHISFUWP, the framework of which is prescribed in the said Decree, still remains a main protection mechanism for health protection for the urban working population in China.

In line with the Decree, the main aspects of the BHISFUWP comprise the following provisions which, compared with the old system, clearly demonstrate the strengthening of financing responsibilities imposed on insured persons, both in forms of contributions and in forms of benefit structure, as well as the low benefit levels provided.

Two-Tiered Structure and Benefit Provisions

Unlike a traditional HI, in China the BHISFUWP is comprised of two components: an individual medical account (IMA) for each insured person, based on self-reliance principles, and a collective health care pooling fund (HIPF), based on social insurance principles. It is prescribed that, in principle, an insured person's annual health expenditures should be charged firstly against his/her personal IMA, provided the overall amount does not exceed 10 percent of the regional average annual salary. Once this amount is exceeded, the major portion of the excess costs will be covered by HIPF up to a ceiling equal to around four times the regional average annual revenues. For any expenditures greater than that amount, the responsibility is then passed either to a state-financed complementary scheme in the case of civil servants or to supplementary schemes, nonprofit or profit-making, if any, or to the insured patients themselves and their families.

Stipulated medical care benefits are subsequently payable separately under the two components, which leaves considerable room for insured persons and their families to top up, also implying the need and necessity for the development of supplementary schemes on either a nonprofit or simply commercial basis. Without the aid of the latter, certain categories of insured persons, such as low-income workers, the aged and patients suffering from serious diseases, would have to pay personally an unbearable percentage of their overall medical expenses when subject to serious illness, thereby incurring the ensuing financial risks.

Contributions and Financing

Besides having responsibility for paying an increasing part of the overall medical cost imposed on insured individuals, insured employees as well as their employers are required to make contributions to the health insurance fund. In keeping with provisions prescribed in the Decree, around 6 percent of a contributory payroll—without imposing a ceiling on the income—should be paid by employers and around 2 percent by workers. In practice, explicit contribution rates by employers and employees are determined by local governments, which may be higher or lower, but the fact remains that workers are required to pay direct contributions to the health insurance funds.

However, two categories of insured persons, i.e., insured retired workers and laid-off workers, can be exempted from paying contributions. For the former, in spite of the exemption, they would further enjoy higher allocations to their IMA and lower co-payment rates, while for the latter, contributions owing, including both those of the employer and themselves, are made by re-employment service centers but calculated on a lower flat rate basis, i.e. 60 percent of the average regional annual wage in the preceding year.

Because of the two-tiered structure of the system, revenues generated are split into two parts as well: for an individual IMA, its financing comes from contributions paid by the insured, equal to 2 percent of his/her salary, plus some credits derived from employers' contributions. It is not entirely clear at this stage whether the second resource is linked to contributions made by the individual employer or by all employers. However, the aggregate percentage of such redistributable employers' contributions could be up to 30 percent. The precise extent and the method of redistribution are again up to the local authorities to determine. But their choice must be in conformity with the defined scope of the first tier in the region and be distributed according to age group. As regards the HIPF, the remainder of the employers' contributions, equivalent to approximately 4.2 percent of the payroll, are earmarked for it.

The Decree further stipulates that no fund transfers between the two tiers and between different IMA's are permitted, but unspent allocations under the same IMA owner's name can be carried over to the following budgetary year and the balance remaining in a deceased member's IMA can be inherited by the designated heir(s).

Apart from employers' and workers' contributions, the government also contributes to the system in the form both of tax exemptions and of subsidies for financing the entire running costs of the BHISFUWP, as well as for financing complementary health insurance schemes for civil servants.

Despite the foregoing provisions, the overall financing level fixed at 8 percent of the payroll is apparently too low: not only potentially and individually inadequate for certain insured groups indicated above, but also too low as a whole for financing the scheme compared with the actual spending for medical care of workers in many regions, which could be as high as 17-18 percent of payrolls. It is clear that the financing gap is extremely large. This further confirms that the strategy and the design of the new BHISFUWP deliberately leave a large part of financing responsibility for health care to insured persons and their families.

Universal Personal Coverage

Universal personal coverage by health insurance was achieved prior to the commencement of the economic reform in 1978, when urban residents accounted for only up to 8 percent of the total population,[1] and urban workers were mainly concentrated in the state and collective sectors. But since the economic reform, coverage under the old system has shrunk considerably: about one-half of urban inhabitants, equaling 15 percent of the whole population,[2] were uninsured in the 1990s. This is because the old HI system has failed to adapt to the market-based economy and the changed labor market. In the first instance, the urban economy no longer consists simply of State Owned Enterprises (SOEs) and Collective Owned Enterprises (COEs), but also includes a rapid growing non-public sector, with a workforce accounting for 29 percent of overall urban employment in 1996,[3] and estimated to rise to more than one-third in 1999, while the overall number and size of urban residents have been growing more than three times over the last two decades, amounting to 379 million and 30.4 percent of the population of 12.5 billion in 1998, respectively.[4] Secondly, employer liability-run schemes have proved to be too fragile in a market-oriented economy; owing to financial difficulties facing their employers, many insured workers do not receive the benefits promised.

The new system is therefore aimed again at achieving universal coverage in terms of the overall urban labor force. The first step is to include—except for retired senior government officers, ex-revolutionaries, war veterans and injured soldiers who are exempted from participating in the BHISFUWP and continue to enjoy privileged entitlement to special provisions financed by the government—the whole range of workers employed in the formal sector, irrespective of the status of the establishments' ownership and of the employment and occupation of workers. In other words, all establishments, be they public or private, profit-making or non-profit-making, national or international, as well as their employees, retired and laid off workers are obliged to participate in the BHISFUWP. The inclusion in the system of urban self-employed persons, and workers in Town & Village Enterprises (TVEs), is up to the provincial, municipal and autonomous regional governments to determine. It is thus estimated that 13 percent of the total population of China[5] (excluding the self-employed and TVE workers), equivalent to approximately 162 million persons, would fall into the compulsory coverage category.

Management and Supervision

As in other social security schemes implemented in the country, responsibility for developing and monitoring the national policy and legislation on health insurance, and for guiding and supervising the administration of the BHISFUWP, comes under the competence of the Ministry of Labour and Social Security (MOLSS) in consultation with other government departments concerned, particularly the Ministries of Public Health and Finance and the Government Auditing Agency. Consultation with social partners is not stipulated in the Decree, but it may take place from time to time. As it is actually organized and operated in each region, the Decree leaves considerable scope on policy to local governments, to enable them to adapt the new system to their own situation. Therefore, the duty of health insurance policymaking is shared between the central and local governments and is somewhat decentralized.

The Decree makes it clear that schemes are to be organized and divided by geographical regions at the prefecture level and above; parallel industrial or occupational schemes are not permitted. They should be administered by health insurance institutions rather than by employers themselves. A supervising organ, comprising representatives from responsible government departments, employers' and employees' organizations, medical providers and external experts, is to be set up at each administrative level to monitor and oversee the performance of the funds. In this respect, the management of BHISFUWP is also rather decentralized.

2. Supplementary HI Programs

Because of the two-component structure of the BHISFUWP, the low level of its financing and the limited benefits it provides, the need for introducing and developing complementary HI schemes is increasingly high. This is already envisaged in a clause of the Decree that in principle allows insured persons to participate in a supplementary scheme financed by up to 4 percent of payroll prior to taxation. Actually, although the new BHISFUWP is still in the course of being formulated, certain supplementary schemes have been developed, or are shortly to be introduced, in three different forms:

State Supplementary Schemes for Civil Servants

It is stipulated in the Decree that civil servants must join BHISFUWP, but will be compensated by state-financed complementary schemes run locally to maintain and ensure the benefit level to which they are entitled under the old scheme. The financing fixed at 4 percent of payroll is to be covered by the government's general revenues.

Nonprofit-making Schemes

Despite the numerous players in this context, the All-China Federation of Trade Unions (ACFTU) presently has a paramount role in running nonprofit-making voluntary HI schemes in China. According to the ACFTU, 10,000 such schemes are currently being implemented by the ACFTU throughout the country, covering a total of 5 million workers. For instance, in Shanghai Municipality, 500 thousand workers participate in two supplementary HI programs run by the Shanghai Workers' Mutual Association of the Shanghai Trade Union, an ACFTU affiliate, which at the same time manages four other complementary old-age, invalidity and survivors' insurance schemes and one social assistance program covering a total of about 2 million urban workers out of the overall workforce of 4 million. More supplementary HI programs are to be designed and implemented to maintain the benefit level provided to the insured and therefore to secure social and political stability during the conversion of the HI system in the region. Following the establishment of the BHISFUWP, the development of such schemes for improving and promoting the overall benefit level of medical care protection is thus becoming one of the top priority tasks of the ACFTU.

Commercial Health Insurance

For the time being, private insurance companies have a small but growing share in the HI market. Having realized that the new BHISFUWP leaves considerable room for supplementary schemes to occupy, certain insurance firms plan in the near future to design more suitable and attractive insurance products for insured persons.

3. Community Health Care Services

In parallel with the restructuring of the urban HI system, the national health care system—the medical supplier of HI—is initiating its own fundamental reform. One of the important aspects thereof is to convert the three-tiered national health services into a two-tiered structure with the Community Health Services (CHS) constituting the basic tier of health protection for the urban population. Although the financing mechanism for such services has not yet been clearly defined and developed, given that the decentralized CHS focus much more on health prevention, education and promotion, are closer to patients and are provided at low cost, they are expected in the long term to have an impact on the restructuring of health services, on the improvement of access to health care services, on the health improvement of the population as well as on medical cost containment.

According to *suggestions on the development of urban community health care services,* jointly issued by ten related ministries, it is envisaged that CHS will be developed over a ten-year period starting from year 2000 and in two stages. In fact, since 1994 when the first CHS centre was set up in Shanghai, out of a total of 668 cities throughout the country, 152 have already established CHS centers for their inhabitants. Following the formulation of the national policy and the development of the CHS strategy, out of 32 provinces, municipalities and autonomous regions, 16 have issued detailed governmental decrees for its implementation within their territories.[6]

4. Conclusion

The trend towards converting the single-tiered state HI into a multi-tiered structure has brought about changes in shares of financing health care services between the government, social insurance and individual persons over the period from 1990 to 1996, with the shares changing from 25 percent to 16 percent, from 48 percent to 27 percent and from 27 percent to 57 percent, respectively.[7] Consequently, even without taking into account the rapid rises in medical costs as a whole in those years, insured workers and their families have had to assume more financial responsibility for health care. Furthermore, there is clear a need for supplementary schemes to fill the gap. The implications of such a reorientation for the development of the health care insurance system in China are considerable.

Notes

1. Statement of State Statistical Bureau, Beijing, reported in *People's Daily*, 6 October 1998, Beijing.
2. *Financing health care: Issues and options for China*, World Bank, 1997, Washington, D.C.
3. *China Statistical Yearbook 1997*, Beijing, China Statistical Informational and Consultancy Service Centre.
4. *Government Bulletin on the Statistics of Economic and Social Development in 1998*, PRC, 26 February 1999, Beijing.
5. Ibid., 1 March 1999, Beijing, China. But according to the *China Statistical Yearbook 1997* (Beijing, China Statistical Publishing House), the population accounted for 1,223 million by the end of 1996; 198 million are urban workers. Of these, 112 million are SOE workers, 30 million COE workers, 23 million self-employed and employees of private enterprises, and 9 million workers employed in other ownership units. Also, in 1996, China had 32 million retired workers, of which 24 million are ex-workers of state and collective enterprises and 10 million urban unemployed. Even taking into account some changes which have occurred in the labor market in China since 1997, it is still difficult to understand how this coverage of 13 percent was calculated, which is inconsistent with the relative provisions stipulated in the Decree and the actual figures.
6. According to Mr. Yao Jian Hong of MOPH, with whom the author had a meeting on 6 July 2000.
7. Ibid.

18

Impacts of Private Sector Involvement in Health Insurance in Indonesia

S. Roesma

1. Development of Health Insurance

Changes in economic and social policy are among the most crucial issues affecting reforms in social health insurance. After Indonesian independence in 1945, as a gesture of appreciation, the government provided free medical care to the military and to civil servants. In the early 1960s, owing to the escalating cost of civil servants and their dependants for the budget of the Ministry of Health, it dispatched members of its staff to the Netherlands and the United Kingdom to carry out a comparative study. In 1968, the first Social Health Insurance (ASKES) State Owned Enterprise was established in Indonesia on the basis of Presidential Instruction No. 230/68, which stated that all civil servants must contribute 5 percent of their basic salary. This contribution was reduced to 2 percent in 1977. In 1991, the community restricted to civil servants was extended to include civil service pensioners, retired military and police personnel and veterans as well as their dependants, covering 13.7 million members. This means that ASKES covers about 7 percent of the population, 20 percent of them above the age of 56, the average retirement age.

In 1992, *Jaminan Sosial Tenaga Kerja* (Jamsostek), a state enterprise providing social security under the Ministry of Manpower established in 1977, became the second such enterprise to provide social health insurance in Indonesia on the basis of Act No. 3/92. Companies were required to pay contributions from the monthly payroll on behalf of their workers amounting to 6 percent for a family and 3 percent for a single person. Although the scheme was compulsory, few companies enrolled. Reasons for this attitude were increased production costs and the fact that many state enterprises and big private companies were already providing health care programs, with some of them even having their own hospitals. Jamsostek has more than 10 million social security members covered for death, pension, and occupational accidents, but only one million covered for health. Workers are required to contribute for their pension only, while the company pays for occupational accidents, death and health.

Meanwhile, in 1993, during the economic boom, ASKES, in need of additional revenues, perceived a profitable market and expanded its company, embracing the private sector by setting up a private network of health facilities. This was authorized by the government through regulation No. 69/91 and, in order to succeed, the scheme had to be competitive and attractive to private companies. Membership was voluntary for companies, associations or groups, consisting of at least 100 persons and the calculation of premiums was based on community ratings. By the year 2000, ASKES had approximately 718,000 voluntary members from 1,799 companies, the largest membership among private health insurance companies. The reasons behind this relatively rapid growth were the competitive premium scheme, community rating and cross subsidy and the absence of age restrictions. Persons retired from companies could enroll via their former employers.

It is regrettable that, during the economic boom in the early 1990s, no effort was made to increase the compulsory contributions made by the government as the employer of civil servants. By then, the growth of inequalities in income and wealth, in conjunction with rising demands, was the cause of increased complaints about social health insurance. The experience of the past decade has shown that increasing contributions to meet the rising demands for health care required a long bureaucratic and legislative process. Because of the rapid growth of economy, people could afford visiting private health facilities on a fee-for-service basis, while the affluent went abroad for their annual checkups. During the financial crisis that swept Asia in 1997, health costs tripled, especially for drugs, so that people fell back upon public facilities and social health insurance. The 2 percent contribution (Rp2,500 equiv. US$0.30 per capita) became inadequate even though ASKES had already taken cost control measures in 1987 by instituting managed care. By mid-1999, ASKES was forced to initiate a policy of cost sharing, which placed an additional burden on its members during these difficult times.

Commercial profit-making health insurance companies in Indonesia were at first confined to the life insurance branch, the reason being that health services were relatively cheap and insurance was not popular. In the early years following World War II, only a few foreign insurance firms entered Indonesia, but during the economic boom in the early 1990s, international insurance conglomerates and small companies, mostly from Australia, invaded the country. The 1 percent out of 210 million people who belong to the high-income group enrolled with well-known international insurance firms. The country's prolonged financial crisis and political uncertainties, plus escalating health costs, have contributed to the people's growing awareness of health insurance. People are indifferent as to whether companies are joint ventures or local, as long as their rates are affordable and they provide good services. At present, 174 general and life insurance firms are registered at the Ministry of Finance, five of them state enterprises. Of the 174 insurance firms, 62 deal in life insurance with some health insurance products, while among the five state-owned enterprises, only Jamsostek and ASKES are concerned with health insurance. ASKES is the only company specializing in health insurance in the form of managed care, both for compulsory and voluntary members. Thirty-five local (city/district) voluntary managed care companies are registered with the Ministry of Health.

It can be observed that health insurance affects the market mechanism by reducing the price and acting as a controlling system. Actually, the emergence of competitive market forces in health has resulted in a fundamental shift in orientation within the health sector, which in turn has affected health insurance. There is no denying that health insurance has an economical and political impact and vice versa.

2. General Situation Before and After the Crisis

Indonesia is the largest island complex in the world, consisting of approximately 17,000 islands with a land area of 1,904,000 square kilometers. The world's fourth most populated country, with a population of 210 millions, it was one of the miracle countries in Asia having dramatic economic growth. In 1996 growth was 7 percent, while in 1997-98 it became minus 2 percent. The per capita GNP in 1987 was US$490, in 1996 more than US$1,000, but after the 1997 crisis it was back down to around US$500.

Health is an essential part of human development. In its latest Development Report 2000 on the Human Development Index (HDI), the UNDP stated that, according to three indicators, i.e., life expectancy, literacy and Gross Domestic Product (GDP) per capita, Indonesia had slid from position 105 to 109, out of 174 countries. This decline was mainly attributable to the country's poor economic situation during the peak of the economic crisis in 1998.

Many Asian and Pacific countries, including Indonesia, are experiencing adverse economic conditions, resulting mainly from currency devaluation in the region, which causes high volatile exchange and interest rates, affecting almost all sectors. Economic and financial pressures are also characteristic of the health sector, with health expenditures of only 2 percent of GDP. This exchange volatility has adversely affected the hospitals and, in turn, the health insurance companies because of their dependence on the import of items such as hemodialysis, non-generic drugs, needles for injections and blood transfusion bags.

Indonesia must cope with demographic changes such as rapid population growth and population aging, and with resurging health problems, namely tuberculosis, leprosy, and malaria. Diseases such as typhoid, dengue, URI's (upper respiratory tract infections) and hepatitis are chronic problems while, during the peak of the crisis, malnutrition of infants and toddlers became a national emergency raising fears of a lost generation. Maternal mortality rates are high, eye cataracts and AIDS are increasing rapidly, forcing the Ministry of Health to set priorities in its budgeting.

Indonesia fortunately has a good health infrastructure, with a three-tier system. People have access to primary and secondary care, while tertiary care is regional. The health care system is run mainly by the government, which has a network of more than 7,000 health centers with 18,000 sub-centers and about 400 public hospitals. The private sector maintains hospitals owned by religious organizations and non-governmental organizations. During the economic boom, additional profit oriented luxury hospitals were established, owned by medical doctors and investors.

Governmental health services are not gratis, except for the poor. Approximately 70 percent of total health expenditure is privately funded, with more than 50 percent of this expenditure going for drug purchases. The worst effect of the financial crisis was the high rate of unemployment, resulting in malnutrition of children. The urban and rural population under the poverty line has increased sharply from 15 percent before the crisis to approximately 40 percent afterwards, causing the World Bank and the government to set up jointly a Social Safety Net covering health and education.

The emergence of competitive market forces in the 1990s has created a health industry. One of the most critical changes adopted by the health industry is a shift in orientation within the health sector. Hospitals and other private institutions moved slowly from a social to a market orientation. Because 15 percent of the population at the time were among the poor, in order to protect them, the Ministry of Health provided health cards enabling them to visit health centers and hospitals for free. The Ministry of Health also issued a regulation that 25 percent of the third-class beds of public and private hospitals had to be free of charge for them. However, the poor seldom went to private hospitals, while the public hospitals were overcrowded.

One of the impacts of the 1997 financial crisis was the trend to privatization causing a shift in both responsibility for, and management of, hospitals from the government to the private sector. In the year 2000, about ten of the largest public hospitals are planning to become private. Singapore, Malaysia and Australia are increasing competition by erecting new high-tech equipped, joint venture hospitals and medical centers for expatriates in Indonesia, mostly in Jakarta and Bali.

The second long-term plan of the Ministry of Health for achieving Health by the Year 2010 gives priority to promotion and preventive care while delivery of health care and its financing will be effected through JPKM (*Jaminan Pemeliharaan Kesehatan Masyarakat*), a managed care approach. Parliament has issued an Act No. 23/92 on Health, stating in one of its articles that JPKM must attain equity, affordable rates, comprehensive care, continuity, quality assurance and cost containment. Indonesia thereby became the first country in the world to have an act on managed care. By decentralizing most of its activities to the autonomous regions, the Ministry of Health is slowly changing from an operational to a more policy oriented entity, starting by the year 2001.

3. Impacts of the Private Sector on Health Insurance

There seems to exist a general rule that reforms will take place after a crisis. During the 1997 financial crisis, reform also took place in Indonesia, affecting private and state-owned health insurance enterprises. As the leading health insurance, ASKES covers approximately 7 percent of the country's population; the present article will therefore lay stress on ASKES.

The first social health insurance state enterprise (ASKES) was established when the Minister of Health was facing serious financial difficulties in providing health care for civil servants and their dependants. The second major change in policy occurred in 1986, when ASKES realized that it needed measures for controlling costs. The favorable results of the Health Maintenance Organizations and Kaizer insurance in the United States induced ASKES to institute Managed Care.

The concept of managed care in Indonesia involves an integration of subsystems for the delivery of health care and for financing respectively. Delivery of health care is comprehensive, comprising promotional, preventive, curative and rehabilitative care. The fee for service method has been gradually abolished and replaced by capitation for primary care doctors/family physicians. The impact of ASKES's ten years of capitation is that about 7,000 health center doctors and 2,000 private family physicians became receptive when other insurance providers entered the scene. Other criteria of managed care have been gradually implemented, the latest item being utilization review, in 1999. When the social security state enterprise (JAMSOSTEK) expanded to health in 1992, it also adopted the managed care approach.

As mentioned above, more than 50 percent of expenditures were going for drugs. Actually, Indonesia can be seen as a major market for drugs, having about 16,000 items of drugs with 1,100 generic names. As a consequence, ASKES, with its scarce funds, compiled its own Drug and Price List in 1987, consisting of about 800 items of drugs with 470 generic names. The list of drugs was agreed upon by specialists from several well-known medical schools in Indonesia and renewed every year. Purchasing selected drugs for 14.5 million people in bulk gave ASKES immense bargaining power, obtaining discounts of up to 40 percent for some drugs. During the ten years, 1987 to 1997, expenses for drugs decreased to 38 percent of total expenditures and then slowly rose to 42 percent. With the devaluation of the rupiah, drug expenses increased to 47/48 percent, which was still less in comparison with those of other health insurance companies. These examples—purchasing in bulk, bargaining power, discounts in price of drugs—are all ingredients of private sector influences on health insurance.

In the early 1990s, owing to the high economic growth rate, existing private life insurance firms in Indonesia expanded their businesses with health insurance products, and new firms entered the picture, mostly in the form of joint ventures. Benefits were offered including hospitalization, heart disease, checkups abroad or travel. People could afford to patronize private hospitals and were insured for treatment in hospitals in the United States, the Netherlands, Australia and Singapore, which were very popular. As mentioned above, no effort was made during this economic boom to increase the contribution/premium of social health insurance. The privatization trend led ASKES to make another major decision, i.e., setting up a private health insurance scheme, thus converting ASKES into a mixed public-private company. In spite of becoming a private company, ASKES practices managed care, such as comprehensive care, community-rating premiums, pre-paid capitation, utilization review, etc., ASKES received the ISO 9002 certificate in 1997.

For decades health was a social institution, but lately, because of market forces, health has become a commodity. The population, nevertheless, continues to regard health as a social issue, expecting it to be free. The change in orientation of hospitals from social to commercial led to increased competition based on price, which had a direct impact on health insurance. Owing to escalating costs in hospital care, drugs and high tech equipment, ASKES implemented total capitation in eight provinces in 1998 (covering 70 percent of ASKES members), replacing a retrospective cost-based reimbursement system with a prospective fixed-rate system. In addition, ASKES introduced the feature of profit sharing with all contractual providers in any one province. The result showed a decline in hospital costs and resulted in less referrals to hospitals along with a shift from in patients to out patients.

The world has experienced a decade of quality and a decade of reengineering. With the new millennium we are now entering the decade of velocity. Computerization has also had its effects in diagnosing diseases and on laboratories for blood and urine tests. Indonesians who travel abroad frequently or view TV series on emergency care are not satisfied with the available health facilities and their service, which are characterized *inter alia* by the absence of prescribed drugs and excessive waiting times. Customer satisfaction has become an important indicator for hospitals and insurance schemes. There has been a shift in demand and people now want swift appointments, no long waiting lines, precise diagnoses, and even quick results. Actually, what is most needed is informed patients so that induced demands can be avoided.

After the peak of the crisis in 1998, the World Bank and the International Monetary Fund (IMF) urged Indonesia to privatize state-owned enterprises. Investors were willing to invest but demanded total control through ownership of at least 51 percent of shares. The Indonesian parliament agreed with privatization but preferred ownership to be in Indonesian hands. The government of Indonesia, through the Ministry of Investment and State Owned Enterprises, decided not to privatize the five existing social insurance state enterprises. ASKES and Jamsostek are often accused of being monopolies, but the question then arises, is social insurance a monopoly?

4. The Future

At the end of June 2000, Clinton and Blair made a joint announcement at the White House on the mapping of the genetic code. This code is really the essence of mankind. The future impact of this genetic code on society will be enormous, in a positive and negative way. In a matter of decades, the medical world will be totally transformed. Scientists believe that medicine will eventually be able to identify from birth the diseases from which a person will potentially suffer, which of course has its positive and negative effects.

Positive, because preventive measures can be taken and treatment can be provided to extend life, and negative because insurance providers can discriminate among people according to their genetic code. The difference between developed and developing countries or between north and south will be pushed to the extreme. Mapping of the genetic code is thus a double-edged sword because it involves not only scientific applications, but ethical, legal and social issues.

The apparent inability of the International Monetary Fund (IMF) to save collapsing Asian currencies, especially that of Indonesia, which has also had to face political and social instability has worsened the situation. Indonesia depends on foreign funding and has a huge debt that will burden future generations for decades. According to the World Bank's country director for Indonesia, since the 1997-98 financial crisis, the government has managed to control inflation and raise the Gross Domestic Product growth rate by over 3 percent, hopefully a basis for a better future.

But as the crisis persists and the deficit grows, building a strong economy is vital to maintaining the health of the population and that of the individual.

While the World Bank and IMF are exhorting Indonesia to privatize its companies, to make them more competitive and transparent, the government is seriously contemplating the creation of a national social security program and discussions are going on in all related ministries. One looming major problem is the high number of unemployed. Many people will not be able to pay contributions while the government is presently unable to offer tax subsidies. Jamsostek appears ready to embark on a scheme whereby all five insurance state enterprises, i.e., *Taspen* (pension), *ASABRI* (military), *Jasa Raharja* (life and accident), ASKES and Jamsostek will be incorporated into one National Body under the supervision of the president.

My personal preference would be to start with a National Health Insurance scheme in the form of managed care, in order to provide at least for basic care. By starting in stages as Korea did, depending on the ability of people to contribute, a national health insurance would gradually materialize after a certain planned period. The government would need to provide social assistance for the poor in defined areas where the scheme was implemented. This would be extended to the whole country when the government was financially strong enough to subsidize all the poor, who by then would hopefully have been reduced in number. According to the Regional Director of WHO, South East Asia Region Office, Uton Muchtar Rafei, the social welfare of a nation is largely dependent upon the number or percentage of elderly people enrolled in health insurance.

One of ASKES's visions, stated by the founders in the 1960s and included in its corporate plan since 1992, was to have a national health insurance scheme. That is why ASKES developed an academic concept in 1998, prepared by the University of Gajah Mada, Indonesia's oldest university, along with the draft of a national health insurance act, prepared in the year 2000 by the social and private health insurance association PAMYAKI. At present, the Ministry of Health is also proposing a JPKM act to parliament, which envisages the setting up of one or two private managed care companies per district, compulsory for their constituents under the supervision of the local health authority, with contributions being expected either from tax revenues or community contributions.

As observed and elaborated above, I would summarize by saying that the impacts of private sector involvement in health insurance in Indonesia are in the fields of economics, politics and culture.

19

Trends in Private Sector Involvement in the Delivery of Workforce Development Services in the United States

S.A. Wandner and J.O. Javar*

1. Introduction

The workforce development system was introduced in the United States as a public responsibility to stabilize the United States economy in the wake of persistently high unemployment rates experienced in the 1930s and the implementation of similar systems in other industrialized nations. The workforce development system, which initially comprised the public employment service (PES) and unemployment insurance (UI), later expanded in the 1960s with the addition of job training programs, including those for welfare recipients. UI was introduced to provide compensation to workers who became involuntarily unemployed while they sought new employment or skills training, with complementary services provided by PES to provide those unemployed individuals with the necessary assistance, tools, and information to seek employment more quickly and effectively. Training programs were later added to provide unemployed individuals with appropriate skills training so that they could attain employable skills and seek employment that offered similar or greater earning than their previous jobs.

* The authors appreciate the comments of David Balducchi, Gerri Fiala, Terry Finegan, Bob Gilham, John Heinberg, Bob Johnston and David Smole. This paper reflects the opinions of the authors and does not represent the policy or positions of the United States Department of Labor.

In early consideration of implementation of a workforce development system, privatized approaches to PES and UI programs were developed and tested, but ultimately rejected. The rejection of these privatized approaches did not, however, signify an isolated relationship of the public system from the private sector in delivering workforce development services. In fact, the workforce development system has always exhibited a role for private sector interest and involvement in service delivery.[1] More specifically, the system has provided opportunities for increased interaction from "intermediaries," defined as public or private organizations that act as brokers between the workforce development system and its customers.[2] The involvement of private sector businesses, including those that act as intermediaries in delivering services for the workforce development system is the primary emphasis of this discussion.

The private sector has traditionally been restricted from delivering "inherently governmental" workforce development services that could significantly impact an individual's life or property, such as determining the receipt of an individual's only source of income (e.g., UI), among other considerations. Services that are defined as inherently governmental functions are therefore exclusively delivered by merit-staffed employees to ensure that unbiased and professional service delivery is given to customers. Merit-staffing has often been used to eliminate or reduce the possibility of outside influences affecting proper service delivery to individuals and employers. Nonetheless, private sector businesses are interactive players in PES, UI, and training programs for delivering workforce development services to customers.

UI is a social insurance program that is not affected by any direct competition from the private sector for similar services. UI has always been provided exclusively through a state-administered program, and delivered exclusively by state merit-staffed employees, with no serious consideration towards privatizing these functions. Notwithstanding, the UI program generally provides for significant private sector involvement, with high levels of interaction from employers and employers' agents (i.e., unemployment insurance management consulting firms that provide unemployment cost control programs and services) to police the system, as well as private banking institutions to manage the flow of tax revenues and benefit outlays. Employers hire private UI management consulting firms to act on their behalf as intermediaries with the state UI programs.[3] These intermediaries are often used by larger employers to outsource the management of a significant amount of their UI responsibilities, such as employer representation at hearing appeals.[4] Similarly, the UI program also outsources to the private sector some of its functions that are not inherently governmental functions.[5]

The PES also delivers services through state merit-staffed employees. However, unlike the UI program, the PES is not isolated from direct private sector competition. Their business of labor exchange—that is, the matching of jobseekers with employers and employers with jobseekers—generates interest and involvement from both public and private sectors. As a result, the PES is open to competition from private employment services offering similar labor exchange services. With national funding decreasing in real terms for public labor exchange services, along with increasing accessibility to labor market information over the Internet, PES staff are relying more heavily on web-based services to assist them with their customers than in the past.[6] To illustrate, the web-based services of America's Job Bank (which posts job openings at a national level to connect jobseekers with employers) and America's Talent Bank (which posts resumes of jobseekers at a national level to connect employers with jobseekers) are public efforts that are large in scale and available free of charge to both jobseekers and employers. Similar automated employment services are offered by a variety of private sector businesses and organizations. Their revenues are generally earned through fees charged to the employer once an employment contract is made between the employer and the jobseeker. Despite direct competition from the private sector, PES staff do not withhold information on private sector services from their customers. PES staff often use those services as another resource for their jobseeking customers so that they can further expand their customers' options for employment. Likewise, private sector employment agencies often use services of the PES to recruit prospective job candidates for employer clients.

The public job training programs, which include services for populations such as welfare recipients, have offered much more flexibility and opportunity for direct private sector involvement when compared to UI and PES programs. With the Workforce Investment Act (WIA) programs superseding the Job Training Partnership Act (JTPA), programs in July 2000, direct training services are no longer provided by the local area's decision-making boards, i.e., the local

Workforce Investment Boards (Local Boards).[7] Under the WIA, Local Boards contract out the operation of One-Stop centers, as well as services provided within the One-Stop centers, to public or private intermediaries, with limited exceptions. With over 1,400 new and existing One-Stop centers operating across the country, the opportunity for using intermediaries has increased as Local Boards contract out their One-Stop operations and training services.[8] A number of Local Boards have exercised the option of contracting out One-Stop operations to private intermediaries, giving Local Boards more flexibility in determining to what extent they are preferring their services to be provided by private intermediaries over public intermediaries.[9] Similarly, for training-related services delivered within the One-Stop centers, a recent study of welfare recipients indicates local areas contracting out to private intermediaries a significant amount of their services that link welfare recipients with jobs.[10] Since WIA and its programs were recently implemented, relatively little is currently known about the extent that local areas have contracted their services to private intermediaries. In addition to establishing One-Stop centers, the WIA also established Individual Training Accounts (ITAs) as a funding mechanism to deliver training services to customers. Since ITAs are a relatively new innovation of the training program, little is known about how private intermediaries will interact with the workforce development system and ITAs to provide training under the WIA.

This chapter provides a brief overview of the relationship between the workforce development system and its customers by focusing on the role of intermediaries that work as brokers between the two. Intermediaries are becoming increasingly more visible in the public workforce development system as a result of a variety of factors, including changes in legislation, technological advances, and decreased funding in real terms for public services. The ensuing discussion describes the different roles emerging for private sector intermediaries as they tailor their approaches in search of their niche in offering services as part of the workforce development system.

2. New Directions in Private Sector Involvement

Unemployment Insurance

When Unemployment Insurance (UI) was implemented in the United States, it was created as a social insurance program, with the provision of benefits administered exclusively by state agency merit-staffed employees. As a result, there is no opportunity for private competition in the delivery of UI to claimants.

Although initial consideration was given to a private administration of UI, the program has not moved in that direction. In fact, during periods of recession, the federal role for UI has expanded, and consideration has actually been given to broadening the pooling of benefits payment. Through the UI program, employer revenues are pooled to provide for six months of potential benefit payments through the "regular UI" state program. By pooling revenues, risk is spread among all businesses, and unemployment shocks are absorbed across the state. Pooling employer revenues only is carried out at the state level for regular UI, with pooling at the state-federal or federal level restricted for recessionary programs. The lesson learned from high rates of unemployment and back-to-back recessions from the mid-1970s through the mid-1980s, when many state trust fund accounts went broke, was the advantages of wide pooling of risk both between states and within states. This resulted in cost equalization proposals to further pool risk across states in the early 1980s, but the issue went away when the United States economy improved in the late 1980s. Nonetheless, half of the funding of the permanent Extended Benefit program comes from the federal portion of the UI payroll tax. In addition, temporary emergency UI programs have been enacted during most recessionary periods, and they have been funded either by federal general revenue or by the federal portion of UI tax. These developments reflect a lack of serious consideration towards implementing a private sector approach in UI administration.

Although UI does not allow the private sector to directly administer the program, the use of UI "experience rating" has opened an avenue for intermediaries. Through experience rating, individual employers have a financial incentive to oversee the UI process. The amount of taxes each employer pays in any given year to the UI system is based on their relative experience with payments of unemployment compensation to their former employees. This tax amount further depends on whether the former employees were laid off, voluntarily quit their job, or were fired for cause. Employers who voluntarily laid off employees are charged additional taxes to the UI system. This UI characteristic was put in place for several reasons:

(a) to provide a financial incentive for employers to stabilize their employment levels; (b) to provide a more equitable means of charging UI costs to those employers responsible for them; and (c) to provide an incentive for employers to police the system through appeals (Advisory Council on Unemployment Compensation, 1996). The financial incentive to employers from policing the system (i.e., ensuring cost control) has encouraged the outsourcing of their UI responsibility to private firms.

As employers seek to manage their financial responsibilities to the UI program, private UI management consulting firms that specialize in unemployment cost control programs have emerged as intermediaries between employers and the workforce development system. Acting as brokers between employers and the UI program, these intermediaries provide services such as: (a) full service claims processing; (b) hearing representation for employers at public unemployment hearings to determine whether workers receive benefits; (c) management reports, including compliance analysis; (d) verification on whether UI claims are charged to their employer's accounts; (e) tax rate verification for corporate entities in each state; and (f) employment verification services.[11] Businesses that employ large numbers of employees tend to use intermediaries to reduce UI taxes. According to the Advisory Council on Unemployment Compensation (ACUC), employer appeals have grown more rapidly than claimant appeals, and representation at hearings affected the outcome by increasing the likelihood of winning the appeal (1996).

Similarly, the UI program uses private sector businesses to outsource allowable administrative functions for providing UI to employers and unemployed individuals. The UI program uses merit-staffing to ensure impartiality in UI administration for proper determination of an individual's unemployment compensation, and to correctly charge employers with UI taxes. While inherently governmental functions are restricted to service delivery by merit-staff personnel, the UI program has often used private sector businesses to fulfill other functions that do not intimately affect the rights and property of individuals, such as developing management information systems.

Public Employment Service

The Wagner-Peyser (W-P) Act of 1933 established a national system of public employment offices that are administered by state agencies. The Workforce Investment Act (WIA) of 1998 amended the W-P Act to require the delivery of PES labor exchange services as part of the One-Stop delivery system. For over 30 years, UI, PES and job training programs often operated through separate delivery structures driven by distinct funding sources. Under WIA, these program services are available in one physical location—the One-Stop center. While the WIA required that PES labor exchange services be delivered through the One-Stop system,[12] it did not affect the W-P Act mandate that staff who actually delivered PES labor exchange services be state merit-staff employees.[13]

From July 1998 through June 1999, the PES served over 17 million jobseeking customers, including those who received UI benefits. Customers who applied for UI benefits without recall dates generally had to register with the PES agency and demonstrate that they would search for work. Of the total customers served, nearly 11 million customers (over 60 percent of the total) received reportable services, including referral to jobs, training, and testing.[14] Other jobseekers and employers who used the public automated job bank and other web-based services result in an even larger number of customers served by the public system.

Technological advances in computers and the Internet have increased the accessibility of information to people, which has sparked an interest for the workforce development system to create and utilize public automated job banks that post job openings and resumes of jobseekers on the Internet. America's Job Bank (AJB) is the public automated web-based job bank that posts job openings throughout the nation, and is one of the most heavily used job banks on the Internet in the United States, with postings of 1.3 to 1.5 million job openings each day. America's Talent Bank (ATB) is another automated web-based public effort that allows jobseekers to post their resumes on the Internet so that employers can access them when they search for potential employees. Employers can review over 400,000 resumes that are available through ATB. Efforts to better inform jobseekers and employers that these employment tools are available to them at no charge are being carried out in a number of ways.[15] AJB and ATB supplement the efforts of PES staff who provide local labor exchange services based on local job openings. These services are now being delivered in One-Stop centers across the country.[16]

In addition to the public services delivered through PES staff, over 31,000 private employment agencies also offer labor exchange services.[17] Private employment agencies range widely in their services, but often fall into the following main categories: (a) employment agencies that charge a fee for bringing the jobseeker and employer together, either for temporary or permanent employment; (b) executive search agencies, also referred to as employment "headhunters," that generally focus on matching jobseekers and employers for professional occupations in specific areas (e.g., finance, health care, human resources, information technology, graphics design, and office support); (c) training and placement institutes that offer their graduates job-search and placement services; (d) individual businesses that maintain their own employment services; and (e) other businesses that link jobseekers to employers for a nominal fee (e.g., newspapers that provide classified help wanted ads by employers).[18] Many of these businesses have also developed their own automated web-based systems on the Internet to link jobseekers with employers.[19]

For the PES, if using local labor exchange services does not result in a job placement for jobseeking customers, then those customers are referred to seek employment through AJB, ATB, and, possibly, private employment services. PES makes a strong effort through the Worker Profiling Reemployment Services (WPRS) system to identify customers who need job search assistance early in their dislocation from work, and then provide them with a combination of job search workshops (which can include self-directed search techniques on how to use automated job banks), labor exchange services, and labor market information. When these services are completed, individuals have the tools to search for work themselves.[20] These services may also be offered to other customers not identified through the WPRS system. While customers may not all be referred to a job by the PES, they can learn how to seek employment on their own, and then utilize AJB, ATB, or private employment services for additional assistance. However, PES and other service providers may not always help transition individuals into new employment, and sometimes this is due to the individual's need for skills training. Eligible individuals for skills training are often referred to the training programs located within the One-Stop center.

Training Programs, Including Those Serving Welfare Recipients

In comparison to the UI and PES, the training programs offered under JTPA, and now under the WIA, have allowed for more flexibility in involving the private sector in delivering services. Under the WIA, the local Workforce Investment Boards (Local Boards) are authorized to contract out the operation of One-Stop centers, as well as formally coordinate or contract out the services delivered within these centers to either public agencies or other for-profit or non-profit private intermediaries. Early observations have revealed that a number of local areas have contracted out to private nonprofit and for-profit intermediaries in place of public intermediaries. For example, Lockheed Martin operates One-Stop centers in several states, including Texas and Florida. Lockheed Martin Corporation had itself experienced several layoffs, and with the assistance of the Department of Labor, initiated unemployment and employment services to those laid-off. It is now expanding its role in providing employment and other related services across the country. Other examples of for-profit private-sector operated One-Stop centers are in Kentucky and Massachussetts. Local Boards may select to contract out to private sector businesses for a number of reasons, including their services to: develop resource management plans; develop service strategies compliant with legislation; develop fee-based services; set up and operate the management information systems (MIS) for data collection; and measure customer satisfaction. Local Boards have the flexibility to select among private and public intermediaries based on their performance, but it is still not known to what extent local areas will seek private businesses, or certain types of businesses, in place of public entities.[21]

In addition to contracting out One-Stop center operations, Local Boards contract out skills training and other training-related services that are delivered within One-Stop centers.[22] Preliminary studies have indicated that using private intermediaries to deliver these types of services may be a widespread occurrence in local areas. For example, under JTPA and the WIA, the Welfare-to-Work (WtW) and Temporary Assistance for Needy Families (TANF) programs have extensively used private intermediaries to provide support in employment services for welfare recipient. The goal of providing these services is to help welfare recipients initially find employment, then help them retain their jobs and advance to better jobs. Under the TANF program, the emphasis has been in moving welfare recipients to work. In a recent study where 20 local areas were selected, 18 of the 20 local areas chose to transfer some responsibility for providing employment-related services to intermediaries.[23] The employment-related services generally included job search, placement assistance, case management, and a range of secondary services (e.g., work experience or short-term training).[24] According to Pavetti, et al., the decision to transfer employment-related services to intermediaries was attributed to one, or a combination of, the following factors: (a) changes in the public sector's administrative capacity, e.g., a hiring freeze that limits the ability to deliver services through state staff; (b) local areas' desire to build on already established relationships with intermediaries; (c) changes in the administrative structure, i.e., welfare services were either shared with welfare offices and intermediaries, or the services were completely transferred out of the welfare office to an intermediary; (d) caseload sizes of rural and urban areas, where urban areas with larger caseloads tended to use intermediaries more than the rural areas with fewer caseloads; and (e) changes in legislative mandates, e.g., Arizona, Arkansas, and Florida encouraged greater use of intermediaries. This study also found that, for welfare services, the use of nonprofit intermediaries appears to be greater than the use of for-profit intermediaries. Pavetti reported that the overwhelming majority of the intermediaries they observed were nonprofit organizations. This was evident in Kalamazoo-St. Joseph counties, Michigan, where service providers for the state welfare Work First program for welfare recipients have been three private nonprofit organizations: Goodwill, Youth Opportunities Unlimited, and Behavioral Foundation.[25]

In general, preliminary observations under the WIA reflect a trend towards a market-based approach of increasing competition for delivering training and training-related services. Since Local Boards, with few exceptions, must contract with public or private intermediaries to deliver these types of services, the use of intermediaries has increased under the WIA. Additionally, Local Boards have moved away from providing training services through class-size training and instead have moved towards a market-oriented delivery of training services through a voucher-type system of Individual Training Accounts using the same types of training providers.

3. Summary and Conclusions

The role of various types of private sector intermediaries involved with the UI, PES, and job training programs generally have been based on how limited—or flexible—each of the programs have been in allowing for private sector interaction. Regardless of the varying administrative structures of each program, intermediaries have been able to find a niche in the public workforce development system. The following observations are made based on the trends of private sector involvement in the delivery of workforce development services:

- *The UI program has not moved towards a privatized administration, but continues to use employers and intermediaries to assist state UI programs administer their programs.* Employers can choose to outsource their UI responsibilities to UI management consulting firms, which act as intermediaries between the UI program and employers. Likewise, the UI program can choose to outsource functions that are not defined as inherently governmental to assist in UI administration. The outsourcing of these UI employer and governmental responsibilities has increased the amount of private sector involvement in the UI program.

- *Wagner-Peyser Act programs face competition from private employment services and the expansion of automated job banks accessible on the Internet.* With over 31,000 private employment service firms offering labor exchange services, the PES faces more competition from the private sector than in the past. While the PES uses many resources to better match jobseekers with employers, and employers with jobseekers—including the use of America's Job Bank, America's Talent Bank, and referrals to other services offered by private sector employment service firms—the PES faces direct competition from private employment services.

- *Workforce development services for training and other services, including welfare-related services, exclusively use intermediaries under the WIA, many of which are private for-profit businesses or nonprofit organizations.* Under the WIA, Local Boards contract out the delivery of training services and operation of One-Stop centers to intermediaries, which can be public, private nonprofit, or private for-profit entities. Little is known to what extent different types of intermediaries are currently being used, or what characteristics they exhibit, but preliminary studies have indicated that the use of private intermediaries for delivering workforce development services may be a widespread occurrence in local areas.

Notes

1. Under the Workforce Investment Act (WIA), planning and oversight of local One-Stop delivery systems are responsibilities of Local Boards that are composed of a business-led majority, and skills training is provided by public and private for-profit and nonprofit service providers. Under previous legislation, the Job Training Partnership Act (JTPA), similar Local Boards were also composed of a business-led majority, with skills training provided by public for-profit and nonprofit providers.

2. This definition is based on the report (Pavetti, Derr, Anderson, Trippe, and Paschal, 2000) on "The Role of Intermediaries in Linking TANF Recipients with Jobs." The definition used in this paper is expanded to include all workforce development customers (both jobseekers and employers), and focuses primarily on the private entities (both nonprofit and for-profit) that serve as intermediaries.

3. The workforce development system considers "customers" as both the employer and the jobseeker. In this case, the "customer" being referred to is the employer.

4. In general, only businesses that employ larger numbers of employees tend to use intermediaries.

5. See Office of Federal Procurement Policy (OFFP) Policy Letter 92-1 (57 *Federal Register* 45096, 30 September, 1992) for more information on definitions of inherently governmental functions.

6. See Balducchi, David E., and Pasternak, Alison J. 2000. "One-Stop Statecraft: Restructuring Workforce Development Programs in the United States". Paper delivered (and to be published) at the Conference on Labour Market Policies and the Public Employment Service, July, Organization for Economic Cooperation and Development.

7. Under certain circumstances, the prohibition on Local Boards to deliver training and other services can be waived.

8. As of 29 June, 2000, there was a reported number of 1476 One-Stop centers operating nationwide. U.S. General Accounting Office, Testimony by Cynthia Fagnoni. Joint Committee Hearing before the Subcommittee on Postsecondary Education, Training and Life Long Learning; and Subcommittee on Human Resources of the Committee on Ways and Means, 29 June.

9. Useful information on these intermediaries will be gathered during a U.S. Department of Labor study on WIA Early Implementation that is currently being conducted, with findings from the study to be published at a later date.

10. See Pavetti, Donna, Derr, Michelle, Anderson, Jacquelyn, Trippe, Carole, and Paschal, Sidnee. 2000. *The Role of Intermediaries in Linking TANF Recipients with Jobs*. Washington, D.C.: Mathematica Policy Research.

11. For more information about the types of services intermediaries offer, visit the Internet sites of the following examples: Frick Company (*www.frickco.com*), Jon Jay Associates, Inc. (*www.jonjay.com*), ADP (*www.adp.com*), UCAC, Inc. (*www.ucac.com*), Accordia Employers Service (*www.accordia.com*), and Gates McDonald (*www.gatemcdonald.com*).

12. Services are available in the One-Stop center, but are not necessarily delivered exclusively through the One-Stop center. For example, UI claims are generally made through remote phones claims at the One-Stop center, It is also possible for other services, such as vocational rehabilitation services, to be made available in a One-Stop center during certain hours or days of the week, and made available full-time at a different location outside of the One-Stop center.

13. In the 1990s, the U.S. Department of Labor authorized demonstrations of alternative PES delivery structures utilizing service providers other that state agency merit-staff employees in three states: Colorado, Massachusetts, and Michigan. In 1998, a federal court upheld the U.S. Department of Labor's interpretation of the W-P Act, affirmed in *State of Michigan v. Alexis M. Herman (W.D.MI, Southern Div.)*, to require the delivery of labor exchange services funded under the W-P Act by state merit-staff employees.

14. See United States Department of Labor. 2000. Annual Report. *Office of Workforce Security U.S. Employment Service Program Report Data: Program Year 1998*. Washington, D.C.

15. The outreach for America's Job Bank has included the following efforts: Internet advertising; magazine and newspaper advertising; cable television ads; commuter rail ads; a national outreach to college students; and state outreach efforts.

16. America's Job Bank can be accessed at *www.ajb.org* and America's Talent Bank can be accessed at *www.atb.org*. These web-based services, along with America's Career InfoNet (*www.acinet.org*) and America's Learning Exchange (*www.alx.org*), are part of America's Career Kit, for which development began in 1995. O*NET has also been developed, and is available on the Internet, to assist jobseekers and employers by providing services such as up-to-the-minute job-related information, tools for building accurate job descriptions, and crosswalk to other popular job classification systems. O*NET can be accessed at www.onetcenter.org or *www.doleta.gov/programs/onet*.

17. See Balducchi, David E., and Pasternak, Alison J. 2000. "One-Stop Statecraft: Restructuring Workforce Development Programs in the United States." Paper delivered (and to be published) at the Conference on Labour Market Policies and the Public Employment Service, July, Organization for Economic Cooperation and Development.

18. There are other types of private employment services, such as overseas employment agencies and agencies for the recruitment and placement of foreigners, but they are not included in this discussion since PES staff generally work with customers who are seeking local or inter-state labour market information. See http://members.aon.at/wapes1/1997_02/journa05.htm for more information on these other types of services being provided by private employment services.

19. The following is a sample listing of automated private employment services that are available on the Internet: (a) examples of employment agencies' websites: *www.monster.com*, *www.careermosaic.com*, *www.snelling.com*, *www.careerbuilder.com*, *www.careercity.com*.; (b) examples of executive search agencies websites: *www.execu-search.com; www.teinc.com, www.emnemn.com* (c) examples of individual business websites: *www.arthurandersen.com* (Andersen Worldwide); *www.levistrauss.com* (Levi Strauss & Co); *www.ups.com* (United Parcel Service); (d) example of a training and placement institute's websites: *www.aplus4u.com;* (e) examples of other businesses (e.g., newspapers) that link jobseekers with employers: *www.washingtonpost*.com (Washington Post)*; www.latimes.com* (*Los Angeles Times*).

20. See Wandner, Stephen A. 1997. "Early reemployment for dislocated workers in the United States," *International Social Security Review*, Vol. 50, No. 4.

21. The Employment and Training Institute operates One-Stop centers in Massachusetts and the Career Resources Institute operates a One-Stop center in Kentucky. Visit *www.cri.com* and *www.eti.com* for more information on types of services offered by these private sector businesses.

22. Local Boards are permitted to waive this requirement.
23. See Pavetti, Donna, Derr, Michelle, Anderson, Jacquelyn, Trippe, Carole, and Paschal, Sidnee. 2000. *The Role of Intermediaries in Linking TANF Recipients with Jobs.* Washington, D.C.: Mathematica Policy Research.
24. In one instance, eligibility determination was also outsourced to an intermediary (Pavetti et al., 2000).
25. See Eberts, Randall W. *The Use of Profiling to Target Services in State Welfare-to-Work Programs: An Example of Process and Implementation.* Kalamazoo, MI: W. E. Upjohn Institute for Employment Research Staff Working Paper.

Bibliography

Advisory Council on Unemployment Compensation. 1996. *Defining Federal and State Roles in Unemployment Insurance.* Washington, D.C.: Advisory Council on Unemployment Compensation.

Balducchi, David E., and Pasternak, Alison J. 2000. "One-Stop Statecraft: Restructuring Workforce Development Programs in the United States." Paper delivered (and to be published) at the Conference on Labour Market Policies and the Public Employment Service, July, Organization for Economic Cooperation and Development.

Barnow, Burt, and King, Christopher. 2000. *Improving the Odds: Increasing the Effectiveness of Publicly Funded Training.* Washington, D.C.: Urban Institute.

Eberts, Randall W. *The Use of Profiling to Target Services in State Welfare-to-Work Programs: An Example of Process and Implementation.* Kalamazoo, MI: W. E. Upjohn Institute for Employment Research Staff Working Paper.

O'Leary, Christopher J., and Wandner, Stephen A. 1997. *Unemployment Insurance in the United States: Analysis of Policy Issues.* Kalamazoo, MI: W.E. Upjohn Institute for Employment Research.

Pavetti, Donna, Derr, Michelle, Anderson, Jacquelyn, Trippe, Carole, and Paschal, Sidnee. 2000. *The Role of Intermediaries in Linking TANF Recipients with Jobs.* Washington, D.C.: Mathematica Policy Research.

United States Department of Health and Human Services. 1999. *The Low-Wage Labor Market: Challenges and Opportunities for Economic Self-Sufficiency.* Washington, D.C.

United States Department of Labor. 2000. Annual Report. *Office of Workforce Security U.S. Employment Service Program Report Data: Program Year 1998.* Washington, D.C.

Wandner, Stephen A. 1997. "Early reemployment for dislocated workers in the United States," *International Social Security Review*, Vol. 50, No. 4.

Workforce Investment Act of 1998. *Public Law*, pp. 105-220, 7 August.

20

Changes in Employment Services through Deregulation

R. Konle-Seidl and U. Walwei

1. Deregulation or Privatization of Employment Services?

The general trend to privatization and deregulation over the last decade—in both the goods and labor market (protection against dismissal, working time, work patterns, etc.)—has not left the employment services untouched. In the early 1990s, the monopoly of public employment services was lifted in most northern and central European EU countries (e.g., Denmark 1990, Netherlands 1991, Sweden 1993, Austria and Germany 1994), followed by the southern EU countries in the mid- to late 1990s (Italy 1995, Spain 1995, Greece 1998/99 for certain occupational groups only).

In this context, deregulation means the abolition of legal restrictions on authorization of private employment agencies. By continuing to provide a public employment service, deregulation is aimed at extending the choice of employment services. Privatization, on the other hand, would mean placement by profit-oriented private, in competition with each other, thus allowing enhanced quality and efficiency through competition. In both cases, however, public employment services can be wholly or partly replaced by private agencies. This could be achieved through:

- reduced public resources for the Public Employment Service (PES) and leaving a larger market share to private agencies, or

- privatization of the PES, which would continue to be publicly financed as before but contracting the employment service out to private agencies (outsourcing),

or a combination of both,

- a (truncated) public labor administration, whose only remaining function is to distribute money to private providers.

In most European countries, liberalization brought in its train the abolition of barriers to entry of service providers into the market, but the overall coverage of the public employment services was retained without any major capping of resources. There is thus so far no question of privatization. Exceptions are Great Britain and recently the Netherlands. In Great Britain, private, professional employment agencies were never banned. Public employment services and private agencies compete for public funding, and the most efficient provider wins the contract. In the Netherlands, the "reintegration service", i.e., services for those difficult to place, were just recently privatized.

2. Why Deregulation of Employment Services?

Image Problems and Customer Dissatisfaction

Alongside the above-mentioned trend towards deregulation in industry and society, image problems and customer dissatisfaction (job-seekers and employers) with the quality of the services provide by the PES has led to changes in the public employment service. Although a fundamental problem of public goods, that they are cost-free, and there is thus an unlimited demand for them that is impossible to satisfy, may perhaps be partly responsible for this dissatisfaction, the legislator sought with the new legislation on job placement to make the operation of the labor market faster and more efficient.

Deregulation in the Implementation of an Active Employment Policy

Trends towards deregulation can be found not only in the core business of public employment services, but also in the implementation of an active labor market policy. In the 70s and 80s, unemployment rose significantly despite increased public resources allocated to employment policy. Rightly or wrongly, there was loud criticism of the performance of the public employment service. Attempts were made in many countries, through budgeting, group targeting, contracting out and decentralization, to improve performance. Welfare state organizations and communities were strengthened through the introduction of active labor market policies. This did not, however, only affect public employment agencies as lone partners, but increasingly involved private agencies in the implementation of active employment policies, such as placement in subsidized employment.

New Forms of Employment

The structural changes in the economy demanded greater flexibility of the labor market. With its emphasis on job placement in unlimited full time, the public employment service did not always have a ready answer to the requirements of business. Temporary work and redundancy have expanded in varying degrees. By deregulation in the form of simplified authorization of temporary employment (temp) agencies, the demands of the market in many places carried a heavy price.[1]

Regulation and Deregulation

Within the European Union a wide range of regulations can be found with regard to the authorization of private agencies, both temp agencies and those not specializing in temporary work. Thus in Denmark, Finland, Sweden and Great Britain, private agencies, with the exception of temp agencies, require no special authorization. However, even in countries where authorization is required, there are great differences in the conditions for the authorization of private temp and employment agencies. Thus, deregulation and liberalization at quasi macro-level (the general authorization of private employment agencies) in many countries (e.g., Belgium, Germany, Austria) is contradicted by more regulation at the micro-level in the form of licensing and professional qualifications (e.g., certificate of minimum professional qualifications, appropriate business premises, etc.). In Great Britain and the Scandinavian countries, state regulation of private agencies is replaced by self-regulation and personal liability.

3. The German Model: Private Employment Services on the Verge of Breakthrough?

For more than sixty years private employment agencies in Germany led a shadow existence. With few exceptions, commercial forms of private employment services were prohibited. In 1994, the picture changed. Private, profit-oriented employment services could now be offered alongside public employment services.

Legal Framework

Until the new legislation in August 1994, the German public employment service, the Bundesanstalt für Arbeit, was virtually alone responsible for placement in employment and traineeships. This did not affect individuals seeking jobs on their own account. There was never any requirement for the employer to publish vacancies. Neither was occasional, unpaid recommendation of workers for placement prohibited. The few exceptions to the public employment service monopoly involved four areas:

- charitable employment agencies;

- commercial theatrical agencies;

- transfer of employees; and

- placement of managerial personnel by personnel consultants.

The law in force since 1 August 1994 provides for an authorization procedure. Thus private employment services can only operate with the authorization of the Bundesanstalt für Arbeit. A condition for the authorization is an application for a licence to provide employment services. A license to provide employment services will be granted if the following four conditions are satisfied:

- personal fitness;

- police certificate that the applicant does not have a criminal record;

- prescribed assets; and

- appropriate business premises.

In operating the employment agency, the licence-holder must also observe a raft of requirements. In particular, he may not require any fee from job-seekers.

Interim Empirical Assessment

The development of private employment agencies has not so far been at all spectacular. The number of private employment agencies making placements over seven days, albeit from a very low base, has risen sharply in volume but is still not of great significance. Private agencies were responsible for a good 7 percent of total agency job placements. In terms of overall job placements, the market share of private employment agencies in West Germany, however, is just over 2 percent (see Figure 20.1). The Bundesanstalt für Arbeit continues to dominate the market for employment services with a share of around 30 percent of all placements.

Of course, certain market segments, such as theatrical agencies and management recruitment, are the particular fief of the private sector. This was true, however, before liberalization. It is noticeable, however, that the new agencies are gaining market share in the area of qualified staff.

According to the business statistics of the Bundesanstalt für Arbeit, since 1994 there has also been the IAB-survey of all job-vacancies in the economy as a whole, and successful job placements. Table 20.1 shows details of forms of job-search and success rates for the years 1994 to 1999 (broken down between West and East Germany). Advertisements in newspapers (especially in West Germany) emerge as the most frequently chosen and most successful method, irrespective of whether the job-seeker is a blue-collar or white-collar worker or the level of qualifications required. Likewise, informal channels also play a not insignificant role. Key figures taken from the private employment services largely support the official statistics of the Bundesanstalt für Arbeit. From the firms surveyed, it emerged that in the period 1994-1999, some 1-2 percent of successful placements were made by private employment agencies.

In other EU countries, too, the quantitative effects of deregulation had remained very limited.[2] Despite a clear tendency to expand, private agencies are playing an increasingly limited role in job-seeking. A significant reason for this is that the employment services continue to be an alternative, and have not lost any of their

Figure 20.1
Market Share[1] of Public and Private Employment Agencies in West Germany
(1979-1999[2])

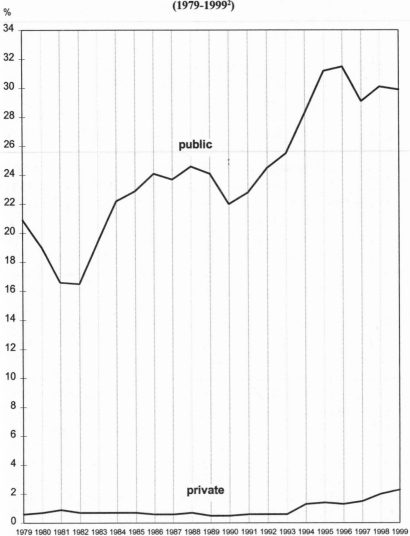

[1] Placements over 7 days as % of all placements.
[2] 1999 estimated.
Source: Bundesanstalt für Arbeit (Labour market in figures).

Table 20.1
Utilization and Results of Various Forms of Job-Search (1994-1999)

Form of job-search	West Germany						East Germany					
	Forms of job-search used			Successful job-searches			Forms of job-search used			Successful job-searches		
	1994	1996	1999	1994	1996	1999	1994	1996	1999	1994	1996	1999
Own advertisements	51	50	55	42	39	35	24	23	25	16	13	13
Replies to job advertisements by job-seekers	6	6	8	3	1	1	6	4	4	2	1	1
Employment exchange	32	38	38	13	13	14	37	49	54	22	34	35
Private Employment Agency	2	2	5	1	2	2	2	1	2	1	1	1
Notice at factory gate	3	4	3	1	1	1	2	1	3	1	0	1
Internal job announcements	14	17	19	2	3	3	7	6	8	2	2	2
Selection of applications on own initiative	18	18	23	12	12	12	18	13	19	17	9	12
Information from colleagues	25	24	29	16	15	18	36	28	30	27	18	17
No details				10	14	8				12	22	18
Total	**151**	**159**	**180**	**100**	**100**	**100**	**132**	**125**	**145**	**100**	**100**	**100**

Source: V/2 (IAB-survey of all job-vacancies in the overall economy).

attractiveness as a result of liberalization. Furthermore, certain employment services in the gray area were not affected by deregulation, but at best legalized.

Outlook for Private Employment Agencies

Despite the limited impact of liberalization so far, it would be premature to conclude that the picture could not change in the future. In the medium and long term, the question arises whether the opportunities for private employment agencies could still grow, if the positive employment trends already visible in the EU and latterly in Germany strengthen. For one thing, unlike almost any other sector, it is dependent on a weak economy. In general, more placements and staff shortages in particular market segments could constitute a turning point as the economic situation improves. Secondly, services provided by private agencies are rarely considered, because in many firms personnel matters are still seen as "a matter for the boss" and only seldom contracted out. This reluctance to outsource could, however, be reconsidered by companies if more private agencies offered comprehensive one-stop services. There could also be more demand from well-qualified job-seekers for professional career advice. Private agencies would benefit from both developments.

4. Deregulation of Employment Services as an Opportunity?

A Contribution to More Employment

As the principal firms and not the agencies decide on recruitment needs and staffing levels, it follows that the contribution of employment agencies to employment is limited. However, under certain conditions, private agencies can, by providing additional services have some positive influence on the labor market. If, for example, private agencies could manage to bring out firms' latent employment needs (e.g., through elimination of skills shortages, conversion of overtime into new jobs or the use of part-time working), they could generate more employment. A similar effect would be achieved, not by creating additional jobs, but by greater involvement of private agencies resulting in faster processing and thus more rapid filling of vacancies. The drag of constantly vacant posts would also be reduced, and the time saved would thus lead to more employment.

Even if the possible direct effects of private employment services is limited with regard to a direct reduction in unemployment, the possibility of indirect effects of private placement activities should not be overlooked. More head-hunting and priority to quality placements (buzzword "cherry-picking") by private agencies should not just be seen as negative. One must always consider the knock-on effect of job placements. If, for example, an undervalued employee finds a better position through a private agency, the need to replace him can lead to an employment opportunity for someone who is unemployed.

Consequences for the Regulatory Mechanism

The historical justification for the predominant monopoly of state employment services in continental Europe up to the 1980s was the shady practices of private employment agencies in the 1920s and 1930s. In Germany, in particular, liberalization recently revived fears, based on historical experience, as a result of which certain aspects of market access and exercise of a profession were regulated by law. The aim of the legislator was to exclude the so-called "black sheep" private agencies by means of specific regulations. However, the regulations do not just bring advantages to the employment services market. They can result in significant management costs and thus create "bureaucratic hurdles" for agencies. In addition, excessively high standards can unnecessarily hinder market access and thus make competition more difficult. It is possible that healthy competition between agencies which depend heavily on their reputation could already lead to pressure on "black sheep." It is frequently the case for private agencies that long-term profitability is an incentive to responsible service provision. Furthermore, private agencies have formed themselves into various associations and subjected themselves to a so-called "Ethical Code."

Consequences for Public Employment Services

The most important effects of private employment agencies should be seen in terms of the ensuing changes in public employment services. Following liberalization, public employment services no longer have to deal with cases which can be much better served by the market (private employment agencies or other forms of job-seeking). They can now devote their limited resources much more to areas where the market has no solution to offer.

More opportunities for the targeted use of scarce public resources also derive from the introduction of job and applicant-oriented self-service systems in many countries. Such computer-based information systems generally follow the "help for self-help principle." They make the market more transparent and make job-seeking easier for the so-called "easy cases." Staff resources (in the form of assistance with job-seeking) can then be concentrated, on both sides of the market, on the "difficult cases."

Public services can also be delegated in part to both commercial and charitable private agencies, where fees are paid for the placement of specific target groups. As well as stronger group-targeting, liberalization opens up a further option for the public employment service. Public and private employment agencies can, at least in certain cases, work together, in the case of a mutual exchange of experience and information. They would thus be in a position to offer their respective clientele more alternatives than would be possible without such cooperation.

Privatization Trends in the Form of Outsourcing

It had been hoped, by allowing private employment services, to achieve stronger competition, and linked to that a better balance in the labor market. Deregulation has, however, led in practice to the coexistence of public employment services and private agencies, with only partly overlapping markets. More competition and better results (meaning good, fast placement) do not therefore happen automatically. Any further moves towards extending market access by private agencies is thus open to debate.

In the light of this, there is certainly no question of full-blown privatization of the public employment service (including the withdrawal of public funding), because that would be likely to have adverse consequences for market access by disadvantaged groups of people.

Some countries have very recently gone over to full (Australia) or part (Switzerland, Netherlands) outsourcing of the public employment service. In the case of Australia, the Public Employment Service no longer provides any services itself, but buys them in from private agencies. In the Netherlands, under the "Reintegration Service," only part, services for those difficult to place, have been outsourced. Experience with outsourced services is being closely watched by international observers.[3] Unlike today, this could lead in the future to new private agencies providing of an enhanced spectrum of employment services (and not just for those difficult to place).

Notes

1.   OECD. 1999. Employment Outlook, Paris.
2.   De Koning; Denys, Walwei. 1999. Deregulation in Placement Services: A Comparative Study for Eight EU Countries, European Commission, Luxembourg.
3.   OECD Conference (3 and 4 July 2000). Labour Market Policies and the Public Employment Service: Lessons from Recent Experience and Directions for the Future, Prague.

21

The Privatization of Accident Compensation in New Zealand

J. Miller

1. Introduction

The election of a social democrat Labor Government in 1999 has halted the privatization of accident compensation in New Zealand.

From 1 July 2000 accident compensation reverts to a system of insurance coverage being provided by a government agency—the Accident Compensation Corporation (ACC).

Prior to the General Election which resulted in a Labor Government a conservative National Government had begun the process of privatization by allowing insurance companies to provide insurance for work place accidents from 1 July 1999.

2. Background

To set this attempt at privatization in context it may be helpful to explain the background to accident compensation in New Zealand.

The first Accident Compensation Act 1972 came into force on 1 April 1974. Prior to that date New Zealand had a system of accident compensation somewhat similar to the present situation in other common law countries.

That system consisted of:

Common law damages claims: Those who could prove an intention to harm or negligence could sue in the courts for damages for their injuries.

Workers compensation: Those injured at work could claim automatic weekly compensation.

Criminal injuries: Those injured by a criminal could claim compensation from the Criminal Injuries Compensation Fund.

Social welfare: Those unable to claim any of the above could obtain a sickness or invalids benefit.

The problem with such a system was that it was "capricious and fragmented."

As is well known, the Common Law Damages system was also expensive, adversarial, and only compensated a small percentage of those injured as it required proof of fault against a defendant. Even after obtaining a court judgment some plaintiffs were still unable to obtain damages as the defendant disappeared or was insolvent.

To overcome the problem of insolvent defendants in motor vehicle accidents, legislation required motor vehicle owners to take out compulsory motor vehicle insurance against personal injury claims. This insurance was provided by private insurance companies.

Most employers and manufacturers also took out liability insurance with private insurance companies in case they were sued for the actions of a negligent employee or a defective product.

There were also problems with workers compensation. Although it did not require proof of fault it only paid low amounts for a 6-year period and only to those who suffered "personal injury by accident arising out of and in the course of employment."

While the workers compensation legislation was intended to provide a simple no fault system the meaning of those thirteen words ensured constant litigation. Again there was the possibility of insolvent or disappearing employers so legislation required employers to take out compulsory workers compensation insurance. This was provided by private insurance companies.

While the Criminal Injuries scheme was the first such scheme in the common-law world it was not widely known or used. It was funded by the government.

As for social welfare this was means tested and only paid low flat-rate benefits which were often inadequate when compared with previous earnings.

3. Royal Commission Report

The dissatisfaction with the low rates and time limits with the workers compensation scheme prompted the then National Government to set up a Royal Commission of Inquiry in 1966 under a judge—Sir Owen Woodhouse. The Royal Commission reported back in 1967 in a report, which is now commonly known as the "Woodhouse Report." Instead of simply recommending improvements in workers compensation the report proposed a no-fault compensation schema for all New Zealanders giving 24-hour-a-day cover against personal injury.

As well as medical and rehabilitation treatment it recommended that compensation be paid at 80 percent of previous earnings for as long as the injured person was incapacitated and also a permanent pension for those with permanent disabilities.

4. Funding

To fund such a scheme the Woodhouse Report recommended the abolition of the right to sue for common law damages in the Courts and the abolition of the other schemes for compensating injured people. In their place a government agency (now known as the Accident Compensation Corporation—ACC) was to be set up. And instead of insurance premiums being paid by motorists and employers to private insurance companies for liability and workers compensation protection those amounts would be directed to the Accident Compensation Corporation.

5. Implementation of Twenty-Four-Hour No-Fault Scheme

The Woodhouse Report was something of a surprise to the then National Government especially as it recommended the removal of private insurance companies and lawyers from the accident compensation system.

Accident Compensation Act 1972

Nevertheless, after some years of further reports and assessments the Accident Compensation Act 1972 was passed to come into force on 1 April 1974.

It differed from the original Woodhouse Report in that as well as compensation based on 80 percent of previous earnings it also provided separate lump sums for disability and pain and suffering.

Accident Compensation Act 1982

The 1972 Act was replaced by the Accident Compensation Act 1982. It was somewhat similar but the lump sums were increased to up to $NZ17,000 for disability and up to $NZ10,000 for pain suffering and loss of amenities.

Accident Rehabilitation and Compensation Insurance Act 1992

In 1992 the National Government repealed the 1982 Act and brought in a much "leaner and meaner" act—the Accident Rehabilitation and Compensation Insurance Act 1992.

This Act abolished the lump sums for compensation and placed strict limits on the amounts payable for assistance and rehabilitation. Nevertheless, the Accident Compensation Corporation (ACC) still remained the sole provider of compensation for accidental injuries. The ACC by now was a large organization and its income for the year ending 30 June 1999 totaled $NZ2,122,594,000, a considerable sum by New Zealand standards.

ACC Income

This income was attained from premiums and government funding and investment income.

The main contributors were:

1.   Premiums paid by employers into the Employers Fund to cover workplace accidents. This brought in $NZ1,047,434,000 for the year ending 30 June 1999.

2.   Premiums paid by earners into the Earners Fund to cover non-work accidents to earners. This brought in $NZ545,345,000 for the year ending 30 June 1999.

3.   Premiums paid by motor vehicle owners into the Motor Vehicle Fund to cover road accidents. This brought in $NZ313,454,000 for the year ending 30 June 1999.

4.   A payment by the government into the non-earners fund to cover accidents to non-earners. This brought in $NZ196,970,000 for the year ending 30 June 1999.

Privatization

Insurance Act 1998. In 1998, however, the then National Government decided to implement a process of privatization of the scheme and the Accident Insurance Act 1998 was passed. This Act repealed the 1992 Act.

From 1 July 1999 private insurance companies were allowed back into the accident compensation scheme for the first time since 1974 but only for workplace injuries. For all other injuries e.g., road accidents, medical misadventure, sporting activities and injuries in the home compensation was still to be provided by the Accident Compensation Corporation (ACC).

The statutory benefits payable under the scheme also remained the same no matter where the accident occurred but the difference now was that employers could take out insurance with private insurance companies and pay premiums to them rather than the ACC for work related injuries.

Despite there being the prospect of $NZ1,047,434,000 in premium income being available for distribution only seven insurance companies including a separate independent company, "At Work Insurance Ltd.," formed from part of the ACC, competed for business.

"At Work Insurance Ltd." was also the default insurance company for those employers who failed to take out an insurance policy under the new Act by 1 July 1999.

The reluctance of many insurance companies to enter the market was probably due to warnings by the then Labor opposition that should they become the government in the forthcoming election they would revert to the status quo of the ACC being the only provider.

6. Labor Government

Accident Insurance (Transitional Provisions) Act 2000

It is clear that had the National Government remained in power the motor vehicle part of the ACC scheme would have been privatized next. However, the Labor Government won the general election and came to power in 1999. It has since passed the Accident Insurance (Transitional Provisions) Act 2000. This Act has removed insurance companies from the workplace injury compensation system.

From 1 July 2000 compensation for work injuries reverts back to the ACC. This does mean that the seven insurance companies remain responsible for the costs of those workplace injuries which occurred between 1 July 1999 and 30 June 2000. Such costs will have to be met from the premiums collected for 1999/2000 year. There will be no further premiums obtainable now until the National Government regains power and reintroduces the insurance companies involvement.

Future of Privatization

In New Zealand the government term is for three years so barring political catastrophes for the Labor Government it will be 2002/2003 before the National Government could ever regain power. There is also the view in New Zealand that the National Government had been in power so long that the Labor Government will probably last at least two three-year terms so it may be 2005/2006 before the question of privatization or of accident compensation resurfaces in New Zealand.

The Labor Government also plans to introduce a completely new Accident Compensation Act later this year to come into force in 2001. As part of their election manifesto they promised the return of lump sum compensation in this new Act but present indications are that in an effort to placate the employers lobby groups with low premiums they will not be reintroducing lump sums.

The Pros and Cons of Privatization

The National Government reintroduced private insurance companies into workplace accident compensation in 1999 in a belief that the market would lead to lower costs, greater efficiency and reduced accidents as insurance companies would offer reduced premiums to companies with good safety practices and fewer claims.

Unfortunately, given that the insurance companies were only allowed to operate for one year from 1 July 1999 to 30 June 2000 this has not been proven.

It is certainly true that the premiums paid by certain mainly large employers did fall dramatically; however, some cynical observers have suggested that there was probably an element of loss leading by insurance companies to obtain business for the first year with the intention of increasing premiums later.

If this is true and the insurance companies hoped to meet the true costs of workplace injuries covered in 1999/2000 by future premiums they are obviously going to be in some difficulty meeting continuing claims now that they have only one year's premiums available.

Premiums

The ACC has just announced the premiums that employers will pay from 1 July 2000 for workplace injuries and they have actually reduced the cost of most premiums charged by the private insurance companies which suggests that there was no real loss leading.

The differences in premiums for employers for the year beginning 1 July 2000 is as follows:

The ACC consider that 70 percent of employers will now receive lower premium rates from ACC than the private insurance companies were able to provide and that smaller employers will benefit the most from these reductions.

Industry	ACC premium per $NZ100 wages	Market premium per $NZ100 wages
Agriculture	1.98	2.18
Hunting and fishing	3.96	4.39
Forestry	4.80	4.97
Mining and quarries	2.54	2.55
Manufacturing	1.60	1.52
Electricity/gas/water	1.17	1.22
Construction	2.58	2.89
Wholesale/retail trade, restaurants and hotels	0.86	1.05
Transport storage and communications	1.64	1.83
Business/financial services	0.48	0.68
Government, community, social and personal services	0.74	0.81
Average premium	1.11	1.23

7. Labor Government Views

The Labor Government returned the Accident Compensation Scheme to its original concept because they considered that profit motivated private insurers had no place in a compensation scheme. They considered it would lead to more expense, more disputes and harsh decisions against injured workers.

They considered that increased expense would inevitably come from seven insurance companies duplicating costs rather than having one organization such as the ACC. They also considered privatization would lead to more litigation and disputes as private insurance companies, to keep up profits, would constantly challenge the acceptability of claims by injured employees or try and shift them off the scheme or on to ACC as non work accidents.

It has to be said that thus far there has been no evidence of increased disputes. Though again cynics maintain the number of disputes was kept low by the insurance companies adopting a generous approach for the first year of claims to create a favorable image for privatization. The cynics consider that disputes are likely to increase now that the insurance companies have been excluded from the scheme.

A rise in disputes may also be inevitable as the premium income collected for the 1 July 1999 to 30 June 2000 year by the insurance companies will not now be able to be increased and they will have to meet all claims arising from that year. It is obviously cost effective for these insurance companies to try and limit the number, or the length or the cost of these claims.

Reducing the length of claims could of course be done by proper medical treatment and extensive rehabilitation being provided to injured workers but this is costly. The cheaper option is to use lawyers and legal loopholes to cancel or reduce claims. It will be interesting to see what transpires.

However, with only one year's privatization experience available and that only with work injuries we will probably never know the answers to the arguments for and against privatization of ACC.

What is clear, however, is that the one-year experimentation with privatization has resulted in the ACC now providing much lower premiums for employers.

It will be interesting to see if these low premiums can be maintained particularly if workers- the natural constituency of the Labor Government demand increased benefits such as lump sums.

The new Accident Compensation Act to be introduced in 2000 and to come into force in 2001 is eagerly awaited.

22

The Advantages of Statutory over Private Employment Accident Insurance: The Example of Germany

G. Sokoll

1. Introduction

Privatization is a magic buzz-word with connotations of cheaper, better and more expeditious solutions. Privatization will make it easier for the state to transfer tasks to the economy, or to the personal responsibility of the individual, with the assent of the general public and thus relieve itself of financial and political burdens. In a profit-oriented context this is conceivable. In the field of social protection, however, and in particular where employers have to bear the entire cost of the system (as in accident insurance), certain considerations as seen from the standpoint of the state must yield pride of place to the interests of enterprises and employees. It is therefore necessary to investigate whether Bismarck's[1] view that employment accident insurance should not become a business is now outdated.

In Germany a discussion which has been going on since 1998 on whether employment accident insurance should be privatized has now come to an end. In both the political and economic spheres the following considerations have been accepted as guidelines.

2. Privatization Would Weaken Prevention

The successes achieved in Germany, confirmed by statistics, as regards the steady reduction of the incidence of accidents over a long period, and the ensuing financial stability of the statutory accident insurance scheme, are attributed, among other things, to a successful and continuing program of prevention "by all appropriate means" (a statutory requirement). It seems likely that privatization would lead to a substantial measure of failure to ensure prevention of a comparable level of effectiveness.

Private insurance companies agree with those they insure on obligations and duties which in concrete individual cases have positive and preventive effects. There are no legislative instruments concerning comprehensive and general prevention which private insurance companies can invoke. However, insurance carriers can, on the basis of their own knowledge of shop-floor situations in enterprises or on that of statistics on prevention, rehabilitation and compensation, react comprehensively and immediately to accident peaks or rises in expenditure. They are not required to initiate the adoption of legislation for the protection of workers by the state. They can supplement state legislation on occupational safety by their own safety rules based on actual situations existing in enterprises, oversee compliance with those rules in member enterprises, advise and support enterprises in every aspect of occupational safety, test tools and personal protective equipment, train occupational safety specialists in enterprises to act as propagators in their places of work and promote, or themselves conduct, research on improvements in occupational safety and health.

The branch-specific organization of the accident insurance carriers ensures particularly close relationships of a technical and specialized nature with the different branches of the economy, each with its specific production relationships and interest groupings. Private insurance companies, which generally cover more than one branch, cannot develop such close relationships. Competitive pressures and the possibility of recourse to competitors in the context of general preventive measures by themselves weaken the economic interest of private companies in promoting and, where appropriate, enforcing preventive measures. In addition, it seems unlikely that the state would extend to private insurance companies powers to influence insured persons and enterprises comparable to those based on legislation.

Thus, if accident insurance were privatized, prevention would in practice become the responsibility of the state alone. However, in these times of financial stringency the state cannot increase its resources for investment in prevention; indeed, it is having difficulty in maintaining those resources at their present level.

In many cases investment in prevention only pays off in the long term. Enterprises competing in the market cannot and will not operate in such a long-term perspective.

3. Cost Control through Quality Safeguards

It is thought that privatization would relieve statutory accident insurance of another thorny problem, namely striking a balance between a targeted control of the medical treatment and rehabilitation of accident victims within the system in order to keep costs down with the endeavor to ensure that the care provided to victims achieves the best possible outcome.

For a private insurance company an insured contingency is generally liquidated with payment of the sum insured. It leaves medical care to the sickness insurance scheme, half of the cost of which is borne by the insured person. This of itself runs counter to the principle of full reparation of the prejudice suffered. In contrast, in the public system insured persons are entitled under statutory provisions to the best possible therapeutic treatment provided in a timely and expeditious manner. In practice this consists of the organization of first aid and a rescue process culminating in the earliest possible provision of medical care and organized cooperation with physicians specializing in accident treatment with up-to-date further training and approved by the insurance carrier; choice of and admission to hospitals specializing in the treatment of accident victims; the establishment by the carrier of its own clinics for accident victims with special departments for seriously injured persons (damage to the transverse section, burns, brain damage, chronic pain); nursing care for victims provided by professional aides, etc. The quality management of service providers can be, and is, influenced by the establishment of guidelines concerning quality standards for structures, procedures and results. Negotiations on charges with individual service providers can be oriented towards both quality safeguarding and cost reduction. Within the therapeutic procedures offered by approved physicians which seem likely to become standard in the event of privatization there is no comparable machinery of control.

4. Assistance with Entry into the Labor Market

Accident victims with permanent disabilities are finding it increasingly difficult to re-enter the labor market, which is becoming steadily more demanding. Private accident insurance offers no services of a vocational character. The statutory accident insurance scheme puts to good use its contacts with the enterprise where an accident occurs and takes appropriate steps to safeguard the victim's job (for instance, through the reorganization of an agricultural enterprise or the alteration of installations, machinery and vehicles), providing specialist personnel to give qualified advice. Dwellings can be adapted for use by disabled persons, or aids to readjustment can be provided. A wide range of opportunities for training for another type of job exists. All these measures are provided within a framework of lifelong, highly personalized and intensive care and counseling provided, according to the circumstances, by specially qualified professionals.

5. Private Insurance Has No Concept of Coverage of Occupational Diseases

It appears that compensation of occupational diseases would create difficulties of both a legal and financial nature for private insurance companies, not only in Germany but also in other European countries (Belgium, Denmark, Portugal).

For instance, problems seem likely to arise on account of the length of the period of latency elapsing before the onset of the disease, which may in some cases be as much as twenty to forty years. In view of existing conditions of competition, the fixing of relevant exposure times during the working life of a patient for purposes of individual private insurers would be inconceivable without official regulation or the establishment of common arrangements.

A further problem which would arise in the event of privatization would be the establishment of a demarcation between occupational diseases requiring compensation and those which are work-related but not compensable. Here we are dealing not only with medical and scientific considerations (and in particular those relating to measurement techniques) but also social and juridical evaluation of causal factors such as the effect of the work environment, genetic predisposition and age-related attrition and the combined effects where more than one of these factors are present. These problems of demarcation, which are already difficult even in a public-law system, will inevitably be aggravated where they have to be dealt with on the basis, not of the obligation of the insurance carrier to conduct an official investigation, but on a basis of civil law where the burden of proof rests on the insured person concerned.

As is clear from the lists of occupational diseases in force in European countries, the problem of demarcation also comprises an element of social policy, namely the demarcation between the general liability of the health care system (sickness insurance) and the specific liability of the employer (accident insurance). The line of demarcation between the two systems of liability coverage is continually being modified and adjusted in the light of social consensus or in accordance with legal or financial remedies or parameters. It is clearly easier to establish a line of demarcation vis-à-vis a public-law accident insurance scheme as part of a social insurance system than vis-à-vis a private accident insurance scheme.

In view of the present difficulty of identifying occupational diseases, to allow the latter to be swallowed up in the ocean of general illnesses would be tantamount to causing a breakdown of the entire system, since the risks to the sickness insurance system arise from the fact that, from both the legal and ethical standpoints, the liability of the employer in respect of both employment accidents and occupational diseases springs from one and the same source.

In the field of occupational diseases, intensive preventive measures are particularly rewarding. In contrast to the environments in which employment accidents occur, they are frequently caused by the working conditions to which small or larger groups of workers are exposed; thus preventive measures taken in respect of a single case may have their uses elsewhere. As stated earlier, private insurance companies cannot react preventively in a comparable manner.

6. Relief from Employer Liability in Civil Law
Makes for Industrial Peace

In any comparison between the respective advantages and drawbacks of an obligation to insure (private insurance) and an obligatory insurance system (statutory accident insurance), relief from employer liability, and its ensuing pacificatory effect in the enterprise when an accident occurs, is an important factor. This is par-

ticularly true in Germany, where in addition fellow-workers are re-
lieved of civil liability towards one another. In systems based on an
obligation to insure, but in which there is no collective relief from
employer liability, victims are inevitably led, in addition to receiving the insured sum, to make further claims under civil law directly
against the employer. In the reality of working life the organizational responsibility of the employer, product defects, incorrect behavior by the worker and other factors, all acting together, are frequently the causes of accidents and provide material enough for
disputes. As is apparent from the experience of private-law compensation schemes, lawyers' and court costs impose burdens on the
economy without contributing to the aims of accident insurance.
Naturally, even within a compulsory insurance system there are cases
which come before the courts—but in comparatively small numbers. In that connection insured persons in Germany can pursue their
claims before the social courts almost free of charge.

The main considerations militating 115 years ago against private
insurance against occupational risks were:

- wariness with regard to private insurance, some elements of which
  were operating on a speculative basis;

- the inability at that time of the insurance sector to assess risks in
  advance.

In view of the efficiently functioning system of regulation of the
private insurance sector and the actuarial techniques and experience
now available in the insurance field, those considerations certainly
no longer apply. However, one critical factor appears to remain unchanged, namely that the obligation of insurance companies to provide insurance depends on the conclusion of policies and the actual
payment of premiums. The fact that every year over 22,000 enterprises go bankrupt in the German economy maintains the interest of
workers in having to deal with a reliably solvent debtor in the event
of employment accidents or occupational diseases. The spectacular
increase in the cost of bankruptcy insurance since 1974 demonstrates
that, today as previously, workers need an insurance which is independent of the legal and financial situation of the individual enterprise.

A "two-pillar" concept of insurance of the kind under discussion
throughout the world for sickness and pension insurance, in which

dynamic basic cover is provided by social insurance and complementary and/or individual insurance by private insurance companies, is difficult to imagine in the field of employment accident insurance, since the latter's structure rests on the basis of relief from liability and reparation of injury; and here a splitting-up of the different levels of insurance could not be explained.

7. General Benefits Deriving from Statutory Accident Insurance

The cash benefits paid by private insurance companies in each individual case compensate in whole or in part the injury sustained.

The prevention measures taken by the statutory accident insurance system are not only directly profitable to the system itself; indirectly private insurance companies also benefit from them to a not inconsiderable degree. The improvements made in tools and techniques in the light of prevention regulations or new discoveries in the field of occupational safety are also making their influence felt in leisure pursuits and in the home, and in those areas influence the incidence of accidents just as much as in enterprises. This spread of influence affects not only the purely technical and mechanical sphere but also the behavior of insured persons. Anyone who has developed a higher degree of safety-consciousness from training imparted by the statutory accident insurance carriers will also demonstrate that safety-consciousness outside the workplace (for instance, while travelling).

In 1996 the prevention function of the statutory accident insurance system was further extended to include the prevention of all work-related health hazards; the system thus became a comprehensive instrument making for prevention in the working environment. This extended prevention mandate offers the social partners an opportunity to make an essential contribution to the social dimension within the framework of the process of European unification. That mandate can offer additional lightening of workload not only to enterprises but also to sickness, pension and unemployment insurance systems. According to an estimate by the German trade unions, the implementation of the extended mandate could by itself, after a running-in period of five to ten years, lead to a saving in Germany of over 50 billion euros yearly—a saving which would be completely lost if the statutory accident insurance system were to be privatized.

With the integration of occupational safety into quality management within the enterprise and into modern entrepreneurial concepts for enterprise restructuring stimulated by the extension of the prevention mandate a potential contribution to the economic strengthening of enterprises is at hand.

Ever-increasingly global competition is reducing the scope for the social and solidarity-based development of insurance systems. The importance of a fully comprehensive set of regulations covering sickness and pension insurance, as found in the German system (with the exclusion of duplication of benefits), is thereby enhanced.

8. From the Standpoint of Insured Persons, the Contingencies Covered and the Range of Benefits Offered by the Statutory Accident Insurance System are Unbeatable

In contrast to private insurance, there is nobody who is uninsurable under the statutory system. Even physically and mentally handicapped persons and persons in need of care are covered if they are in an insured occupation. There are no exclusions based on age—a possibility admitted in new policies concluded with private insurance companies.

One example: a private insurance system would not be a suitable vehicle for the insurance of seasonal workers against employment accidents.

In the statutory system persons who act "like" insured persons are also covered. Even persons who on request undertake a particular activity for a short period—or even for a few moments—can while so doing enjoy protection as employees within the meaning of accident insurance legislation; for instance, a neighbor of the owner of an enterprise is covered while taking a letter to the post for the latter; so is a holiday guest on a farm who offers to take their midday meal to the harvesters.

Private insurance typically offers only cash benefits in the form of lump sums which can be commuted into pensions. They do not provide benefits in kind or, above all—as previously emphasized—preventive benefits. The insurance benefit consists of the agreed sum insured. An insured person not only has the problem of correctly assessing the degree of need for insurance but also that of complying with the prescribed rules of conduct and ancillary obligations when in a situation where the insurance applies in order not to jeopardize his entitlement to benefit. In contrast, the obligatory and compulsory nature of compulsory insurance ensures that the insured persons is immediately and comprehensively covered, even if, for instance, the entrepreneur has not paid his premiums.

Again in contrast to private insurance, the statutory system generally pays cash benefits in the form of pensions (disability and survivors') on which there is no ceiling except for that relating to insurable annual earnings set by law or in the internal rules of the insurance carrier. These cash benefits are designed to maintain the standard of living attained during the period preceding the accident. Moreover, with this aim in mind the benefits—again, in contrast to those of private insurance—are adjusted annually. This also applies to cases of allowances for continuing care, provided either at home or in an institution; private insurance does not provide any benefits in cases where continuing care is required.

Both statutory and private insurance protect the insured person "in his present condition." However, private accident insurance schemes treat earlier illnesses and health impairments as grounds for deductions in the event of a subsequent accident; no such deductions exist in the statutory scheme.

In addition, the benefits provided by private insurance companies are subject to certain restrictions with regard to time. For instance, benefit in respect of a fatal accident is payable if the death occurs within one year of the date of the accident. No comparable restrictions exist in statutory insurance.

Private insurance legislation allows reductions in benefits where the effects of an accident combine with those of factors unrelated to the accident. Certain contingencies are excluded (for example, an accident arising from partial or total loss of consciousness due to the influence of alcohol). The statutory system withholds protection only if in law that was the sole cause of the accident.

In the statutory system the time elements in the concept of an accident are generously interpreted. A sudden incident limited in time is envisaged as an incident taking place over a relatively short space of time (at most the duration of a shift); in private insurance an incident which lasts two and a half hours is no longer deemed to be "sudden."

The differences in the aims of the two systems are important. Statutory insurance provides full reparation for the injury suffered. In private insurance the only link of dependency between a specific injury suffered and the amount of the insurance benefit paid resides in the agreed amount payable in respect of that injury. In contrast, the range of benefits provided by statutory accident insurance is influenced by considerations of prevention, rehabilitation and compensation, all of which are provided within the one system. Admittedly, the amount of income-based cash benefits is indirectly determined by contributions based on annual earnings; but the provision of prevention and rehabilitation benefits is based on actual need.

9. Advantages in the Fields of Organization and Costs

The public-law accident insurance system permits self-administration, which is provided on a joint basis by the two groups of social partners. This arrangement distances the system from the state and gives it in particular the possibility of acting as a provider of services to enterprises. The management of the system by the social partners has brought visible benefits, in particular in the field of occupation-specific prevention, organized in close contact with individual enterprises. With the mandatory principles of economic strength and cost containment in mind, it leads in the context of occupational safety at enterprise level to optimum resource allocation, productivity, economic functioning and efficiency.

The financing system is also used for the creation of incentives to achieve higher standards of prevention. In this field a contribution structure based on branches and risks will tend to have a neutral effect on competitiveness, since all enterprises in a particular branch will bear the same cost burden. In contrast, private accident insurance companies put together insurance "packages" and use the premium income from accident insurance to cover deficits in other branches of insurance through transfer payments. Thus there will be a tendency to avoid excessive transparency with regard to premium income and expenditure. The situation is different in statutory accident insurance, where transfer procedures are designed to ensure coverage of additional needs. However, it has been established that the pay-as-you-go system ensures that some 80-85 percent of premium income is spent on the provision of benefits to victims, whereas in private insurance the proportion is sometimes considerably less then 50 percent.

If the system were to be privatized, the method of financing would have to be changed; pay-as-you-go systems would have to be replaced by one based on funding. This would give rise to enormous conversion costs. It is not only the normal anticipated expenditure needed to fund all new pensions which would have to be funded. In addition, it would be necessary to continue payment of all current pensions which formed part of pension expenditure in earlier years. If these were also to be funded, the ensuing costs would be of the order of several years' pension fund contributions. Moreover, entrepreneurs favor the pay-as-you go system, since it is unaffected by movements in capital markets; furthermore, it is their view (and in their interests) that any additional sums for funding payable to insurers would be put to better use in their enterprises than in the coffers of an insurer.

As is illustrated by the mining industry, and as is likely to become increasingly apparent in a globalized economy in which frontier barriers have disappeared, the economy is being subjected to major structural changes. Where the cost burden of pensions awarded earlier exists, a public-law system seems better placed to organize financial equalization arrangements among the different branches. The taking over and integration of 270,000 accident-related pensions from the former German Democratic Republic in 1991 could not have been effected on a private-law basis.

As is apparent from the competition in the field of sickness insurance, a tendency exists to select "good" risks. In a public-law system selection is avoided. Consequently an ability to cover its costs is an essential precondition for acceptance of a social insurance system; where there is risk selection, it is threatened.

In the arguments for and against privatization, costs are not a legal consideration. As privatized solutions are generally regarded as incomparably cheaper than public-law solutions, it seems justifiable to make the following point: although the statutory accident insurance system in Germany provides comprehensive benefits of high levels on a no-fault basis in cases of employment accidents and occupational diseases, the average financial burden on enterprises in all branches of the economy is currently (1999) 1.33 percent of contribution wages. This average gradually declined from 1.53 percent in 1976 to 1.36 percent in 1990. After the incorporation of the new Länder beginning in 1991, the average climbed again, reaching 1.46 percent in 1995. Since then the average contribution rate has declined significantly every year; in 1999 it reached its lowest level since the end of the 1939-45 war. Private insurance, notwithstanding favorable ratios and earnings from reserves, has to spend a considerable proportion of its contribution income on administrative, marketing and acquisition costs and on dividend payments to its shareholders; this explains the comparatively low proportion of premium income spent on benefit payments. On the basis of information available in states with private accident insurance schemes it can be affirmed that the administrative costs of statutory accident insurance systems are at least 10 percent lower.

10. Conclusions

The fundamental difference between private and statutory accident insurance systems resides in the fact that the statutory accident insurance system in Germany pursues a goal of economic efficiency within its compensation system by promoting comprehensive prevention and rehabilitation by all appropriate means. To that end the mutual feedback among the three functions of compensation, rehabilitation and prevention is exploited. Even the financing aspect is used to create incentives to prevention.

In order to change over to a private-law approach it would be necessary to clarify who would pay the pensions awarded over the past decades, since private insurance companies are interested in new business, not in taking over old burdens. In view of the size of the amounts involved, it can be foreseen that the state will even be forced to subsidize a financial transition to a private accident insurance system from taxation.

In the light of its closeness to the economy the statutory accident insurance system itself can further improve the efficiency of its operations and introduce practices taken from the private sector such as customer orientation, shorter processing times, the simplification of hierarchies, closer study of profit sectors and recourse to controlling and bench marking.

Note

1.   On 15 March 1884, during the discussions on the 1884 Bill concerning accident insurance, Bismarck said: "I take this opportunity of bringing up immediately the subject of competition from private insurance companies. The Honourable Member

Mr. Bamberger has raised objections to the proposed text precisely on this point... I want to put forward the principle ... that we should not in any circumstance treat accidents of any kind as providing a suitable operating basis for the securing of high interest payments and dividends (cheers from the Right); that we must make insurance for workers against this and other evils as inexpensive as possible; and that we should consider it our duty to bring the cost of that insurance down to the lowest possible level, this in the interests of both workers and industry, and of employers as well as workers. I do not believe that anyone can set a price as low as that which can be achieved through an insurance system based on the principle of mutual benefit and which proscribes all considerations of return, through the State; through the *Reich*."

Bibliography

Breuer, Joachim. 1995. "Die private Unfallversicherung im Vergleich zur gesetzlichen Unfallversicherung," *Die BG*, No. 3, pp. 138 ff. and No. 4, pp. 198 ff.

Deisler, Harald. 1999. "Landwirtschaftliche Unfallversicherung— Unternehmerpflichtversicherung oder teilprivatisiert?," *Soziale Sicherheit in der Landwirtschaft*, No. 3, pp. 223 ff.

von Heinz, Hans-Michael. 1973. "Entsprechungen und Abwandlungen des privaten Unfall- und Haftpflichtversicherungsrechts in der gesetzlichen Unfallversicherung nach der Reichsversicherungsordnung," *Schriftenreihe zum Sozial- und Arbeitsrecht*, Vol. 9, Berlin, Duncker & Humblot.

Leichsenring, Christian, and Petermann, Olaf. 1998. "Gesetzliche Unfallversicherung—öffentlich-rechtlich oder privat?" *Die Sozialversicherung*, pp. 14 ff.

Möller, H. 1964. "Soziale und private Unfallversicherung—Vergleich und Wechselbeziehungen," Berufsgenossenschaftstag, *National Federation of Industrial Employment Accident Insurance Funds*.

Sokoll, Günther. 1997. "Private versus staatliche Systeme für Betriebsunfall- und Invaliditätsversicherungen–die deutsche Lösung," *The Geneva Papers on Risk and Insurance, Die Genfer Hefte*, No. 84, July.

23

The Danish Experience with Privatization:
New ways of Solving Tasks

K.S. Christensen

1. Interaction between the Public and Private Sectors in the Social Services Area

Over the years, the Danish model for social welfare has developed in a manner that has resulted in most social services tasks being both defined and handled in a public sector context.

It has so far been a characteristic of social policy that the solving of any social problems that arise is by definition a task solely for the public sector.

In the current debate on the future of the Danish welfare state, questions are now being raised as to whether the Danish model is always the most appropriate, or whether the private sector can or must increasingly be included in dealing with the tasks traditionally handled exclusively by the public sector. The discussion concerning the interaction between public and private service providers thus constitutes part of the debate on the ways in which the Danish welfare society may be modernized and reinvigorated so as to meet the demands and needs of the future.

Among other considerations in the background of this debate is the expectation that citizens will become increasingly demanding and conscious consumers, especially as regards the service provided.

In this context it is important to bear in mind that the Danish welfare model is rooted in a decentralized system, in which the vast majority of tasks are managed locally (at municipal level) or at regional level (county level), and hence are carried out in close proximity to the citizens.

The Danish welfare model is furthermore built on the basis of collective responsibility for welfare tasks such as child care and care for the elderly. In addition, Danish welfare services are subject to democratic control, that is, in practice it is the politically elected representatives of the local and regional political entities that are responsible for and exercise control over the welfare services provided. This basis secures the influence of all interested parties on the way in which the different and often conflicting interests and concerns are weighed and priorities are set.

All this takes place within the framework provided by the Danish parliament, Folketinget, by virtue of current social legislation.

At the same time there is a political consensus that growth of municipal service costs must be kept low as compared to the strong growth of recent years.

Thus, on the one hand, stand the highly differentiated needs and demands of the citizens and their wish for a wider range of free choice and concerns for the weakest groups of the population, and, on the other hand, concerns for responsible expenditure growth.

Cooperation between the public and private sectors may be one means among many others of accepting this challenge, and there is therefore also an ever-increasing debate on ways in which private sector service providers may be included in handling the relevant tasks.

However, a good deal of uncertainty and reluctance exists towards ceding welfare tasks to private sector service providers, especially tasks relating to care.

2. Knowledge on the Interaction between the Public and Private Sectors

Involving private contractors in the handling of social tasks is nothing new, but there is no tradition of extensive interaction with private companies. Thus, no comprehensive overview of the extent of this practice, and no systematic collection of experience in the field exists.

A review of the relevant legal basis shows that there are not a great many hindrances to increasing cooperation between the public and private sector in the area of social services.

The barriers to be found in Denmark against increased cooperation are largely of an ideological and emotional character. There is a widespread perception, including politically, that care for the weakest groups should be handled by the public authorities, since this offers the greatest security for these citizens, while this requirement may be relaxed somewhat when dealing with groups that are less weak.

This attitude presumably reflects the perception that by definition the public authorities guarantee the quality of the service provided as well as satisfaction among the citizens.

The question might be asked whether the quality of service is not the most important thing. If the services are of adequate quality, it would presumably be of little concern to most whether public authorities or private contractors carry out the tasks.

The fact is, however, that an overview is lacking of both the extent of and the experience with cooperation between the public authorities and private sector companies in the area of social services. The task of collecting and ordering this experience, good as well as bad, and of making it visible, is therefore an important one. It may then be seen which barriers still exist to increasing cooperation between the public authorities and private contractors, and to what extent an effort can and must be made to remove such barriers.

3. Arguments in Favor of Increased Cooperation with Private Sector Contractors

The most important factor must not be who carries out the tasks but how, and how cooperation may be approached, including determination of the extent to which the public authorities should retain an obligation to carry out inspections.

It is my opinion that cooperation between public authorities and private sector contractors can have a positive effect on the development of the quality of the service provided. High quality of service will be a competition parameter when there are several providers of services, not least of all when we look at flexibility in relation to the needs of the users. Increased cooperation will also mean more options from which to choose for citizens, and thereby increased user influence and participation in decisions. This constitutes a quality in and of itself, even if the options are not exercised. This may also lead to greater efficiency in the actual performance of the task. If there is competition among several providers, more service may be achieved at no extra cost, or services of the same quality may be achieved at a lower price. The latter possibility may be the most interesting, given that managing growth of expenditures is a major concern.

4. Prerequisites for Cooperation between the Public and Private Sectors

From the general viewpoint of social policy, certain conditions and prerequisites must be met, irrespective of whether the service providers are public authorities or private contractors.

It will be of decided importance that exercise of authority is not ceded to the private sector and, as stated earlier, the local authorities must retain the ultimate responsibility for social services including, not least, inspections carried out to ensure that the legal requirements are met and that the standard of quality is not lowered.

One central problem will be ensuring that there will always be relevant offers for the weakest groups; requirements must therefore exist for quality standards, inspection visits and contact with the users.

5. Privatization Means More Than Contracting Out Services

Denmark has a long-standing tradition whereby both administration and service authority are close to the citizens. The public sector is not based on central government, and the Danish welfare state must be deemed to be more community orientated than what is seen internationally.

The perception of the citizens as an important element of the welfare state has been institutionalized in Denmark in the form of democracy for its users. In part, a user democracy has been established through formal rules providing for user representation on the board and influence with respect to schools and day-care, for instance. Further, there is a not insignificant network of persons in the individual communities who have considerable influence on service institutions and the provision of service. The term used to describe many of these areas is *development from government to governance*, particularly in individual communities.

6. Strengthening of Voluntary Social Efforts

The Danish government has decided to give priority to the question of strengthening voluntary social efforts. Based on the realization that the voluntary organizations hold, and have assumed, social responsibilities, the government wishes to create a better framework for carrying out these efforts.

New regulations were recently introduced on local authority cooperation with voluntary social organizations and societies, and on funding support for these organizations. The aim was to strengthen voluntary organizations and the coordination of volunteer efforts at the local level. Because, as previously stated, the municipalities are responsible for the lion's share of concrete public efforts, they have a decisive role to play. Strengthening interaction involves both strengthening cooperation and providing greater financial support.

The decisive element is the fact that funds have been set aside to support voluntary work, obtainable by applying, from a pool of funds. Another significant element is that annual accounts of these efforts must be submitted, which will contribute to the development of knowledge about local voluntary work.

Preliminary information concerning this new initiative shows that DKr100 million have been appropriated for this purpose. Preliminary surveys further show that there has been great diversity among the approaches to cooperation chosen, for the legislation also presupposes and specifies that the way in which the cooperation should be structured is a matter of local decision.

Some municipalities have set up regular contact committees with representatives of the municipalities and the voluntary organizations. The voluntary organizations select their own representatives, and the representation of all sectors of volunteer work is ensured. Other municipalities have a looser form of cooperation; a few have chosen a form so loose that it must be said that it does not live up to the intentions of the legislation.

7. The Perspectives on Cooperation between Public Authorities and Private Organizations

The perspective on strengthened voluntary social efforts and the ensuing stronger cooperation with the public authorities is the development of preventive efforts by strengthening the social network, which in the long term contributes toward creating a more solid society, in which a greater number of social problems are identified and dealt with as they arise, and in which the need for efforts on the part of the public authorities is thereby reduced.

However, it is equally important that voluntary social initiatives function as an extension of public sector endeavors, thus ensuring improved general social welfare.

It is also important to note that, through their counselling among other activities, voluntary organizations can strengthen the individual user in interacting positively and negatively with the efforts of the public authorities. There are great expectations concerning cooperation, but also understanding that the autonomy and freedom of action of the voluntary organizations must be ensured to show respect for the special character of voluntary efforts.

8. The Accommodating Labor Market, a Special Public/Private Initiative

The accommodating labor market is the aim of a special effort, which is to prevent exclusion, hold on to individuals who may have health problems and (re)integrate individuals who have difficulties finding their place on the labor market. The concept of the "accommodating labor market" implies the notion that the labor market should have room not only for fully able people but also for people with limited work capacity, in order to keep the highest possible number in employment and improve the possibilities for them to have an active life.

The accommodating labor market is an expression of political thinking based on the idea that individuals, especially those who possess full work ability, should not receive public benefits unless they in fact use their abilities.

This task falls to companies, which through retraining, job rotation and other means can contribute toward keeping people with health problems in their work position, as part of the social responsibilities of companies.

This is also a task for the parties in the labor market, who through "social chapters" in the labor market agreements may now create possibilities for more flexible terms of employment. There are now "social chapters" in most collective agreements in the Danish labor market, that is, rules on social responsibility on the part of companies toward employees who become ill or have their work capacity reduced for other reasons.

Lastly, it is also a task for the public authorities. Some of the central areas of the accommodating labor market lying within the area of social responsibility are activation/ restart, retraining, maintaining an individual in a job, flexible jobs, sheltered jobs and the social co-responsibility of companies. Even though the areas of effort have to a certain extent been known for some time, the shift in focus from public support to a more accommodating labor market has caused a development within the areas of effort.

This development which presupposes that private participants back up initiatives and assume their share of responsibility for implementing them.

9. Conclusion

It has been shown that the development moves in the direction that it is not always up to the public authorities to solve social problems. The social policy objective has changed. The aim now is for an increasing number of people to manage on their own and each other's resources, and by being part of social communities.

The role of the public authorities in Danish social policy will not likely be cut back or reduced, but they will assume a different role.

The public authorities still have overall responsibility for social security, but others share that responsibility. The public sector (the government) has been effective at redistributing economic means to people who find themselves in distress materially, and has thereby largely removed all the material distress that was part of reality merely a few decades ago. However, there are a number of challenges facing Danish society today that the public authorities are not necessarily in the best position to alleviate, such as loneliness, isolation, lack of social network and low self-esteem.

One way to solve social problems is to create greater human accommodation in all sectors, be it the labor market, the educational system, the housing area, etc. In these areas the private actors may play a significant role in creating a positive development.

However, when we consider the weakest groups it is my clear opinion that the public authorities must step in and make an appropriate effort.

In this case there can be no doubt who holds the responsibility.

List of Authors

Robert Basaza   Senior Health Planner, Ministry of Health, Uganda, and associated with the Makerere University Institute of Public Health, Uganda

Ewa Borowczyk   Vice-President, Social Insurance Institution, Warsaw, Poland

Théopiste Butare   Programme Manager, International Social Security Association, Geneva, Switzerland

Guy Carrin   Senior Health Economist, Global Programme on Evidence for Health Policy, World Health Organization, Geneva, Switzerland

Karen Sejersdal Christensen
Director General and President, Social Appeals Board, Ministry of Labour, Denmark

Martinus Desmet   Country Office, World Health Organization, Uganda, Adviser for health planning and financing, Ministry of Health, Uganda

Walter Geppert   Director General, Federation of Austrian Social Insurance Institutions, Vienna, Austria

Dik Hermans

Director, Social Security Supervisory Board, Zoetermeer, Netherlands

Robert Holzmann

Director, Social Protection Sector, Human Development Network, The World Bank, Washington, DC, United States

Dalmer D. Hoskins

Secretary General, International Social Security Association, Geneva, Switzerland

Aidi Hu

Social Security Specialist, International Labour Office, Geneva, Switzerland

Jürgen Husmann

Alternate Chairman of the Governing Body, Federation of German Pensions Insurance Institutions, Frankfort, Germany

Janet O. Javar

Researcher, Division of Research and Demonstration, Employment and Training Administration, U.S. Department of Labor, Washington, DC, United States

Mohamed Ridha Kechrid

President-Director General, National Social Security Fund, Tunis, Tunisia

Regina Konle-Seidl

Federal Employment Institute, Nuremberg, Germany

Christiane Kuptsch

Research Officer, International Social Security Association, Geneva, Switzerland

Carmelo Mesa-Lago

Distinguished Professor Emeritus of Economics, University of Pittsburgh, and Professor and Research Scholar Florida International University, United States

John Miller Barrister, Senior Lecturer in Law, Dean of Students, Victoria University of Wellington, Wellington, New Zealand

Alicia H. Munnell Peter F. Drucker Professor of Management Sciences, Boston College Carroll School of Management Director, Center for Retirement Research at Boston College, United States

Robert Palacios Senior Pension Economist, Social Protection Sector, Human Development Network, The World Bank, Washington, DC, United States

Edward Palmer Professor of Social Insurance Economics, Uppsala University and Chief for Research and Evaluation, National Social Insurance Board, Sweden

Julio Pilón Treasurer, Union of Mutual Benefit Societies of Uruguay, Montevideo, Uruguay

Monika Queisser Department for Social Policy, Organization for Economic Cooperation and Development, Paris, France

Sonja Roesma Consultant, former President Director, PT (PERSERO) Asuransi Kesehatan Indonesia (ASKES), Jakarta, Indonesia

Xenia Scheil-Adlung	Programme Manager, International Social Security Association, Geneva, Switzerland
Günther Sokoll	Director General, National Federation of Industrial Employment Accident Insurance Funds, Sankt Augustin, Germany
Monica Townson	Independent economic consultant working in the field of social policy and former member of the Canada Pension Plan Advisory Board, Canada
Ulrich Walwei	Counselor, Federal Employment Institute, Nuremberg, Germany
Stephen A. Wandner	Director, Division of Research and Demonstration, Employment and Training Administration, U.S. Department of Labor, Washington, DC, United States

Index

Accident insurance. *See* Germany, accident insurance; New Zealand, accident insurance

Africa. *See also specific countries*
overview, xiv
social security system
administration, 32, 35-36, 39
contributions, 31, 34, 36
coverage, 31, 39
privatization impact, 32, 34, 35-36, 39, 40n.8
reform agenda, 38-40
social solidarity and, 39
structural adjustment impact, 34, 35, 38-40
structural adjustment programs
economic impact, 32-33, 34-35, 36-38
education and, 37, 38
gross domestic product (GDP), 37-38
gross national product (GNP), 32-33
International Monetary Fund (IMF), 33
poverty impact, 35, 36-37
privatization and, 33-34, 35
public expenditure and, 38
sector impact, 37, 38
social impact, 33, 35, 36-37, 38
social security impact, 34, 35, 38-40
unemployment and, 37-38, 39
World Bank, 33

Aging population
Germany, 95
individual accounts and, 51-52
United States
dependency ratio, 65, 67t
fertility rate, 65, 66t
international comparison, 64t, 66t
life expectancy rate, 65, 66t

Argentina, pension reform
impact of
administrative cost, 162
capital accumulation, 163
commissions, 161
competition, 162-63
compliance, 161
coverage, 160
entitlement, 162
fiscal cost, 166
individual choice, 160
portfolio diversification, 164
real investment yield, 163-64
mixed model
administration, 159
benefits, 158
contributions, 158
defined, 158
financing, 159
implicit pension debt (IPD), 159-60

Artificial privatization, 11

Australia
employment services, 256-57
health insurance, 12
Lifetime Health Cover, 12

Austria, employment services, 247, 249

Austria, pension insurance
funded schemes
as alternative, 181-82
pros/cons, 180-81
government responsibility, 178
international perspective
competition, 175
demographics, 175
economic development, 175-76
pay-as-you-go system
divisions of, 176-77
legislative impact, 176, 177-78
overview, xvi, 176-77

reform proposals, 182-83
reforms (1997/2000), 177-78
World Bank proposals
    elements of, 178-79
    reaction to, 177, 179-80

Bangladesh, health insurance
    contributions, 133
    coverage, 132-33, 134
    development factors, 134-35, 136-37
    government responsibility, 145-47
    overview, 135*t*
Belgium, employment services, 249
Bolivia, pension reform
    impact of
        administrative cost, 162
        capital accumulation, 163
        commissions, 161
        competition, 162
        compliance, 161
        coverage, 160-61
        entitlement, 162
        fiscal cost, 166
        individual choice, 160
        portfolio diversification, 164
        real investment yield, 163-64
    substitutive model
        administration, 159
        benefits, 158-59
        contributions, 158
        defined, 158
        financing, 159
        implicit pension debt (IPD), 159

Canada Pension Plan (CPP)
    contribution increase, 83, 84-85
        legislative impact, 86
        steady-state rate, 85-86
    elderly income and
        equality goal, 84, 90
        poverty, 84, 90
        sources of, 84, 92
    international comparison, 84
    overview, xv, 83
    partial privatization and
        costs of, 84, 86
        Investment Board, 86
        market investment, 83, 86-87
        pension fund growth, 87
    privatization debate
        financial costs, 89-90
        investment taxation, 87-89

plan for, 85
Registered Pension Plans (RPPs),
    87
Registered Retirement Savings
    Plans (RRSPs), 88-89
    social costs, 90
public confidence in, 89
Quebec Pension Plan (QPP), 90n.1
World Bank and, 85, 89
Chile, pension reform
    impact of
        administrative cost, 162
        capital accumulation, 163
        commissions, 161
        competition, 162-63
        compliance, 161
        coverage, 160
        entitlement, 162
        fiscal cost, 166
        individual choice, 160
        national savings, 165
        portfolio diversification, 164
        real investment yield, 163-64
    substitutive model
        administration, 159
        benefits, 158-59
        contributions, 158
        defined, 158
        financing, 159
        implicit pension debt (IPD), 159
China, health insurance
    Basic Health Insurance System for
        Urban Working Population
        (BHISFUWP)
        administration, 219-20
        benefits, 216
        contributions, 217-18
        coverage, 218-19, 222n.5
        Decree reform, 215, 216, 217,
            219-20
        government responsibility, 218,
            219-20
        health insurance pooling fund
            (HIPF), 216
        individual medical account
            (IMA), 216, 217
        Ministry of Labour and Social Se-
            curity, 219
        self-employed, 219
        supervision, 219-20
        Township/Village Enterprises
            (TVEs), 219

two-tiered structure, 216
overview, xvii, 215, 222
supplementary programs
All-China Federation of Trade
Unions (ACFTU), 220-21
commercial schemes, 221
Community Health Services (CHS),
221
government responsibility, 220
nonprofit schemes, 220-21
Civil society, xiii
Colombia, pension reform
impact of
administrative cost, 162-63
capital accumulation, 163
commissions, 162
competition, 162-63
compliance, 161
coverage, 160
entitlement, 162
fiscal cost, 166
individual choice, 160
portfolio diversification, 164
real investment yield, 163-64
parallel model
administration, 159
benefits, 158
contributions, 158
defined, 158
financing, 159
implicit pension debt (IPD), 159
Commercialization, 14-15
Competition. See Market competition
Competitive government responsibility,
6
Constitutional influence, 6
Costa Rica, pension reform
impact of
administrative cost, 162
commissions, 161
competition, 162-63
compliance, 161
coverage, 160
individual choice, 160
portfolio diversification, 164
real investment yield, 163-64
mixed model
administration, 159
benefits, 158
contributions, 158
defined, 158
financing, 159

implicit pension debt (IPD), 159
Creeping privatization, 8-9
Cultural influences, xii-xiii, 3, 4

Democratic Republic of Congo, health
insurance
Bwamanda Plan
contributions, 133
coverage, 132-33
development factors, 134-37
government responsibility,
145-47
National Health Policy, 135-36
nonprofit health insurance
schemes (NPHIS), 130
objectives, 135, 149n.27
overview, 135t
systemic approach, 135, 149n.28
Grameen Plan
contributions, 133, 134, 149n.24
coverage, 133-34
overview, 135t
Denmark, social welfare
employment, 247, 249
overview, xviii, 289
private/public cooperation
accommodating labor market,
288-89
advantages of, 285-86
barriers to, 284-85
prerequisites for, 286
service contracting, 286
service quality, 285-86
service supervision, 285, 286
voluntary organizations and,
287-88
private/public interaction
collective responsibility, 284
cost reduction, 284
decentralization model, 283-84
democratic control, 284, 286
knowledge regarding, 284-85
service quality, 283, 285
voluntary organizations and
funding of, 287
private/public cooperation, 287-88
sector representation, 287
Deregulation. See Employment services,
European deregulation; Government
deregulation
Disability insurance
Jordan, 8

United States, 11-12, 13-14

Economic impact
    Africa, 32-33, 34-35, 36-38
    Austria, 175-76
    Germany, 97
    individual accounts and, 49-51,
        59n.7, 73-74
    Indonesia, 226, 231
    Poland, 171-73
    Tunisia, 207
    United States, 72-74
El Salvador, pension reform
    impact of
        administrative cost, 162
        capital accumulation, 163
        commissions, 161
        competition, 162-63
        compliance, 161
        coverage, 160
        entitlement, 162
        individual choice, 160
        portfolio diversification, 164
    substitutive model
        administration, 159
        benefits, 158-59
        contributions, 158
        defined, 158
        financing, 159
        implicit pension debt (IPD), 159
Employment services, European deregu-
    lation. *See also* United States, em-
    ployment services
    Australia, 256-57
    Austria, 247, 249
    Belgium, 249
    consequences for
        private agency contribution,
            254-55
        privatization achievement, 247-48
        public employment services,
            255-56
        regulatory mechanism, 255
        service outsourcing, 256-57
    Denmark, 247, 249
    deregulation defined, 247
    Finland, 249
    Germany, 247, 249
        privatization assessment, 251-54
        privatization authorization
            (1994), 250-51
        privatization outlook, 254

Great Britain, 248, 249
Greece, 247
Italy, 247
Netherlands, 247, 248, 256, 257
overview, xvii, 247-48
rationale for
    employment policy, 248-49
    employment restructurization,
        249
    micro-level regulation, 249
    service image, 248
    service quality, 248
    temporary employment, 249
Spain, 247
Sweden, 247, 249
Switzerland, 256
Exclusive government responsibility, 6

Family benefits, 13
Finland, employment services, 249
Formally identified privatization, 7-8
Formal privatization, 11

Germany
    dependency insurance, 99
    employment services, 99, 247, 249
        privatization assessment, 251-54
        privatization authorization
            (1994), 250-51
        privatization outlook, 254
    health insurance
        legislative impact, 10-11
        reform measures, 98-99
    legislative impact
        health insurance, 10-11
        pension insurance, 95-96
Germany, accident insurance
    administration and
        privatization, 278-80
        statutory system, 278-80
    benefits and
        privatization, 275, 276-78
        statutory system, 275-78
    cost reduction and
        privatization, 271, 278-80
        statutory system, 271, 278-80
    coverage and
        privatization, 276
        statutory system, 276
    employer liability and
        privatization, 273-75
        statutory system, 273, 274-75

employment re-entry and
    privatization, 272
    statutory system, 272
financing and
    privatization, 278-80
    statutory system, 278-80
occupational diseases and
    privatization and, 272-73
    statutory system, 273
overview, xvii, 269, 280
prevention effectiveness and
    privatization, 270-71
    statutory system, 269-71, 275-76
Germany, pension insurance
    legislative impact, 95-96
    partial privatization and
        economic development, 97
        employee costs, 98-99
        employee taxation, 98
        employer responsibility, 97
        social policy guidelines, 96, 99
    social policy challenges
        aging population, 95
        employee costs, 95-96, 98
        employee taxation, 96
    social policy guidelines
        economic development, 97
        employer responsibility, 97
        individual choice, 96
        partial privatization and, 96, 99
        social solidarity, 96
        subsidiarity principle, 96

Government deregulation. *See also*
    Employment services, European de-
    regulation
    liberalization, 14
    privatization synonym, 14
    Sweden, 194
Government regulation
    individual choice and, 24, 25, 26, 27
    privatization and, 6-7, 16n.7
    Sweden, 186-87
    United Kingdom, 28
    Uruguay, 211-12
Government responsibility
    Argentina, 10
    Australia, 12
    Austria, 178
    Bangladesh/Gonoshashthya Kendra
        (GK), 145-47
    Bolivia, 9-10

Chile, 9-10
China
    Basic Health Insurance System
        for Urban Working Population
        (BHISFUWP), 218, 219-20
    supplementary programs, 220
Colombia, 9-10
Democratic Republic of Congo,
    145-47
employment services and
    Austria, 178
    United States, 234-35, 237, 238
Germany, 10-11
health insurance and
    administration information,
        141-42
    alternative health packages,
        140-41
    Bangladesh/Gonoshashthya
        Kendra (GK), 145-47
    capacity identification, 143-45
    China, 218, 219-20
    co-financing, 142-43
    contracts, 144, 150n.45
    Democratic Republic of Congo/
        Bwamanda Plan, 145-47
    development time, 145, 150n.49
    Germany, 10-11
    Indonesia, 223-24, 225, 226-28,
        230, 231-32
    information, 140, 141-42
    monitoring protocol, 142
    privatization, 10-11, 12-13
    Tunisia, 201, 202, 203
    Uganda, 147
    Uruguay, 210-13
Hong Kong, 8
individual choice and
    contributions, 27
    failure outcomes, 28
    guaranteed funds, 25, 27, 28
    information requirement, 25
    mandatory basic protection, 24,
        25, 27
    market competition, 27
    market discrimination, 27
    market regulation, 24, 25, 26, 27
    market supervision, 24, 26, 27
    moral hazard, 20
    resource redistribution, 20
Indonesia
    financial crisis (1997), 226-28

health insurance development,
223-24, 225
health insurance future, 231-32
privatization and, 230
information and
health insurance administration,
141-42
health risks, 140
individual choice, 25
Iran, 8
Japan, 8
Jordan, 8
Mexico, 9-10
Panama, 7-8
Peru, 9-10
privatization and
accident insurance, 10
administrative reorganization,
11-12
artificial, 11
civil society, xiii
competitive responsibility, 6
constitutional influence, 6
creeping, 8-9
cultural influences, xii-xiii
disability insurance, 11-12, 13-14
exclusive responsibility, 6
family benefits, 13
financing reorganization, 12-13
formal, 11
formally identified, 7-8
health insurance, 10-11, 12-13
institutional reorganization, 9-11
invalidity insurance, 13
legislative impact, 6, 7-8, 10-11,
16n.4
market regulation, 6-7, 16n.7
task redistribution, 5-7
welfare states, xii, 6
Tobago, 8
Trinidad, 8
Tunisia, 201, 202, 203
Uganda, 147
United States
employment services, 234-35,
237, 238
privatization, 10, 11-12, 13-14
Uruguay, 10
cost reduction, 210-11
future trends, 212-13
regulation, 211-12
Social Security Administration,
210, 211

Great Britain
employment services, 248, 249
pension insurance, 28
Greece, employment services, 247
Gross domestic product (GDP)
Africa, 37-38
United States, 72-73
Gross national product (GNP), Africa,
32-33

Health care market
overview, xv, 122-23
privatization development, 113-15
contemporary, 114
developing countries, 114
European model, 114
historically, 113, 114
United States model, 114
variations in, 114
provision development
disease management, 115, 116
evidence-based medicine, 115,
116
globalization impact, 116-17
managed care organizations,
115-16
professional migration, 117-18
treatment guidelines, 115, 116
provision development effects
access inequality, 118-19
infrastructure impact, 120-21
medical ethics, 121
service quality, 119-20
treatment inequality, 119
unprofitable markets, 121-22
recommendations for, 122-23
Health insurance, low-income countries.
See also China, health insurance; Indonesia, health insurance; *specific
countries*; Tunisia, health insurance;
Uruguay, health insurance
Bangladesh/Gonoshashthya Kendra
(GK)
contributions, 133
coverage, 132-33, 134
development factors, 134-35,
136-37
government responsibility,
145-47
overview, 135*t*
characteristics of
compulsory membership, 127
contributions, 126-27, 148n.6

low-income defined, 148n.1
social insurance concept, 126-27
taxation financing, 125-26
Democratic Republic of Congo/
Bwamanda Plan
contributions, 133
coverage, 132-33
development factors, 134-37
government responsibility,
145-47
National Health Policy, 135-36
nonprofit health insurance
schemes (NPHIS), 130
objectives, 135, 149n.27
overview, 135*t*
systemic approach, 135, 149n.28
Democratic Republic of Congo/
Grameen Plan
contributions, 133, 134, 149n.24
coverage, 133-34
overview, 135*t*
government responsibility, 130, 131,
132, 138-43
administration information, 141-42
alternative health packages,
140-41
Bangladesh/Gonoshashthya
Kendra (GK), 145-47
capacity identification, 143-45
co-financing, 142-43
contracts, 144, 150n.45
Democratic Republic of Congo/
Bwamanda Plan, 145-47
development time, 145, 150n.49
health risk information, 140
monitoring protocol, 142
Uganda, 147
implementation limitations, 127-29
administration, 128
benefit consensus, 127-28
benefit deliverance, 128
political stability, 128
implementation recommendations,
137-38
administration, 138
benefit consensus, 138
benefit deliverance, 138
nonprofit health insurance schemes
(NPHIS)
cooperatives, 131
coverage, 129-31, 132, 137
credit schemes, 131
defined, 128-29

Democratic Republic of Congo/
Bwamanda, 130
financial risk, 129-30, 131, 132
government responsibility, 130,
131, 132, 138-43
international performance,
129-32
sector organization, 131-32
self-financed, 131
UMASIDA/Tanzania, 132,
149n.19
overview, xv, 125-26, 147-48
Uganda
contributions, 133, 134
coverage, 132-33, 134
government responsibility, 147
overview, 135*t*
Hong Kong, 8

Individual accounts. *See also* United
States, individual accounts
defined benefit/contribution plans,
46-48, 58n.2
aging population impact, 51-52
employment impact, 52
funding impact, 53-54
overview, 47*t*
risk factor, 47-48
funded/privately managed plans,
54-57
funded/unfunded plans, 48
funding impact, 53-54
overview, 47*t*
International Monetary Fund and, 50
international trend
funded/privately managed plans,
55*f*, 56*f*, 57
overview, 45-46, 58
plan distinctions, 47*t*, 48, 49, 50,
51
overview, xvi, 58
publicly/privately managed plans,
48-49
overview, 47*t*
support of
aging population impact, 51-52
employment impact, 52
family pattern impact, 52-53
political economy impact, 49-51,
59n.7
types of
defined benefit/contribution
plans, 46-48, 58n.2

funded/unfunded plans, 48
overview, 47*t*
publicly/privately managed
plans, 48-49
World Bank and, 50
Individual choice
consumer rational for
consumption patterns, 23
contribution level, 22
service preference, 22-23
defined, 19
dimensions of
within system, 20-21
system opt-out, 21
government rational for
group targeting, 23-24
provision efficiency, 23
provision level, 23
government responsibility and
adverse selection, 20
contributions, 27
failure outcomes, 28
guaranteed funds, 25, 27, 28
information requirement, 25
mandatory basic protection, 24,
25, 27
market competition, 27
market discrimination, 27
market regulation, 24, 25, 26, 27
market supervision, 24, 26, 27
moral hazard, 20
resource redistribution, 20
information requirement
consequences, 25-27
costs, 20, 26-27
government responsibility and,
25
options, 25-26
overview, xiv, 19-20
provider rational for, 24
rational for, 20-24
administrative system, 21
consumer perspective, 22-23
cost efficiency, 21
government perspective, 23-24
market system and, 21
provider perspective, 24
system efficiency, 21-22
Indonesia, health insurance
development of
contributions, 223, 224-25
coverage, 223, 224

government responsibility,
223-24, 225
independence (1945), 223
Jamsostek (1992), 223-24, 225
privatization (1993), 224, 225
Social Health Insurance State
Owned Enterprise (1968),
223, 224, 225
financial crisis (1997)
demographics, 226
economic indicators, 226
government responsibility,
226-28
health infrastructure, 226-27
human development, 226
managed care emergence, 227-28
post-crisis conditions, 225-27
pre-crisis conditions, 225-27
privatization trend, 227
future trends
contributions, 231, 232
economic development, 231
genetic code mapping, 230-31
government responsibility,
231-32
International Monetary Fund and,
231
Jamsostek, 231
managed care, 231-32
Social Health Insurance State
Owned Enterprise, 231, 232
World Bank and, 231
government responsibility
financial crisis (1997), 226-28
health insurance development,
223-24, 225
health insurance future, 231-32
privatization and, 230
Jamsostek (1992)
development of, 223-24, 225
future trends, 231
privatization impact, 228, 230
managed care
financial crisis (1997), 227-28
future trends, 231-32
privatization impact, 228
overview, xvii
privatization impact
benefits, 228-29
contributions, 228, 229
cost reduction, 229-30
drug expenditures, 228-29

government responsibility, 230
International Monetary Fund
    (IMF), 230
Jamsostek, 228, 230
managed care, 228
private/public integration, 229
quality care, 230
Social Health Insurance State
    Owned Enterprise, 228-30
World Bank, 230
Social Health Insurance State Owned
    Enterprise (1968)
    development of, 223, 224, 225
    future trends, 231, 232
    privatization impact, 228-30
Information
    government responsibility and
        health insurance administration,
        141-42
    health risks, 140
    individual choice, 25
    individual choice and
        consequences, 25-27
        costs, 20, 26-27
        government responsibility, 25
        options, 25-26
    Netherlands, 107
International Labour Office, 5
International Monetary Fund (IMF)
    Africa, 33
    individual accounts and, 50
    Indonesia, 230, 231
International Social Security Associa-
    tion (ISSA), xv
Internet, employment services, 235, 239,
    240, 243, 245n.19
Invalidity insurance
    Netherlands, 13, 102, 111n.2
    privatization and, 13
    Tobago, 8
    Trinidad, 8
Iran, retirement age, 8
Italy, employment services, 247

Japan, retirement age, 8
Jordan, disability insurance, 8

Latin America, pension reform
    Argentina
        administration, 159
        administrative cost impact, 162
        benefits, 158

capital accumulation impact, 163
commission impact, 161
competition impact, 162
compliance impact, 161
contributions, 158
coverage impact, 160
entitlement impact, 162
financing, 159
fiscal cost impact, 166
implicit pension debt (IPD), 159
individual choice impact, 160
mixed model, 158
portfolio diversification impact,
    164
real investment yield impact, 163-
    164
Bolivia
    administration, 159
    administrative cost impact, 162
    benefits, 158
    capital accumulation impact, 163
    commission impact, 161
    competition impact, 162
    compliance impact, 161
    contributions, 158
    coverage impact, 160
    entitlement impact, 162
    financing, 159
    fiscal cost impact, 166
    implicit pension debt (IPD), 159
    individual choice impact, 160
    portfolio diversification impact,
        164
    real investment yield impact, 163-
        64
    substitutive model, 158
characteristics of
    long-run impact, 165-67
    overview, xvi, 9-10, 157
    private vs. public system, 157-58
    structural reform, 157
Chile
    administration, 159
    administrative cost impact, 162
    benefits, 158
    capital accumulation impact, 163
    commission impact, 161
    competition impact, 162
    compliance impact, 161
    contributions, 158
    coverage impact, 160
    entitlement impact, 162

financing, 159
fiscal cost impact, 166
implicit pension debt (IPD), 159
individual choice impact, 160
national savings impact, 165
portfolio diversification impact,
    164
real investment yield impact, 163-
    64
substitutive model, 158
Colombia
administration, 159
administrative cost impact, 162
benefits, 158
capital accumulation impact, 163
commission impact, 161
competition impact, 162
compliance impact, 161
contributions, 158
coverage impact, 160
entitlement impact, 162
financing, 159
fiscal cost impact, 166
implicit pension debt (IPD), 159
individual choice impact, 160
parallel model, 158
portfolio diversification impact,
    164
real investment yield impact, 163-
    64
Costa Rica
administration, 159
administrative cost impact, 162
benefits, 158
commission impact, 161
competition impact, 162
compliance impact, 161
contributions, 158
coverage impact, 160
financing, 159
implicit pension debt (IPD), 159
individual choice impact, 160
mixed model, 158
portfolio diversification impact,
    164
real investment yield impact, 163-
    64
El Salvador
administration, 159
administrative cost impact, 162
benefits, 158-59
capital accumulation impact, 163

commission impact, 161
competition impact, 162
compliance impact, 161
contributions, 158
coverage impact, 160
entitlement impact, 162
financing, 159
implicit pension debt (IPD), 159
individual choice impact, 160
portfolio diversification impact,
    164
substitutive model, 158
Mexico
administration, 159
administrative cost impact, 162
benefits, 158
capital accumulation impact, 163
commission impact, 161
competition impact, 162
compliance impact, 161
contributions, 158
coverage impact, 160
entitlement impact, 162
financing, 159
implicit pension debt (IPD), 159
individual choice impact, 160
portfolio diversification impact,
    164
real investment yield impact, 163-
    64
substitutive model, 158
mixed model
administration, 159
administrative cost impact, 162
benefits, 158
capital accumulation impact, 163
commission impact, 161
competition impact, 162
compliance impact, 161
contributions, 158
coverage impact, 160
defined, 158
entitlement impact, 162
financing, 159
fiscal cost impact, 166
implicit pension debt (IPD), 159
individual choice impact, 160
portfolio diversification impact, 164
real investment yield impact, 163-
    64
Nicaragua
administration, 159

administrative cost impact, 162
benefits, 158
commission impact, 161
competition impact, 162
compliance impact, 161
contributions, 158
coverage impact, 160
financing, 159
implicit pension debt (IPD), 159
individual choice impact, 160
portfolio diversification impact,
   164
substitutive model, 158
parallel model
administration, 159
administrative cost impact, 162
benefits, 158
capital accumulation impact, 163
commission impact, 161
competition impact, 162
compliance impact, 161
contributions, 158
coverage impact, 160
defined, 158
entitlement impact, 162
financing, 159
fiscal cost impact, 166
implicit pension debt (IPD), 159
individual choice impact, 160
portfolio diversification impact,
   164
real investment yield impact, 163-
   64
Peru
administration, 159
administrative cost impact, 162
benefits, 159
capital accumulation impact, 163
commission impact, 161
competition impact, 162
compliance impact, 161
contributions, 158
coverage impact, 160
entitlement impact, 162
financing, 159
fiscal cost impact, 166
implicit pension debt (IPD), 159
individual choice impact, 160
parallel model, 158
portfolio diversification impact,
   164
substitutive model

administration, 159
administrative cost impact, 162
benefits, 158
capital accumulation impact, 163
commission impact, 161
competition impact, 162
compliance impact, 161
contributions, 158
coverage impact, 160
defined, 158
entitlement impact, 162
financing, 159
fiscal cost impact, 165-66
implicit pension debt (IPD), 159
individual choice impact, 160
portfolio diversification impact,
   164
real investment yield impact, 163-
   64
Uruguay
administration, 159
administrative cost impact, 162
benefits, 158
capital accumulation impact, 163
commission impact, 161
competition impact, 162
compliance impact, 161
contributions, 158
coverage impact, 160
entitlement impact, 162
financing, 159
fiscal cost impact, 166
implicit pension debt (IPD), 159
individual choice impact, 160
mixed model, 158
portfolio diversification impact,
   164
real investment yield impact, 163-
   64
Legislative impact
Austria, 176, 177-78
Canada, 86
Germany
   health insurance, 10-11
   pension insurance, 95-96
government responsibility and
   competitive, 6
   exclusive, 6
Panama, 7-8
Sweden, 186-87
United States, 16n.4
Liberalization, 14

Managed care
  health care market, 115-16
  Indonesia and
    financial crisis (1997), 227-28
    future trends, 231-32
    privatization impact, 228
Market competition
  employment services and, 235
  individual choice and, 27
  Netherlands and
    coalition agreement, 105, 106
    privatization background, 102,
      103-4
    privatization rejection, 107
    reorganization limitations, 104-5
  pension insurance and
    Argentina, 163
    Austria, 175
    Bolivia, 163
    Chile, 163
    Colombia, 163
    Costa Rica, 163
    El Salvador, 163
    Mexico, 163
    Netherlands, 102, 103-5, 106,
      107
    Nicaragua, 163
    Peru, 163
    Uruguay, 163
  privatization synonym, 13-14
  United States, 235
Market deregulation. See Employment
  services, European deregulation;
  Government deregulation
Market regulation. See Government
  regulation
Mexico, pension reform
  impact of
    administrative cost, 162
    capital accumulation, 163
    commissions, 161
    competition, 162-63
    compliance, 161
    coverage, 160
    entitlement, 162
    individual choice, 160
    portfolio diversification, 164
    real investment yield, 163-64
  substitutive model
    administration, 159
    benefits, 158-59
    contributions, 158

defined, 158
financing, 159
implicit pension debt (IPD), 159

Netherlands, employment services, 247,
  248, 256, 257
Netherlands, insurance administration
  coalition agreement
    advisory board, 106, 112n.3
    amendments, 109-10, 111n.8
    government recommendations,
      106
    market competition, 105, 106
    Piloting Model, 106-7, 112n.5
    public administration, 105, 106,
      112n.4
  future trends, 110-11
  health insurance, 13, 101, 107
  invalidity insurance, 13, 102
  overview, xv, 101
  privatization background
    administration amendments,
      103-4
    invalidity insurance, 102, 112n.2
    market competition, 102, 103-4
    political factors, 102
    social factors, 102
    unemployment rates, 102, 112n.1
  privatization distinctions, 101
  privatization rejection
    cost benefit analysis, 108
    information privacy, 107
    legal irregularities, 108
    market competition, 107
    personnel risks, 108
    reintegration activities, 109,
      112n.7
    structure complexity, 108
  reorganization limitations, 104-5
    market competition, 104-5
  Sickness Benefit Acts, 101
New Zealand, accident insurance
  background
    Accident Compensation Act
      (1972), 259, 261-62
    Accident Compensation Act
      (1982), 262
    Accident Insurance Act (1998),
      263
    Accident Rehabilitation and
      Compensation Insurance Act
      (1992), 262, 263

"At Work Insurance Ltd.," 263
benefits, 260, 261-62, 263
common law damages, 259, 260, 261
contributions, 260, 261, 262, 263
criminal injuries, 260
motor vehicles, 260, 262, 263
National Government, 259, 261-63, 264-65
social welfare, 260
Woodhouse Report (1967), 261
workers compensation, 260, 261
future trends, 264
overview, xvii, 259
privatization pros/cons, 264-65
privatization rejection
Accident Compensation Act (2001), 264, 267
Accident Compensation Corporation (ACC), 259, 261, 262, 263, 264, 265-67
Accident Insurance (Transitional Provisions) Act (2000), 263-64
benefits, 264, 266-67
contributions, 264-67
Labor Government (1999), 259, 263-67
Nicaragua, pension reform
impact of
administrative cost, 162
commissions, 161
competition, 162-63
compliance, 161
coverage, 160
individual choice, 160
portfolio diversification, 164
substitutive model
administration, 159
benefits, 158-59
contributions, 158
defined, 158
financing, 159
implicit pension debt (IPD), 159

Panama
formally identified privatization, 7-8
legislative impact, 7-8
Peru, pension reform
impact of
administrative cost, 162
capital accumulation, 163

commissions, 161
competition, 162-63
compliance, 161
coverage, 160
entitlement, 162
fiscal cost, 166
individual choice, 160
portfolio diversification, 164
parallel model
administration, 159
benefits, 158-59
contributions, 158
defined, 158
financing, 159
implicit pension debt (IPD), 159
Poland, pension reform
benefits of, 171-72
contributions
Demographic Reserve Fund, 170
pay-as-you-go, 170
economic development and, 171-73
limitations of, 171, 172
overview, xvi, 169-70
privatization elements
contributions, 170-71
open pension funds, 170
Social Insurance Institution, 170
Political impact
individual accounts and, 49-51, 59n.7, 74-75
low-income countries, 128
Netherlands, 102
United States, 74-75
Poverty
Africa, 35, 36-37
Canada, 84, 90
Privatization
defined
concepts, xi
cultural influences, 3, 4
as effects, 3-4
International Labour Office, 5
privatization, 4
social protection, 4
social security, 5
starting-point process, 4, 6, 15
government responsibility and
accident insurance, 10
administrative reorganization, 11-12
Argentina, 10
artificial privatization, 11

Australia, 12
Bolivia, 9-10
Chile, 9-10
civil society, xiii
Colombia, 9-10
competitive responsibility, 6
constitutional influence, 6
creeping privatization, 8-9
cultural influences, xii-xiii
disability insurance, 11-12, 13-14
exclusive responsibility, 6
family benefits, 13
financing reorganization, 12-13
formally identified privatization,
  7-8
formal privatization, 11
Germany, 10-11
health insurance, 10-11, 12-13
Hong Kong, 8
institutional reorganization, 9-11
invalidity insurance, 13
Iran, 8
Japan, 8
Jordan, 8
legislative impact, 6, 7-8, 10-11,
  16n.4
market regulation, 6-7, 16n.7
Mexico, 9-10
Panama, 7-8
Peru, 9-10
task redistribution, 5-7
Tobago, 8
Trinidad, 8
United States, 10, 11-12, 13-14
Uruguay, 10
welfare states, xii, 6
overview, xii-xiii, xiv, 3-4
social security branches, xi-xii
  accident insurance, 10
  disability insurance, 11-12, 13-14
  family benefits, 13
  health insurance, 10-11, 12-13
  invalidity insurance, 13
synonyms for
  commercialization, 14-15
  competition, 13-14
  deregulation, 14
  liberalization, 14

Regulation. See Government regulation

Spain, employment services, 247

Sweden, employment services, 247, 249
Sweden, pension insurance
  overview, xvi, 185, 190, 198-99
  privatization development
    banking deregulation, 194
    earnings ceiling, 192-93, 199n.9
    individual retirement accounts
      (1994), 195
    insurance providers, 196-98,
      1963-1982, 192-93
    1980s, 193-94
    1990s, 194-98
  privatization elements, 193
  public system reform (1994), 195
  regulation legislation (1904),
    186-87
  stock market investment, 194
  supply-side restrictions, 191-92,
    199n.7
  tax deduction utilization, 195-96,
    197
  unit-link insurance (1993), 191,
    194-95, 196-98
  widow's benefit (1989), 193, 194
  public system evolution
    defined benefits, 185-86
    defined contributions (1990s),
      189, 191
    earnings-related ATP (1960),
      186-88, 199n.1
    earnings-related ATP (1990s),
      188-89
    notational defined contributions
      (1992), 189-91, 199n.6
    quasi-mandatory agreements
      (1960), 187-88, 199n.3
    quasi-mandatory agreements
      (1993), 191
    unit-link insurance (1993), 191
Switzerland
  employment services, 256
  health insurance, 10

Taxation
  Canada, 87-89
  Germany, 96, 98
  low-income countries, 125-26
  Sweden, 195-96, 197
  United States, 75-76
Tobago, invalidity insurance, 8
Trinidad, invalidity insurance, 8
Tunisia, health insurance

achievements
    hospital infrastructure, 203
    professional employment, 203
integration and
    agreed tariffs, 205
    benefits, 206
    quality improvement, 206
overview, xvi, 201
reform of
    motivation for, 204
    principles, 204-5
regional indicators
    economic, 207
    social, 207
structure of
    government responsibility, 201,
        202, 203
    Ministry of Public Health, 202,
        203
    National Pension and Social In-
        surance Fund (NPSIF), 202
    National Social Security Fund
        (NSSF), 201, 202

Uganda, health insurance
    contributions, 133, 134
    coverage, 132-33, 134
    government responsibility, 147
    overview, 135t
United States
    disability insurance, 11-12, 13-14
    family benefits, 16n.4
    health insurance, 10
    legislative impact, 16n.4
    Ticket to Work and Self-Sufficiency
        Program, 11-12, 13-14
United States, employment services
    job training
        development of, 233
        Individual Training Account (ITA),
            236, 242
        intermediary brokers, 236, 241-42,
            245n.24
        Job Training Partnership Act
            (JTPA), 235, 241
        One-Stop centers, 236, 239, 240,
            241-42, 244n.8, 245n.21
        privatization and, 235-36, 241-42,
            243
        Temporary Assistance for Needy
            Families (TANF), 241-42
        welfare recipients, 235-36,
            241-42

Welfare-to-Work (WtW), 241-42
Workforce Investment Act
    (1998), 235-36, 241, 242, 243
Workforce Investment Boards,
    235-36, 241-42, 243
overview, xvii, 243
privatization and
    intermediary brokers, 234-36,
        237-38, 241-42, 244n.2
    job training, 235-36, 241-42, 243
    merit-staffing, 234-37, 238, 239
    program development, 234
    public employment service
        (PES), 235, 238-40, 243
    rejection of, 234
    service delivery, 234, 243n.1
    unemployment insurance (UI),
        234-35, 236-38, 243
program development
    job training, 233
    privatization and, 234
    public employment service
        (PES), 233
    unemployment insurance (UI),
        233
    welfare recipients and, 233
public employment service (PES)
    America's Job Bank (AJB), 239,
        240, 243, 245n.16
    America's Talent Bank (ATB),
        235, 239, 240, 243, 245n.16
    development of, 233
    Internet usage, 235, 239, 240,
        243, 245n.19
    labor exchange, 240
    market competition and, 235
    merit-staffing, 235
    One-Stop centers, 239, 240,
        244n.12
    privatization and, 235, 238-40,
        243
    Wagner-Peyser Act (1933),
        238-39, 243
    Worker Profiling Reemployment
        Services (WPRS), 240
    Workforce Investment Act
        (1998), 238-39
unemployment insurance (UI)
    development of, 233
    experience rating, 237-38
    Extended Benefit, 237
    government responsibility, 234-35,
        237, 238

intermediary brokers, 234-35,
    237-38, 244n.4
merit-staffing, 234, 236-37, 238,
    239, 244n.13
One-Stop centers, 239, 244n.12
privatization and, 234-35,
    236-38, 243
welfare recipients and
    job training, 235-36, 241-42
    program development, 233
    Temporary Assistance for Needy
        Families (TANF), 241-42
    Welfare-to-Work (WtW), 241-42
United States, individual accounts
opposition factors
    administration, 77, 81n.8
    automatic annuitization, 77,
        81n.7
    costs, 77, 81n.7
    long-term implications, 78-79
    low-income workers, 78-79
    means-tested benefits, 78-79
    mixed system, 78
    pre-retirement access, 76-77
    risks, 76-77
overview, xiv, 63-64, 79-80
supportive factors
    contribution returns, 73-74,
        75-76
    economic, 73-74
    market returns, 75-76, 81n.6
    political, 74-75
    savings increase, 74
    system deficit, 73
    taxation and, 75-76
    Wall Street investment, 74
    wealth inequality, 74
United States, pension insurance
aging population and
    dependency ratio, 65, 67t
    fertility rate, 65, 66t
    international comparison, 64t, 66t
    life expectancy rate, 65, 66t
benefits/earnings ratio, 69-70
    international comparison, 69-70
inflation adjustment, 70-71
    international comparison, 70-71
international comparison
    aging population, 64t, 66t, 67t
    benefits/earnings ratio, 69-70
    contributions, 71-72
    dependency ratio, 67t

early retirement benefits, 68-69
fertility rate, 66t
full benefit retirement, 68-69
gross domestic product (GDP),
    72-73
inflation adjustment, 70-71
labor force participation, 66-69
life expectancy rate, 66t
program costs, 71-73
replacement rates, 69-70
system financial status, 72-73
labor force participation and
    early retirement benefits, 68-69
    full benefit retirement, 68-69
    international comparison, 66-69
overview, xiv, 63-64, 79-80
program costs
    contributions and, 71-72
    gross domestic product and,
        72-73
    international comparison, 71-73
    system financial status, 72-73
replacement rates, 69-70
    international comparison, 69-70
Uruguay, health insurance
background
    contributions, 209-10
    health insurance introduction,
        209
    mutualist cooperatives, 209-10
future trends, 212-13
government responsibility
    cost reduction, 210-11
    future trends, 212-13
    regulation, 211-12
    Social Security Administration,
        210, 211
institutional responsibility, 211-12
    future trends, 212-13
overview, xvi, 210-11
Uruguay, pension reform
impact of
    administrative cost, 162
    capital accumulation, 163
    commissions, 161
    competition, 162
    compliance, 161
    coverage, 160
    entitlement, 162
    fiscal cost, 166
    individual choice, 160
    portfolio diversification, 164

real investment yield, 163-64
mixed model
    administration, 159
    benefits, 158
    contributions, 158
    defined, 158
    financing, 159
    implicit pension debt (IPD), 159

Welfare. *See also* Denmark, social wel-
    fare
    government responsibility and, xii,
        6
    New Zealand, 260

United States
    job training, 235-36, 241-42
    program development, 233
    Temporary Assistance for Needy
        Families (TANF), 241-42
    Welfare-to-Work (WtW), 241-42
World Bank
    Africa, 33
    Austria, 177, 178-80
    Canada, 85, 89
    individual accounts and, 50
    Indonesia, 230, 231
World Labour Report 2000, 5